THE TWINS STORIES

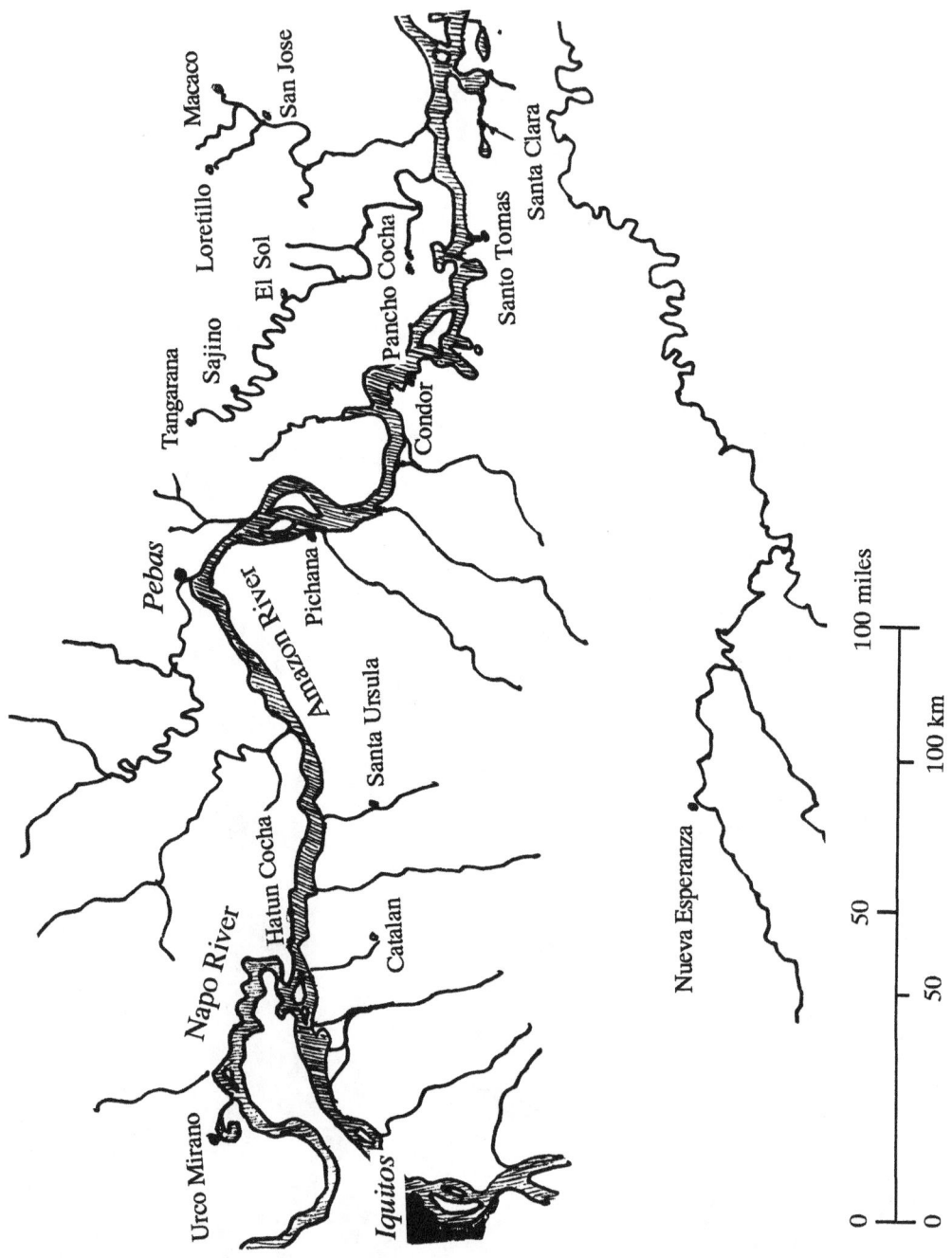

Figure 1. Distribution of Yagua communities (major non-Yagua communities are in italics)

The Twins Stories

Participant Coding in Yagua Narrative

Thomas Edward Payne

UNIVERSITY OF CALIFORNIA PRESS
Berkeley • Los Angeles • Oxford

UNIVERSITY OF CALIFORNIA PRESS
BERKELEY AND LOS ANGELES, CALIFORNIA

UNIVERSITY OF CALIFORNIA PRESS, LTD.
OXFORD, ENGLAND

©1993 BY THE REGENTS OF THE UNIVERSITY OF CALIFORNIA
PRINTED IN THE UNITED STATES OF AMERICA

Library of Congress Cataloging-in-Publication Data

Payne, Thomas Edward, 1951–
    The twins stories: participant coding in Yagua narrative / Thomas
Edward Payne.
        p.   cm. — (University of California publications in
linguistics; v. 120)
    Includes bibliographical references.
    ISBN 0-520-09774-2 (alk. paper)
    1. Yagua language—Grammar. 2. Yagua language—Discourse
analysis. 3. Yagua Indians—Folklore. I. Title. II. Series.
PM7263.P39   1992   92-23632
498'.4—dc20   CIP

The paper used in this publication meets the minimum requirements of American
National Standard for Information Sciences—Permanence of Paper for Printed
Library Materials, ANSI Z39.48-1984. ∞

To the memory of
the first daughter of Robinson
of the Red Macaw Clan

Born 1980, died May 1982 of chronic pneumonia

Contents

Acknowledgments

This work was initially conceived in the dry season of 1981 during a workshop on "discourse and grammar" at Yarinacocha, Perú. The primary consultants for that workshop were Joseph Grimes and Desmond Derbyshire, both of whom planted seeds that eventually took root and gave rise to the present work. For technical and logistical help in Perú I wish to thank the members of the Summer Institute of Linguistics. Paul Powlison deserves special recognition, not only for his careful comments on my work, but also for his pioneering work on Yagua and for his logistical help in getting my family and me established with the Yagua people and language.

For technical consultation at later stages of preparation of this work, I wish to thank William O. Bright, Pamela Downing, John W. Du bois, T. Givón, Paul Kroskrity, Pamela Munro, Doris Payne, David Perlmutter, Paul Powlison, and Sandra A. Thompson, all of whom read and commented on early drafts. Sandra Thompson in particular has been a consistent source of encouragement and a stimulus to better scholarship. The world's greatest authorities on Yagua are my wife, Doris Payne, and Dr. Paul Powlison, both of whom have read versions of this work ad nauseam. I thank them heartily for their help. As might be expected, there are points where my analysis differs from those of Doris and Paul, but I claim full responsibility for all errors that appear in this work.

For software and hardware support I thank the members of the JAARS computer services department, and the SIL Language Data Processing department. Shirley Hooge and Jan Tyhurst keyed in some of the texts that appear in the appendices.

The University of Chicago Press is to be thanked for permission to use the English translation of Laureano Mozombite's version of the Twins Cycle, which appeared in Dorson (1975). However, I have retranslated the tale from the Yagua, and so the version that appears in Dorson's work (which was contributed by Paul Powlison) is not identical to that which appears as appendix 4 of this work.

The Peruvian Ministry of Education, the Graduate Division of the University of California at Los Angeles, and the Linguistics Department at U.C.L.A. have all provided resources essential to the completion of this work.

Of course none of this work would have been possible without the openness and cooperation of the Yagua people. In particular, I would like to thank Pedro Díaz, Mamerto Macahuachi, Hilario Peña and many others who served as language consultants; Manungo Díaz and Arámi Sarco who contributed folk stories; Alchico Jápiiryá and Estela Múcatyuriryá who allowed us to stay in their home and who put up with our unorthodox behavior; and finally Eleazar Pano and Celina Tello who were our friends, counselors, guides and teachers through many joyous, as well as difficult times.

Abbreviations

1SG	=	First person singular
1DL	=	First person dual
1PLINC	=	First person plural inclusive
1PLEX	=	First person plural exclusive
2SG	=	Second person singular
2DL	=	Second person dual
2PL	=	Second person plural
3COL	=	Third person collective (same form as 3SG)
3SG	=	Third person singular
3DL	=	Third person dual
3PL	=	Third person plural
ANIM	=	Animate (specifies kinds of classifiers and nominalizers)
ANTIC	=	Anticipation
ARR1	=	Arrival #1 (action takes place as subject arrives on current scene -- no scene change implied)
ARR2	=	Arrival #2 (action takes place as subject arrives on new scene -- scene change implied)
AUX	=	Auxiliary
CL	=	Classifier
COM	=	Comitative
COMPL	=	Completive
COND	=	Conditional
CONT	=	Continuative
COP	=	Copula
COR	=	Coreference
DAT	=	Dative
DAY	=	Discourse particle (see footnote 5 of chapter 2)
DEMO	=	Demonstrative
DEP	=	Departure (action takes place as subject departs)
DETRANS	=	Detransitivizer
DIM	=	Diminutive
DIR	=	Direction towards
DIST	=	Distributive
EVID	=	Evidential
EXCL	=	Exclamatory particle
FEM	=	Feminine
FRUST	=	Frustrative (auxiliary indicating action is unsuccessful)
HABIT	=	Habitual
HC	=	Head coding
INST	=	Instrumental
INTS	=	Intensifier
IMPRF	=	Imperfective

INAN	=	Inanimate
IRR	=	Irrealis auxiliary (also referred to as AUX:IRR)
IT	=	Iterative action (single location)
ITM	=	Iterative movement (locomotion implied)
JIITA	=	Discourse particle (see chapter 1, section 1.3.3)
LOC	=	Locative (to, at, in)
MALF	=	Malefactive auxiliary (also referred to as AUX:MALF)
MASC	=	Masculine
NEG	=	Negative
NEUT	=	Neutral (marks some classifiers and nominalizers)
NIY	=	Semantically 'empty' morpheme following a left-dislocated pronoun (see chapter 2, section 2.1.5)
NOM	=	Nominalizer
NP	=	Noun phrase
PART	=	Participle (a nominalizer which includes among its uses something like the participial uses of *-ing* in English)
PAST1	=	1st past tense (Action occurred a few weeks ago)
PAST2	=	2nd past tense (″ ″ a few months ago)
PAST3	=	3rd past tense (distant past)
PERF	=	Perfective
PL	=	Plural (rare nominal suffix)
PNP	=	Pre-predicate or pre-head noun phrase
Post-NP	=	Post-posed noun phrase
POT	=	Potential (subsumes desiderative and abilitative)
PPRO	=	Pre-predicate pronoun
PRO	=	Pronoun
PROX1	=	1st degree of proximity (when attached to verbs indicates that action occurred earlier in the day of speaking. When attached to other elements, including predicate nominals, indicates that action occurred in a location close to the speaker.)
PROX2	=	2nd degree of proximity (on verbs indicates action occurred a day or so ago, on other elements indicates action occurred farther away from speaker.)
QP	=	Yes/no question particle
RD	=	Referential distance
REFL	=	Reflexive (second paradigm only)
REL	=	Relativizer
REP	=	Repetition (enclitic meaning "again" or "also")
SW	=	Sound word (idiophones, or onomatopoeic expressions)
TRNS	=	Transitivizer
VC	=	Verb coding

Chapter 1

INTRODUCTION

1.1. Aims and organization

This study concerns Yagua, a lowland language of Perú, and the choices speakers make as to how they refer to or "code" participants in discourse. The body of the work is organized into two parts, corresponding to these two general concerns. In the first part, consisting of Chapters 2 and 3, I describe the formal devices used to code participants in Yagua. This part partially meets the need for accurate descriptive data on Yagua, a relatively unstudied Amazonian language. In the second part, Chapters 4 through 7, I examine the use of a subset of those devices in a body of folkloric narrative texts, developing and refining certain hypotheses emerging in the functional analysis of discourse. As starting point for the textual study, I take the framework and methodology developed by Givón (1983a, b, c, d) for measuring topicality in terms of the indices of REFERENTIAL DISTANCE and PERSISTENCE. Deviations from the general predictions of Givón's framework are then examined in some detail. In Chapter 4 the methodology is outlined and the basic findings presented. Chapter 5 gives specific examples that seem to violate claims made in the general theory of topic continuity; in Chapter 6 the discourse function of one particularly interesting clause type is examined, and in Chapter 7 the use of pre-predicate pronouns is discussed. Finally, in Chapter 8, I summarize the findings of the previous chapters and present some possible directions for future research.

The general conclusion made in Chapter 8 is that the two indices of topicality considered in Chapter 4 in fact measure two independent functional domains. Referential Distance is sensitive to the functional domain properly termed CONTINUITY, i.e., the pragmatic availability or givenness of a participant at any given point in a text. Persistence, on the other hand, measures DEPLOYABILITY, i.e., the likelihood of that participant's being repeatedly mentioned in subsequent text. Whereas continuity looks backward to previous mentions of a participant, deployability looks forward to subsequent mentions. Though these domains are related, they are logically distinct: high continuity does not imply high deployability, and vice versa. In fact, the formal coding scale of phonological size (Givón 1983a) is reversed for these two domains: highly continuous participants are coded with phonologically smaller devices, while highly deployable participants are coded with phonologically larger devices. Therefore it is hardly appropriate to consider the two indices (Referential Distance and Persistence) as refering to a single functional domain such as "topicality."

Within the domain of continuity, it is found that statistically there is really only a two-way distinction between the functions of various coding devices, rather than a true continuum. The distinction is between "long-range" and "short-range" devices. The reason that more than two devices exist is that functional pressures other than

1

continuity impinge upon the system. In particular, contrastiveness, deployability, thematic groupings (such as episodes and locational scenes), and episodic climax are discussed at some length.

In the remainder of this Chapter, I briefly introduce the reader to the Yaguas, and to previous work relevant to the concerns of this study. I also outline theoretical assumptions that underlie this work at every stage.

1.2. The Yagua people: demography and sociolinguistic context

Currently, the Yagua live in some 30 communities dispersed throughout a section of the Peruvian and Colombian Amazon basin which can roughly be described as a rectangle 330 km wide and 580 km long (191,000 km^2) extending southward from the 2nd to the 5th parallels and westward from the 70th to the 75th meridians (Paul Powlison 1969; see Figure 1). As for the present-day population, I estimate that approximately 3,000 people would identify themselves as Yaguas; and of these perhaps 75% of the women and 25% of the men are monolingual in Yagua, the rest being bilingual in Spanish to varying degrees.

There are two possible etymologies for the term 'Yagua,' both of which originate outside of the Yagua language. First, the Quechua term *yawar* meaning 'blood' or 'the color of blood' is a likely possibility because of the Yaguas' custom of painting their faces with *achiote*, the blood-red seeds of the annatto plant (*bixa orellana*). During the pre-conquest period the Yaguas were undoubtedly in close contact with the Incas, as to this day there are far more Quechua (Inca) words in Yagua than there are Spanish words. The term in Quechua would have been something like *yawar runa*, 'the blood-red people,' which could easily have been assimilated into Spanish as *yagua*. Second, *yagua* in Spanish means 'royal palm,' and this term might have been applied to the Yaguas by the Spanish explorers since much of the Yagua traditional clothing is made of palm fiber. Unfortunately, as there is no data on whether a name resembling *yagua* was first used by the Quechuas or the Spanish, there is no principled way to distinguish between these two possible etymologies. The only native term that might be thought of as a self-referent is *nijyąąmíy* 'people.' This word is often used in contrast with *mááy* 'white people' and *munuñúmiy* 'savages,' 'enemies,' or 'non-Yagua Indians.' However, *nijyąąmíy* is also clearly the generic term for all human beings. Currently the term 'Yagua' is recognized by all Yaguas and is for all intents and purposes the contemporary self-referent.

The earliest documented European contact with the Yaguas was probably made by the Spanish explorer Francisco de Orellana in January of 1542. While exploring in the area of modern-day Pebas, Orellana encountered a village called Aparia and captured two chiefs named Aparia and Dirimara, as well as some others (Medina 1934:257). These names could conceivably have come from the Yagua words *(j)ápiiryá* 'red macaw clan' and *rimyurá* 'shaman', respectively. The former could very well be a village name as well as a name applied to an individual; clan names are still used by many Yaguas as family names. The word for shaman might also be used to refer to an individual, especially one singled out as a "chief." Regular European contact began in

1686 with the establishment of a Jesuit mission at San Joaquín de los Omagua, on an island in the Amazon river probably near what is now the mouth of the Ampiyacu river (Jean-Pierre Chaumeil 1981:18). Though this mission was established to serve the Omagua people, there was undoubtedly contact with the Yaguas as well. From the 17th century to the last half of the 19th century, European contact with the Yaguas was mainly through the Jesuit and Franciscan missionaries. In the early 18th century, Portuguese raiding parties attacked the Spanish missions throughout the Amazon region, causing much dispersion of the tribes that were in contact with the Spanish and inflicting severe casualties (Espinosa 1955).

The present extreme geographic dispersion of the Yaguas, however, is due largely to the effects of the "rubber boom" in the late 19th and early 20th centuries. At that time Europeans arrived in large numbers from Brazil and began to exploit the indigenous people to extract natural latex from the jungle. Many Yaguas died in conflicts with these Europeans, as well as by exposure to European diseases. Others were exploited as slave labor. Still others fled to remote regions of the jungle. Ever since the rubber boom, the Yagua sense of unity and of common culture has declined. The tremendous distances between villages make it very difficult for Yaguas to have consistent interaction with Yaguas from other villages. All economic activity outside of the village is with non-Yagua peoples, usually Spanish-speaking "mestizos." Thus there is economic and social pressure to learn Spanish and assimilate to the general Peruvian culture. Villages are also characteristically small (2 to 30 families). This fact further limits the breadth of interaction with other Yaguas and increases the tendency to want to reach out beyond one's village for social and economic advantages.

However, the Yagua culture and language do continue to be viable, especially in some of the larger and more isolated communities. Many children grow up speaking only Yagua, and native artistry is a significant economic activity. Approximately 20 women and nearly the same number of men wear traditional Yagua clothing on a daily basis. There is no doubt, however, that because of geographic dispersion combined with economic and sociolinguistic pressures, the use of the Yagua language is declining. I estimate that the children now growing up in monolingual homes will speak Yagua for the rest of their lives, but I doubt that their children will. For this reason, I informally estimate that the language will continue to be a medium of everyday communication in at least some communities for approximately 60 years.

1.3. The Yagua language

1.3.1. Genetic classification

Greenberg (1960), Loukotka (1968), and Voegelin and Voegelin (1977) all classify Yagua as the only extant member of the Peban or Peba-Yaguan language family of the Ge-Pano-Carib Phylum. Kaufman (1990:42) places Yagua within the "Yawan" family, possibly a member of the Sáparo-Yawa stock of his Northern Foothills region of Amazonia. The only closely related languages that have been documented are Peba (Rivet 1911) and Yameo (Espinosa 1955), both of which are now extinct. Greenberg's classification of Peba-Yaguan as part of the Ge-Pano-Carib phylum (on which both Loukotka's and Voegelin and Voegelin's seem to be based) is not supported by any concrete evidence, and thus is not to be considered authoritative. In fact, the very existence of the Ge-Pano-Carib and Andean-Equatorial phyla has not been sufficiently documented, and therefore offers no real help in identifying the more distant genetic relations of Yagua. Doris Payne (1984) has made some intriguing observations indicating a possible connection with the Zaparoan languages, purportedly part of the Andean-Equatorial phylum, but these observations have yet to be corroborated by an in-depth research program. Even if Yagua and the Zaparoan languages were shown to be related genetically, the relationship would certainly be very distant. Historical reconstruction and genetic classification of the languages of the Amazon region are definitely areas where much research is needed (cf. Kaufman 1990, Doris Payne 1990). This research will require much more consistent and accurate descriptions of these languages than are now available. For the purposes of this study, I assume that Yagua has no extant relatives, and further issues of genetic classification will not be considered.

1.3.2. Dialects

Data discussed in this study come primarily from two dialect areas: (1) "downriver" dialects, spoken in the vicinity of Caballococha, near where the Amazon River crosses into Colombia, and (2) "upriver" dialects, spoken from about Pebas up to about Iquitos. There is a certain degree of homogeneity within these two general dialect areas, though they are quite distinct from each other, especially if opposing extremes are compared. Dialect differences lie mostly in the phonology and in the phonetics of specific lexical items, though certain grammatical differences have been noted. Detailed dialect comparison will not be attempted in this study, but significant dialectal variations will be noted when appropriate.

1.3.3. Transcription and morphophonemics

The transcription used in Yagua examples is a modification of the current official Yagua orthography used for educational purposes by the Ministry of Education. The primary modifications I introduce are the specification of vowel length and tone, both of which are important to the phonology of the language. Other modifications are the use of *k* for the voiceless velar stop instead of the Spanish qu/c, and consistent specification of the phoneme *y*. The latter sound is omitted in certain environments in the official orthography, because in some of those environments it is practically inaudible and in others it is predictable from the context. I have retained the use of *v* for the labiovelar approximate and the Spanish-based use of *j* for the pharyngeal approximate simply because I am used to these transcriptions, and they are completely consistent (unlike the use of *qu/c* for the velar stop).

The following conventions are observed in presenting Yagua examples: (1) Four lines of information appear with most examples: (a) a surface phonemic representation, without morpheme divisions; (b) a morphemic representation giving the underlying forms of all the morphemes and the boundaries between them; (c) a morpheme-by-morpheme English gloss; and (d) a free English translation. To save space, line a is omitted when morphophonemic alteration of the underlying forms is nonexistent or minimal. The texts given in Appendices 1 and 2 present only three lines of data: a surface phonemic representation with approximate morpheme boundaries indicated, a gloss line, and a free translation. (2) Morpheme boundaries in the Yagua morphemic representations and the English glosses are indicated by hyphens (-). (3) When more than one English word must be used to indicate the meaning of a single Yagua morpheme, a colon (:) is inserted between the English words. (4) Most morphemes are glossed in such a way that their approximate meanings are transparent. However, common recurring forms are given abbreviated glosses indicated in upper-case letters; a list of these abbreviations is given in the introductory pages of this work.

I would like to emphasize that the morpheme glosses are meant only as a help to the reader. They do not necessarily represent an all-inclusive analysis of the meanings of morphemes. I have attempted, insofar as possible, to gloss morphemes in such a way that the most general meanings are represented in the glosses, e.g., "proximity" seems to be the most general concept that unites the tense and locational meanings of the PROX1 and PROX2 morphemes. However, it is not always possible to determine the "basic" meaning of a form by looking at all its various uses. Also, the morphemic representation (the second line of data in most examples) assumes that morphemes are isolatable "chunks" of phonological material corresponding in a direct way with chunks of meaning. I recognize that this assumption cannot be made for all languages, as Anderson (1982) demonstrates. There are situations even in Yagua where this assumption breaks down. However, for the most part Yagua morphology can be adequately and insightfully analyzed as consisting of strings of meaningful formal units. Because of the various phonological and morphophonemic processes that alter the shapes of morphemes in those strings, I have elected to include the morphemic representation in order to aid the reader in understanding the examples.

Three forms remain unglossed in the examples. These are *jįįta*, *day*, and *niy*. *Jįįta* is a discourse-structuring particle that correlates highly with thematic breaks at various levels (Doris Payne 1989). Day is discussed briefly in footnote 6 of Chapter 2. *Niy* is described in Chapter 2, section 2.1.5. I have not been able to gloss these forms in a satisfying way with terms available within linguistic tradition. As an interim convention I have simply repeated these forms in capital letters in the morpheme-by-morpheme glosses. Doris Payne (1989) provides a comprehensive analysis of the use of *jįįta* from a discourse perspective. The same sort of study with respect to *niy* and *day* is certainly in order. However, since these forms clearly function outside of the domain of participant coding, I will not attempt such a study here.

The orthographic symbols used in the Yagua examples are given in charts A and B:

Chart A: Consonant Phonemes					
	Bilabial	Dental	Palatal	Velar	Pharyngeal
Vcls stops	p	t	ty	k	
Vcd stops	b	d	dy		
Nasals	m	n	ñ		
Fricatives		s	ch		
Approx.	v				j
Glide			y		
Flap		r			

Chart B: Vowel Phonemes			
	Front	Central	Back
High	i	ï	u
Mid	e	o	
Low		a	

Phonemic vowel nasalization is indicated by a nasal hook (ą). Vowel length is indicated by orthographic doubling. In the surface phonemic representation, high tone is indicated by an acute accent (á) and low tone by no accent. In the morphemic representation, three vowel types are distinguished on the basis of tone: (1) vowels which always carry low tone, indicated by a grave accent (à); (2) vowels which always carry high tone, indicated with an acute accent (á); and (3) vowels whose surface tone varies, indicated by no diacritic. The phonological and morphophonemic analysis assumed throughout this study is found in T. Payne (1983b).

1.4. Data base of the study

Insofar as possible, all data in the study are from texts, though elicited material is used to fill in certain crucial gaps and to illustrate simple, completely straightforward forms. Textual data are from texts collected either by Doris Payne and myself during our two years with the Yaguas, or by Paul Powlison, primarily between 1952 and 1956. The former texts comprise approximately 934 clauses or nonclausal conversational turns, and are primarily from the downriver dialect area. These data have all been entered onto computer disk in a linguistically oriented data-base format. Most are folkloric or personal-experience narratives, though there are some conversational, hortatory, and procedural texts. The Powlison texts consist of over 7,000 clauses of folkloric and personal-experience narratives, and are primarily from the upriver dialect area; an exhaustive morpheme-based concordance provides excellent accessibility to relevant examples. Additional data sources include the unpublished Yagua-Spanish and Spanish-Yagua dictionaries produced by the Powlisons (2,889 and 3,529 entries respectively), supplementary dictionaries produced by ourselves (Yagua-Spanish, 502 entries; Spanish-Yagua, 501 entries), and our personal field notes.

Four texts appear in the appendices of this work, two in Yagua with glosses and translations and the other two in a fairly literal English clause-by-clause translation. These last two, the One-Eyed Warriors and the Twins Cycle, are long, and the Yagua text of the Twins Cycle (Appendix 4) is given by Paul Powlison (1969), who describes both tales in some detail. For these reasons, I have elected not to include the full Yagua versions of these last texts; I consider the English translations to be sufficient for illustrating thematic structure. Examples in the work that come from any of the appended texts are labeled with a reference in parentheses to the text and the clause number within the text. For example FSQ10 is clause 10 of the First Squirrel text (Appendix 2). Examples from other sources, including other texts, are not so labeled.

1.5. Previous research

Because this study involves two general areas of interest, there are essentially two broad categories of previous research that I will draw from: (1) descriptive work and (2) more theoretical work. The first category is further divided into previous descriptive work on Yagua and a descriptive framework within which the data is organized. The second category pertains to the tradition of discourse analysis that forms the basis for Chapters 4 through 7. In the following two sections of the present chapter I briefly review the literature and attempt to outline my assumptions relevant to the two major divisions of this work.

1.5.1. Background to Chapters 2 and 3

1.5.1.1. Previous work on Yagua

The major anthropological treatments of the Yagua are Tessmann (1930) and Fejos (1943). Both works are comprehensive and generally reliable. Neither one, however, deals in any depth with the topic of folklore and/or mythology, much less linguistics.

Paul Powlison (1969, and an abridged version in 1987) is undoubtedly the most comprehensive and reliable source on Yagua folklore and mythology. His 1969 work contains transcriptions and translations of two tales in the standard orthography as it stood at that time. The Twins Cycle (Appendix 4 of this work) is a retranslation of one of these tales. Powlison's work is based on a much larger body of texts collected in situ over a period of about four years. His hypothesis is that Yagua folklore exhibits characteristics of true epic literature, as defined in the classical tradition, and he cites various structural and conceptual similarities between Yagua folklore, as represented by his sample, and classical epic literature such as the Iliad and the Odyssey as proof. Powlison concludes that all that is needed for Yagua folklore to be considered truly epic would be for one author to codify the various recurring episodes into one, unified whole. This is essentially what Homer is presumed to have done in the Greek tradition. Powlison is pessimistic, however, of this ever happening in the Yagua context, because of the lack of education among the Yaguas and the general cultural decline that is currently taking place.

Paul Powlison's published linguistic work on Yagua consists of one paper on palatalization (1962), another applying Propp's (1958) principles of paragraph analysis to a Yagua folktale (1965), and a third in collaboration with Esther Powlison on the number system (1958 and 1961). Esther Powlison has also published one paper on Yagua suprasegmental phonology (1971). Various unpublished works by the Powlisons are listed in the bibliography of the Summer Institute of Linguistics, Perú branch (Wise and Shanks 1977). One of these is a tagmemically-oriented grammar sketch by Paul Powlison, which, though it contains many significant details about the language, remains a tentative, unpolished description. Everett (1989) gives an account of constituent order and related syntactic phenomena in terms of the Principles and Parameters approach of Government and Binding theory, based entirely on data obtained from unpublished versions of my work and that of Doris Payne.

Josette and Jean-Pierre Chaumeil and Annemarie Seiler-Baldinger are other scholars who have worked extensively with the Yaguas, and have still-unpublished work in the area of folklore and belief. The published joint work of the Chaumeils includes a valuable bibliography (1976a) and several other short works in Spanish. Jean-Pierre Chaumeil's major published contribution to date is a detailed monograph on Yagua migrations since the 17th century (1981). He is currently working on a book of Yagua mythology which also promises to be a major contribution. Annemarie Seiler-Baldinger has contributed much in the area of material culture (1979), and somewhat to the migratory question (1976). She is currently continuing her research on Yagua migrations, and is reportedly collaborating with the Chaumeil's on a work relating the Yagua belief system to the material culture (J-P. Chaumeil, pers. comm.).

1.5.1.2. A descriptive framework

In discussing Yagua clause structure, the descriptive framework adopted is that which is emerging within the subfield of typological-functional linguistics. In this section a few terms from that tradition that will be essential to the following discussion are defined.

A PARTICIPANT, as used in this work, is a typically animate entity referred to in discourse. In a sentence such as 'John kissed Mary,' the referents of the terms John and Mary are participants. In practice, we will be concerned primarily with animate participants that are referred to repeatedly. A PARTICIPANT CODING DEVICE (sometimes termed simply "coding device") is any concrete linguistic expression (including the conspicuous absence of any phonetic material) that serves to mention, i.e., CODE, a participant. This term subsumes both full noun phrases and abbreviated forms such as pronouns, agreement markers and zeros. Occasionally the term "participant coding system" will refer to the set of devices, and their various possible combinations, that are available in a particular language. Participant coding is thus presented in conceptual opposition to other conceivable kinds of coding, such as perhaps "event" or "time" coding, and will delimit the domain of investigation of this work.

Throughout the study the terms A, O, S_a and S_o are used to refer to the "semantico-syntactic" roles associated with participants. The terms A, O, and S were first used by Silverstein (1976), but taken up and refined somewhat by Dixon (1979), who, as far as I know, first used the terms S_a and S_o. Dixon's definitions of these terms rest on several assumptions, mostly implicit, which I will attempt to list and explicate in the following paragraphs.

Dixon's first assumption that underlies the terms A, O, S_a and S_o is that the syntactic clause is the relevant unit of structure within which linguistic primes can be isolated. This assumption is consistent with the view taken here that the clause is the concrete linguistic expression of the discourse SCENE (Fillmore 1977), i.e., a verb and its associated participant mentions (see section 1.5.2.3).

Second, even as the clause is the linguistic instantiation of a scene, so an ARGUMENT is the linguistic instantiation of a participant. The terms A, O, S_a and S_o presuppose that clauses have CORE ARGUMENTS and PERIPHERAL ARGUMENTS. This assumption is consistent with the notion that a language user can only primarily attend to a very limited amount of information at a time (Chafe 1987). Many participants may be on stage, but it is an empirical observation across languages that at most three participants can be attended to at once. Core arguments are traditionally termed subjects, objects, and indirect objects, while peripheral arguments are any obliques.

Third, these terms assume the existence of two prototypical clause types, those with one core argument (traditionally termed INTRANSITIVE) and those with more than one core argument (traditionally termed TRANSITIVE).

Finally, these terms assume that in any clause that has more than one core argument, one of the arguments is more agent-like, by virtue of either its inherent semantic features (e.g., animates are more agent-like than inanimates) and/or the semantic similarity of the verb to other verbs which activate similar scenes that clearly contain an agent role (e.g., the experiencer of the verb 'see' is more agent-like than the perceived item because the experiencer of functionally similar verbs such as 'watch,' 'scan,' etc., is also agentive).[1]

Given these assumptions, Dixon defines A, O, S_a, and S_o as follows: A is the most agent-like argument of a multi-argument clause, O is the next most agent-like argument (and in fact is not normally agent-like at all). The category of S arguments (i.e., S_a and S_o) encompasses all unique core arguments of single-argument clauses. S_a arguments are those that exert volition and control over the event expressed by the verb, e.g., 'John' in 'John ran.' S_o arguments are those that exert no such volition or control, e.g., 'John' in 'John died.'

The difference between the way I intend to use the terms A, O, S_a and S_o and the way Dixon uses them is rather minimal, and will not in any crucial way affect the presentation of the data. Dixon distinguishes the terms S_a and S_o semantically, whereas for Yagua it will be convenient to use the terms as labels for specific structures before drawing conclusions as to the semantic import of each structural type. That is, for Dixon, all S participants which are in fact agents are S_a; all S participants which are not agents are S_o. Particular languages (though not many, according to Dixon) make a morphosyntactic distinction based on this semantic distinction, though every such language has lexically determined exceptions. In Yagua, however, it is clearly not the case that the morphosyntactic distinction between S_a and S_o is always, or even predominantly, based on the semantic roles of the participants. Therefore, in Yagua the term S_a refers to unique arguments of intransitive clauses that are referred to by the same set of participant-coding devices as are A arguments, and S_o refers to unique arguments of intransitive clauses that are referred to by the same set of participant-coding devices as are O arguments. This phenomenon will be illustrated in Chapter 2, section 2.2.1.

1.5.1.3. Previous topic-continuity studies of lowland South American languages

There are at least two topic-continuity studies available on lowland South American languages: Aberdour (1985) on Apuriná (Arawakan, Brazil), and Derbyshire (1986) on Hixkaryana (Carib, Brazil). In Chapter 7 I discuss these works in the context of the functions of nondemonstrative free pronouns in discourse. It appears that Yagua and Hixkaryana are similar in that in both languages free pronouns are used rarely in discourse, and then only to code participants that are being contrasted with other possible referents. In Apuriná, on the other hand, pronouns are very common and serve a simple anaphoric, as opposed to contrastive, function.

1.5.2. Background to Chapters 4 through 7

It is difficult in principle to know where to begin in describing the evolution of a tradition. Traditions have no specific, easily observable starting points. Rather, they materialize out of a pool of ideas and evolve little by little into something definable as a tradition. In thinking about the theoretical tradition in which this study is cast, three works stand out: Joseph Grimes (1975), Chafe (1976) and Fillmore (1977). Clancy (1980) and Givón (1983a, b, c, and d) represent specific methodological and technical developments which hold deep significance for the present study. In this section I will attempt to describe the tradition that these works represent and how my work elaborates on that tradition.

1.5.2.1. The discourse as a structural unit

I will begin the discussion with Joseph Grimes' Thread of Discourse (1975). This work, like any other, is the product of a conglomerate of traditions, with strong influence from Generative Semantics, Systemics, and Tagmemics. Grimes, following Pike (1971), defines a discourse as a verbal "behavioreme," i.e., something that is recognized as a cohesive unit by a particular culture, and as such has definable beginning and end-points as well as internal structural characteristics. *The Thread of Discourse* is essentially an inventory of the ways in which discourses begin, end, and exhibit internal structure. One crucial contribution of Grimes' work, then, is the notion that discourse does have structure, and that linguists should not in principle avoid investigations of the structural characteristics of whole discourses simply because the field is too vast, or the principles appear to be too nebulous.

A recurring theme in Grimes' work is the interrelation of two principles which govern the structure of discourses: COHESION and PROMINENCE. Structural characteristics of discourses, be they semantic or morphosyntactic, can generally be divided into those that provide cohesion and those that provide prominence. Without cohesion a list of sentences would not be perceived as a text. Without prominence bits of information in a text would blur together into a hopeless mush. All research in discourse analysis recognizes that discourse is most naturally continuous (see, e.g., Givón 1983a, c, d). That is, we expect that any text will "hang together" in some way or another. We need to be able to link what is said in one sentence to what comes before it and what comes after. Speakers use various semantic and syntactic devices to establish such links. On the other hand, there must also be ways in which discontinuity is expressed. Even as cohesion allows discourse to flow smoothly, prominence (or discontinuity) provides rhythm, texture, and depth.

1.5.2.2. Givenness and participant-coding

In discussing the use of various participant-coding devices, both Grimes and Chafe (1976) observe that more "attenuated"[2] forms of reference are used for items that the speaker perceives the hearer already has "available" in his or her consciousness. Thus, for example, the use of a pronoun rather than a full noun phrase conveys to the hearer that the speaker is referring to something that should already be available at some near-surface level of consciousness. A pronoun is therefore a cohesive device in that it provides a link between the sentence in which it occurs and something that has already been established (i.e., made "available"). Both authors propose a categorical either-or notion of availability: pronouns are used for entities that are available (or given), and full noun phrases are used for entities that are not available (or new). Neither of these works takes these ideas to the point of postulating an explicitly defined scale of availability corresponding to a scale of attenuation. This is precisely what Givón (1983a, c, d) has done.

In Givón's view, availability is a scalar notion: participants are more or less available at any given point in a discourse. The more available a particular bit of information is in memory, the easier it is to retrieve. The easier something is to retrieve, the more "attenuated" the form of the device used to retrieve it is likely to be. This line of reasoning is based on the universal "principle of least effort": "Expend only as much energy on a task as is required for its performance" (Givón 1983c:18). Full noun phrases are assumed to require more effort to produce than pronouns since noun phrases are "larger," both semantically and phonologically.

Chafe (1976:32-33) has the following to say regarding the ways in which one might approach a systematic examination of the effect of "givenness" on the choice between full noun phrase and pronominal reference in discourse:

The question of what causes the speaker to believe that an item has left the addressee's consciousness needs systematic examination (Chafe 1974:127-32). It would not be difficult to examine tape recorded speech with this question in mind, and to look for instances where something previously treated as given is later treated as new. The number of intervening sentences in which the item was not mentioned is one obvious variable, but more interesting would be the effect of such discourse boundaries as a change of scene, where a whole new set of items can be assumed to enter the consciousness of the addressee, presumably pushing out old ones.

Clancy (1980), working under Chafe, takes up the challenge represented in the above quote and actually measures the discourse distance in sentences and clauses between the various references to a participant in Japanese and English narratives, and calculates mean values for the degree of distance for noun phrases, pronouns (for English), and ellipsis (for Japanese). Furthermore, Clancy makes a serious attempt to come to grips with higher-level discourse structure (sometimes referred to as "thematic structure"), in that she also measures the effects of various kinds of high-level discourse boundaries on the choice of coding devices. Finally, Clancy also measures the number of mentions of other participants between one mention and another of a given participant, and records the effects of this measurement on coding choices. This measurement she terms "interference". Thus Clancy is the first to empirically validate, using quantitative data from actual texts, the intuitive claims of Grimes and Chafe concerning the effect of givenness (or "availability") on the choice between noun phrases and more attenuated coding devices. Givón (1983a,c,d) builds on Clancy's methodology for assigning quantitative values to the degree of availability of various participants. His central contribution, however, is that he provides functional principles that predict exactly the results that the quantitative studies in Clancy (1980), Givón (1983b) and elsewhere show (see Chapter 4, sections 4.1 and 4.2 for a more detailed discussion of Givón's theory and methodology).

1.5.2.3. Some recurring metaphors

I believe that we must choose our metaphors carefully, since they to a large extent determine our view of reality. A metaphor can help us understand a phenomenon by putting limits on our conceptualization of its nature. However, we must always keep a metaphor in perspective, and be willing to exchange it for a new way of approaching a phenomenon when our understanding reaches the limits of that metaphor's usefulness. For example, in trying to understand how a pocket calculator works, we could use the metaphor of an abacus. We might be able to explain a good deal of the output of the calulator by supposing, at least temporarily, that it functions like an abacus. However, there must come a point at which the abacus metaphor will fail us, and we must either revise our metaphor or be content with a limited understanding of the calculator.

The phenomena that Chafe, Clancy, Givón and others are concerned with are the cognitive processes involved in discourse production. More specifically, these and the present work are concerned with the process of keeping track of participants in discourse. Many metaphors have been used to describe aspects of this process, most of them based on mechanico-computational phenomena. For example, Du Bois

(1980:220) uses the metaphor of a filing system. When a participant is introduced into the discourse, a "cognitive file" may be opened for that participant. Some coding devices serve to introduce participants, but without opening a cognitive file for them. Once a file has been opened for a participant, however, that participant can be referred to at will with attenuated coding devices. This particular metaphor has been used by several other writers, including Chafe and Givón.

Givón (1983a, c, d) uses the metaphor of a discourse "register." Whenever a participant is mentioned it is "registered," to some degree or another, in memory. Different coding devices may register participants more strongly than others, and each mention establishes a given participant more firmly in the register. If a participant is not mentioned in a given clause, it begins to "decay," i.e., its prominence decreases. Prolonged lack of mention renders a participant "absent from the register," and any subsequent mention must treat that participant as if it were being introduced as new information.

Chafe (1987) uses the terms "already active" in place of "given" information, and "previously inactive" in place of "new" information. This terminology is adopted in order both to clear the air of much confusion of terminology in this area and also to capture the sense that givenness has ultimately to do with the status of information in the mind. Various morphosyntactic coding devices are said to shuttle information among three stages of activation: (1) previously inactive, (2) previously semi-active, and (3) already active information. Hence Chafe assumes a view of discourse as an ongoing computational process which includes the assessment and assignment of various activation states to pieces of information.

The major metaphor and recurrent theme of the present study is that discourse depicts a world that can metaphorically be described as a stage on which a play is being acted out. This view is consistent with that of Fillmore (1977), who claims that verbs with their unique case frames activate "scenes" (another dramaturgical metaphor) in the minds of language users. This metaphor appeals to me for several reasons. First, it is especially appropriate for the description of narrative discourse. In narrative the story teller creates and manipulates a "story world" (Clancy 1980) in which participants come, go, and interact. This is very similar to what happens in a formal drama; the house-lights dim and the audience is transported to another "world" in which events are manipulated by others. Second, it seems to me that "presence on stage" is a more appropriate metaphor than, e.g., "presence in the register" in that participants can be on or off stage independently of the number of times they have been mentioned previously. For example, a narrator may shunt a participant "off stage" by the use of a clause like 'he left,' or 'he died.' The content of such a clause renders the participant less likely to be mentioned again in the next clause, even though that participant may be very strongly registered at that point. Finally, storytelling has more in common functionally, it seems to me, with formal dramatization than with computerized data processing. The narrator of a story accomplishes socio-cultural tasks that are very similar to those accomplished by the formal dramatist, e.g., entertainment, instruction, socialization, etc. If we view storytelling as similar, even metaphorically, to the process involved in formal dramatization, we are closer to the functional roots of the cognitive process we are trying to describe than if we use a mechanico-computational metaphor.

All of the above views are no more than metaphors. They are all useful in their own ways in helping us to understand something about the cognitive processes involved in discourse comprehension and production. However, we err if we take any of these metaphors so seriously as to mistake them for reality. The human mind does not necessarily function like a computer any more than a hand calculator functions like an abacus. We will never fully understand the workings of the human mind until and unless we develop the technology to examine the cognitive and biological systems involved with appropriate scrutiny and detail.

1.6. Summary

The Amazon region represents a significant gap in current knowledge of languages of the world. Although approximately 6.5% of the living languages of the world are spoken in lowland South America (Barbara Grimes 1984:xv), typological studies rarely include languages from this region. Yagua is one of the many languages of lowland South America for which little in the way of descriptive material is available. It is hoped that the present work will partially fulfill this need for solid descriptive material.

Research in the quantitative analysis of texts, and the use of anaphora in discourse, has advanced to the stage where cross-language comparison of participant-coding systems is now possible. The present work contributes to this area of investigation by providing further empirical text-based data from a previously little-studied language. It is also hoped that refinements to the methodologies proposed in this study will allow more exact measurements and incorporation of previously problematic data, such as reported speech, in future studies.

Notes to Chapter 1

[1] In fact, research by Du Bois (1981) shows that in actual discourse, subjects (A together with S in Dixon's terminology) are only occasionally agentive, or even agent-like. It may be a true generalization that if there is an agent (or an agent-like participant) in a clause, that participant is typically the subject, but from this we cannot infer the oft-proposed converse: subjects are typically agents. This kind of finding suggests that perspectivization is really closer to the actual conceptual basis for subjecthood than is agentivity -- and this, to me, is reasonable if we take the view that the categories we propose for a language should correspond to the categories that are relevant to the users of that language in actual discourse. If syntactic categories were based even loosely on semantic categories speakers would have a very difficult time assigning participants to the correct syntactic categories, given the range and complexity of semantic roles that participants play in events. Perspectivization, on the other hand, is a variable that the speaker can control, deciding which participants are going to be prominent and which peripheral in any given clause. It stands to reason that formal categories such as "subject" should be based on criteria that language users are actually sensitive to. Perspectivization is definitely more elusive than semantic roles to the linguist constrained by traditional linguistic methodology, i.e., analysis of texts as artifacts of behavior. However, recent studies by Tomlin (1985), and others are attempting to empirically verify such categories through psycholinguistic experimentation. I have no doubt that future work in this area will uncover many new methodologies and hypotheses involving the relationship between perspectivization and syntactic categories.

[2] The term "attenuated" here refers to both semantic and phonological attenuation. For example, a pronoun is semantically attenuated in that it codes only a limited number of semantic features of its referent, typically person and/or number. Pronouns are also phonologically attenuated in that they are characteristically "smaller," i.e., have fewer phonemes, than full noun phrases.

Chapter 2

CODING DEVICES

The term coding devices (Givón 1983a) will refer here to all formal devices used to code participants. These include noun phrases, pronouns, verb coding ("agreement"), head coding (for possessors and oblique objects), enclitics (for O and S_o arguments), zero, and all combinations and ordering permutations thereof. Zero as a coding device refers to the conspicuous absence of any morphological material in a position where mention of a participant is clearly implied. In this chapter I will introduce and illustrate these coding devices in simple constructions. Not all of the devices presented here will enter into the discussion of the use of coding devices in discourse in Chapters 4 through 6, as not all are represented in the corpus in sufficient numbers to make significant discourse-based generalizations.

Attributive nouns (i.e., "modifiers" including numerals, demonstratives, and descriptive adjectives) can serve as heads of noun phrases when accompanied by a noun classifier (Doris Payne 1986):

(1)   a.   Súduu-bii-numáá-ra.
            ripe-CL:sprout-now-INAN
            'The sprout/stalk is now ripe.'

        b.   Naada-júúrįį   ru-nu-jųy.
            3DL-arise:early   DEMO-CL:HUMAN-DL
            'Those two (people) arose early.'

In 1a, the classifier -bii can be thought of as the only reference to the head of the predicate nominal súduubii, with súduu functioning as a modifier. Similarly, in 1b, the form -nu can be thought of as anaphorically designating the head of the noun phrase, with the other components serving as kind of an ambifixal modifier. This phenomenon is described as an anaphoric use of classifiers by Doris Payne (1986 and 1987). In the present study, attributive nouns combined with classifiers are not distinguished from other full noun phrases.

2.1. A and S_a coding

As mentioned in Chapter 1, A is defined as the most agent-like argument of a multi-argument (transitive) clause, and S is defined as the unique argument of a single-argument (intransitive) clause. S_a arguments in Yagua are those S arguments that take the same set of coding devices as do A arguments. The devices that code A and S_a arguments in Yagua are: verb coding (VC), pre-predicate noun phrase (PNP), verb coding plus post-predicate noun phrase (VC+NP), zero, pre-predicate pronoun (PPRO), right-dislocated pronoun (RDPRO, often occurring with the enclitic -day), and right-dislocated noun phrase (RDNP). The right-dislocated PRO and NP are marked devices that occur very rarely, and then only in combination with one of the other devices. All of these coding devices will be illustrated in the following subsections.

2.1.1. Verb coding (VC)

The basic forms of the verb-coding prefixes are identical to the head coding prefixes used on nouns to code possessors (section 2.3.1) and on postpositions to code their objects (section 2.4.1). These basic forms are illustrated in Chart C:

		1st		2nd	3rd	COR	inan
	excl.		incl.				
Sg.		ray-		jiy-	sa-		
Dl.	nááy-		vu̧u̧y-	sá̧a̧da-	naada-	jíy-	rá-
						(no number	
Pl.	núúy-		vu̧u̧y-	jiryey-	riy-	distinction)	

Chart C: Verb-coding Prefixes[1]

The prefix *jíy-* is used when the argument is coreferential with the subject of a preceding verb or head of a preceding NP or postposition. This prefix is glossed as COR for "coreferential"; its functions are described in more detail in Chapter 3. Both *jíy-* and the inanimate prefix *rá-* do not vary for number.

There are four major classes of stems distinguished by the form of the initial syllable. Class I stems are all those whose initial syllable is a consonant other than *j* plus any vowel, or *j* plus the vowel *o*. The three other classes exhibit the initial stem syllables *ja*, *ji*, and *ju* respectively. No stems begin with the syllable *je* in their underlying form, and stems in *jo* inflect as class I stems.

The following examples illustrate the VC device with verb stems from each class:

(2) **Rañikyéé.**   'I speak.' (S$_a$)
     ray-nikyee   (class I, regular)
     1SG-speak

(3) **Sa̧atu   buyá̧á̧.**   'S/he drinks manioc beer.' (A)
     sa-jatu   buya̧a̧   (class II)
     3SG-drink manioc:beer

(4) **Vuryiimíy.**   'We eat.' (S$_a$)
     vurya-jimyiy[2]   (class III)
     1PLINC-eat

(5)   Suутúra.   'S/he carries it.'
        sa-jutú-rà   (class IV)
        3SG-carry-INAN

These prefixes may also occur on preverbal auxiliaries. In example 6, the first-person-inclusive prefix occurs with the irrealis auxiliary *a*, while in 7 the third-person-singular prefix occurs with the malefactive auxiliary -*niy*:

(6)   **Vuryaa**   jatú   buyáá.
        vurya-a   jatu   buyaa
        1PLINC-AUX:IRR   drink   manioc:beer
        'We will drink (or let's drink) manioc beer!'

(7)   **Saniy**   jiryiy   yímújura.
        sa-niy   jiryiy   yí-mu-jù-rà
        3SG-AUX:MALF   grab   COR-LOC-AL-INAN
        'He grabbed it to himself (to his own detriment, or with evil intentions).'

2.1.2. Pre-predicate noun phrase (PNP)

A full noun phrase that codes an A or S_a argument may precede the verb. Verb coding then may not code the same argument, as illustrated by the ill-formed strings following examples 8 and 9:

(8)   **Sa-munaa-dee**   kúútya.   'His placenta[3] whispers.'
        3SG-placenta-DIM   whisper (S_a)

        *Samunaadéé sakúútya.   'His placenta he whispers.'

(9)   **Jíryoonú**   súúyanníí   'A bushmaster (snake) bit him.'
        jíryoonú   súúy-janu-níí   (A)
        bushmaster   bite-PAST3-3SG

        *Jíryoonú sasúúyanníí.   'A bushmaster he bit him.'

2.1.3. Verb coding plus (post-predicate) noun phrase (VC + NP)

When verb coding is accompanied by the overt expression of a coreferential noun phrase within the clause, that NP must follow the verb:

(10)   **Sa**-suvúúy   **Anita**.   'Anita is afraid.'
        3SG-afraid   Anita (S_a)

(11)   **Sa**-nááyi   **Alchíco**-rà.   'Alchico presses it.'
        3SG-press   Alchico-INAN   (A)

Conversely, when a full NP coding an A or S$_a$ argument follows the verb, a verb-coding prefix is obligatory.[4] Thus it is not necessary to annotate the coding device here termed VC + NP as to whether the NP occurs postverbally or preverbally. It is a syntactic requirement that when an NP alone codes an A or S$_a$ argument, it must be preverbal. When the NP occurs in combination with a coreferential VC prefix, however, the NP must be postverbal.

A preliminary hypothesis regarding the use of the postverbal NP in addition to the VC prefix would be that the NP is uttered as an "afterthought" when the speaker judges that VC was not sufficient to uniquely distinguish the correct participant. However, there are four arguments against this analysis: (1) An inspection of texts reveals that the VC + NP forms are used more commonly, and in less marked discourse contexts than the simple NP constructions (see section 4.5.1). This would hardly be an expected characteristic of afterthought constructions. (2) VC + NP constructions are normally uttered under a single intonation contour, suggesting that they code a single focus of consciousness and therefore do not involve a reconsideration and partial restatement. (3) As illustrated in example 11, when an O argument occurs in the clause it must follow any overt subject NP. This indicates that the overt subject NP is at least as closely tied syntactically to the verb as is the O argument, which again is not a reasonable characteristic of afterthought subjects. (4) Finally, there is another device - right dislocated NP - that does, in fact, code afterthoughts, as evidenced by the fact that it is normally uttered under a new intonation contour and occurs very rarely in discourse (see section 2.1.7). Thus it appears that the afterthought hypothesis does not explain the function of the VC + NP constructions, at least as far as the synchronic grammar is concerned. In Chapter 5 I will attempt to distinguish the function of VC + NP coding devices from that of the others.

2.1.4. Zero

Zero as a coding device for A and S$_a$ arguments is rare in discourse. It occurs in nominalized complement clauses whose subjects are coreferential with the subject of another conceptually closely tied verb (see Chapter 3), but with independent verbal predicates it is quite rare. Oddly enough, when zero is used for A or S$_a$ arguments it does not necessarily indicate interclausal coreference. For example in clause 489 of the Twins Cycle (12b below), Placenta, transformed into a woodpecker, is trying to steal a pifayo seed from Grandfather. In example 12a there is no mention, overt or covert, of Placenta. Grandfather is just shooting in general, not specifically at Placenta:

(12)   a.   Váriy   sa-duu   vári-dyéy.
              then   3SG-shoot   then-DAY
              'Then he (Grandfather) shoots.' (TC488)

b. Múúy diiyą́ą́sityéé   pariché rííva   rátaditéé.
   múúy diiy-yąą-siy-téé   pariché rá-íva   rá-tadi-téé
   there find-DIST-DEP-INTS   finally INAN-DAT   INAN-seed-INT
   'There (Placenta) finally finds its seed.' (TC489)

In 12b there is absolutely no overt reference to Placenta, though he is clearly the agent of *diiy* 'find.'[5] Interestingly, this story continues with another couplet of clauses very similar to that illustrated in 12, but with Placenta receiving overt mention, and Grandfather being coded with a zero:

(13)   a. Sa-niy   maa-sii-ñumáá-ta   ruumu-síy,
            3SG-AUX:MALF   exit-run-now-when   there-from
            'When he (Placenta) rushes out of there (to his own detriment), (TC490)

        b. jásiy 0 dúúntyéé   váricharą́jųdañíí.
            jásiy 0 duu-ntyéé   váriy-sarąjų̀-day-níí
            there 0 shoot-right:there then-immediately-DAY-3SG
            right there (Grandfather) immediately shoots him.' (TC491)

Again, the use of zero coding for the A of 13b is not explainable in terms of an interclausal constraint on coreference, since the antecedent of the zero does not appear in the previous clause. However, the context of these clauses makes it clear who is acting upon whom, and thus no more specific coding device is, strictly speaking, necessary.

2.1.5. Pre-predicate pronoun (PPRO)

The forms of the independent pronouns in Yagua are quite similar to the forms of the verb-coding prefixes illustrated in Chart C. Chart D illustrates the independent pronouns:

	1st		2nd	3rd	COR	INAN
	ex	inc				
SG.		ráy	jíy	níí		
Dl.	nááy	vų́ų́y	sąądá	naadá	--	--
Pl.	núúy	vų́ų́y	jiryéy	ríy		

Chart D: Forms of Independent Pronouns

These pronouns can occur as integral clause constituents in prepredicate position, or right-dislocated (see section 2.1.6). In this section I will illustrate pre-predicate independent pronouns functioning to code A and S_a arguments.

Independent pronouns are used quite rarely in Yagua discourse as integral clause constituents. I hypothesize that they function in situations of EXCLUSIVE CONTRAST (see Chapter 7), as in the following examples. In example 14, two wasps have tried to spear a boa, using their stingers as spears, but are not able to penetrate his skin. So the hero of the story, a human being, grabs a real spear and says:

(14) **Ráy**   **jį́į́**   **rą**   **jachiñį́í,**   **rá.**
      ráy   jį́į́ta   rą   jachiy-nį́í   ra
      1SG:PRO   JIITA   IRR   spear-3SG   EXCL
      'I will spear him!' (KT65)

Here the 1st-person-singular pronoun *ráy* is used to indicate that the speaker will spear the boa where the other two have failed. An English translation with a stressed first-person pronoun roughly captures the flavor of this sentence.

In the following excerpt (from the Hunter's Narrative; see Chapter 4), the PPRO device is used twice. The immediately preceding context concerns a group of Yaguas who come upon a group of non-Yagua Indians. They wonder how they can speak with the non-Yaguas, since they don't know their language. Then another participant is introduced, a Yagua who happens to be with the group of non-Yaguas. He is contrasted with the other Yaguas because of his knowledge of Spanish:

(15)   a.   There is a certain Yagua person with them too.

        b.   **Nííniy**   **jį́į́ta**   **dáátyara**   **mááñikyeejadá.**
             níí-niy   jį́į́ta   dáátya-rà   maay-nikyee-jada
             3SG:PRO-NIY   JIITA   know-INAN   non:indian-speak-PART
             '**HE** (this new participant) knows Spanish.'

        c.   **Nííniy**   **nikyeetaríy**   **nijyąavay . . .**
             níí-niy   nikyee-ta-ríy   nijyąą-vay
             3SG:PRO-NIY   speak-TRNS-3PL   Yagua-PL
             '**HE** says to the Yaguas . . .'

The existential clause in 15a introduces the new participant, while 15b contrasts him with the other Yaguas, and 15c contrasts him with the other non-Indians. The basic form of the 3SG pronoun is *níí*. The clitic *-niy* in these examples is a second-position special clitic whose function is still under investigation. From a sentence grammar perspective, it seems to be semantically empty, in contrast to other clitics that may appear in the same position and which add various modal and adverbial senses to the clause. There is a homophonous auxiliary *niy* (see example 13a above) which I have termed "malefactive" since it implies that the action was carried out in anger or to the detriment of the subject. However, this malefactive form is clearly an auxiliary, since it takes verb coding (3SG = *sa-*), whereas the *-niy* in examples 15b and 15c follows the pronoun. Furthermore, there are no malefactive connotations to the latter two examples.

It is also significant that when the PPRO device is used, verb coding is precluded. In example 14 above the irrealis auxiliary is in the bare form *rą* which, the initial *r* notwithstanding, does not code the 1SG subject. Similarly, the verbs *dáátya* in example 15b and *nikyee* in 15c are uninflected for subject. This constraint also holds when the subject is coded by a preverbal NP, as discussed in section 2.1.2.

2.1.6. Right-dislocated pronoun *(+day)*[6]

A right-dislocated pronoun is never the primary coding device for a participant in a clause. Rather, it always recapitulates a previous mention within the same clause. Right-dislocated pronouns may occur under a different intonation contour from that of the clause with which they are associated. This intonational break is symbolized in the examples by a comma. Often, however, there is no noticeable intonational break, as in example 16 below. In these cases the particle *-day* typically occurs.

(16)   Tomáása   jį́į́ta   rą   jiyá,   néé   rąą   jiyá   **radyéy**.
       Tomáása   jį́į́ta   rą   jiya   néé   ra-ą   jiya   ray-day
       Tom   JIITA   IRR   go   NEG   1SG-IRR go   1SG-DAY
       'Tom is going; **I'm** not going.' (i.e., Tom is going instead of me.)

The right-dislocated pronoun device is common in information questions, e.g.:

(17)   Tą́ą́ratanaa   saduunúúyada
       tą́ą́ra-ta-numaa   sa-duu-núúy-jada
       what-INST-now   3SG-kill:blowgun-CONT-PAST3

                rajyę́ę́beñíí   javąądá,   **tą́ą́ratá**?
                ray-ją́ą́y-bay-níí   javąąda   tą́ą́ra-ta
                1SG-father-deceased-3SG   meat/animal   what-INST

       'With what did my father shoot animals, with what?'

(18)   Chį́į́   deenú   jų naachara   nááváy,   **chį́į́**   **deenú**?
       chį́į́   dee-nu   jų naay-sara   nááváy   chį́į́   dee-nu
       who   DIM-CF   cry-NOM   above   who   DIM-CF
       'Whose children are always crying above, whose children?'

In example 18, the possessor of 'children' is the participant being questioned. The right-dislocated echo is a full NP, though the question pronoun *chį́į́* is what is significant. The form *-deenu* just goes along for the ride.

2.1.7. Right-dislocated noun phrase (RDNP)

Occasionally a participant is coded with a full noun phrase occurring after all other clause constituents. Like right-dislocated pronouns, these noun phrases always recapitulate a mention of that participant inside the clause itself. For example:

(19)   Nííntyéé   súútyéé   jiyudáy,   **nuuvá**.
       níí-niy-téé   súúy-téé   jiyu-day   nuuvá
       3SG:PRO-NIY-INTS   call-INTS   here-DAY   toucan
       'HE really calls, the toucan.' (FSQ129)

(20) Rájaavyemáá,   yunúúy,   **mukutyunú**.
      rá-jáávye-maa   jiy-junúúy mukutyu-nú
      INAN-grow-PERF   2SG-see   pachaco-CL:tree
      'It had already grown, you see, the pachaco tree.'

These examples illustrate what I intuitively see as a true afterthought construction.

The right-dislocated NP device is also used for added detail, as in the following example:

(21) Jánnaridyeenú   siichíy,   **núútyįįdeerá**.
      jánnariy-dee-nú   siiy-siy   núúy-tįį-dee-ra.
      deer-DIM-MASC   run-DEP   spot-NOM:having-DIM-NOM
      'A little deer ran away, a little spotted one.'

In example 21, the recapitulating NP is not an afterthought in the usual sense of this term, since the reference to the deer is perfectly established by the pre-predicate NP. There are no other deer in the story that might compete as the referent of the subject NP. Rather the speaker simply wishes to describe the deer more fully, and so qualifies the clause with a right-dislocated NP which adds detail to the reference of the subject NP. See section 2.2.8 for examples of an RDNP device used for added detail with O arguments.

2.2. O and S_0 coding

As discussed in section 1.5.1.2, the term O refers to the syntactic role of the non-agent-like argument of a transitive clause. In traditional terms these can be thought of as transitive objects. In Yagua, subjects of predicate nominals, predicate locatives, etc., as well as certain intransitive verbal predicates (discussed in Chapter 6), receive the same morphosyntactic treatment as transitive objects. Such predicates have been termed S_0 PREDICATES following Dixon (1979), and the subject of such predicates is termed the S_0 argument. In Yagua, the devices which code O and S_0 arguments are: enclitic (E), post-predicate noun phrase (NP), enclitic plus NP (E+NP), zero, pre-predicate pronoun (PPRO), pre-predicate NP (PNP), pre-predicate NP plus enclitic (PNP+E), and right-dislocated NP (RDNP). The following sections illustrate each of the coding devices for O and S_0 arguments.

2.2.1. Enclitic (E)

O and S_0 arguments in Yagua may be coded with an enclitic attached to the last postverbal constituent. If no constituents (other than an NP coding the O or S_0 itself) occur after the verb, the enclitic occurs on the verb itself. If a coreferential full NP also occurs, it immediately follows the enclitic (see section 2.2.3). Chart E illustrates the paradigm for O and S_0 enclitics:

	1st		2nd	3rd	COR	INAN
	ex	inc				
Sg.		-ráy	-jíy	-níí		
Dl.	-nááy	-vų́ų́y	-sąądá	-naadá	-yù	-rà
					(no number	
Pl.	-núúy	-vų́ų́y	-jiryéy	-ríy	distinction)	

Chart E: Forms of O and S$_o$ Enclitics

Examples 22, 23, and 24 illustrate the enclitic device used to code O arguments of verbal predicates:

(22)   Ravyą́ą́ta-**jíy**.
        1SG:want-2SG
        'I like/love you.'

(23)   Sa-nááyi   Alchíco-**ra**.
        3SG-press   Alchico-INAN
        'Alchico is pressing it.'

(24)   Sa-jáátya   sínu-mu-**níí**.
        3SG-toss   land-LOC-3COL
        'He tosses them on the shore' (i.e., fish; hence
        the animate 3COL enclitic).

As mentioned above, subjects of predicate nominals and related constructions are treated morphosyntactically as direct objects, in that they also may be coded with an enclitic. The following examples illustrate some simple predicate nominals:

(25)   a.   Maésturu-**níí**.   'He is a teacher.'
              teacher-3SG

        b.   Maésturu-**ríy**.   'They all are teachers.'
              teacher-3PL

Examples 25a and 25b illustrate the simplest kind of predicate nominal construction. In these examples, the predicate nominal is *maésturu*, and the subject is coded with an enclitic. In the following example, the "copula" *day* appears. This particle may or may not be classifiable as the same *day* that functions as a discourse particle (see section 1.3.3). It is certainly not a verb since it has none of the properties characteristic of true verbs. However, it does frequently occur in predicate nominal constructions such as 26, and so I have glossed it "copula" following Powlison (1969) in such contexts.

(26)   Tomáása   báárya   dá**rya**.
        Tomáása   báárya   day-rà
        Tom   thing   COP-INAN
        'It is Tom's thing.' (It belongs to Tom.)

In example 26, the form *day* is fairly strongly demanded, though in isolation the sentence is acceptable to native speakers without the *day*. In 25a and b, *day* could occur immediately following the predicate nominal with no change in truth conditions or referential meaning.

Examples 27 and 28 illustrate the use of enclitics to code the subject of predicate locative clauses:

(27)   Vóóka-ncha-**níí**.
        cow-upon-3SG
        'He is on the cow.'

(28)   Rá-tuunu-dee-numaa-téé-**naadá**.
        INAN-beside-little-now-INTS-3DL
        'They (2) are right beside it now.'

In example 27, the predicate locative is *vóókancha* 'on the cow,' and the subject is coded with the 3SG enclitic *-níí*. In 28, the predicate locative is *rátuunudee* 'right beside it' and the subject is coded with the 3DL enclitic *-naadá*. The formative *numaa* is a second-position special clitic that modifies the sense of the predication. *Numaa* and several other second-position clitics are also used in verbal predicates (cf. example 13a; see Doris Payne 1990 for a detailed discussion of clitic placement in Yagua).

In addition to predicate nominals, many intransitive verbal predicates in Yagua can appear with S$_o$ coding, though S$_a$ coding is always allowed as well.

(29)   a.   Pariché **naada**-siimyaasíy   ráviïmusíy.   (S$_a$)
              pariche   naada-siiy-maasiy   rá-viïmu-siy
              finally   3DL-run-exit   INAN-inside-from
              'Finally they (2) rush out from inside.' (KT43)

        b.   Múúy   siimyaasityéé**níí**.
              muuy   siiy-maasiy-téé-níí
              there run-exit-INTS-3SG
              'There he really rushes out.' (FSQ106)

In example 29a, the compound verb stem *siimyaasíy* occurs with the VC prefix *naada-*, while in 29b the same stem occurs with an enclitic. Contrary to observations concerning S$_o$ coding on verbs in other languages, there is no necessary semantic difference between them such that 29a implies volition and control on the part of the subject whereas 29b does not. Both of these sentences clearly imply volition, action, and control.

When verbs occur with S$_o$ coding, they are formally parallel to nonverbal predications in that they may not indicate time reference. Certain time-reference suffixes may appear in S$_o$ predicates, but the meaning of these suffixes is then no longer that of time reference. For example, consider the following:

(30)   Nuuñííto̯o̯**jásiy**   musajomú.
        nuudya-jíto̯o̯-jásiy   musa-jo-mu
        1PLEX-arrive-PROX1   descend-NOM-LOC
        'We arrived (earlier today) at the port.'

(31)   Siijééñuveejá̯a̯**siy**   Mokáyu   sṵtajyariñaadá.
        siiy-jáa̯y-nuvee-ja-jásiy   Mokáyu   sṵtay-jariy-naada
        run-enter-ARR2-o'land-PROX1   Mokayu   shelter-into-3DL
        'They 2 run there (close by) into Mokayu's shelter on arrival.' (KT44)

In example 30, the PROX1 suffix *jásiy* expresses the time reference of 'earlier in the
day of speaking.' Notice that this is a single-argument clause with the VC prefix
indicating the S_a argument 'we.' Example 31, however, is an S_o predicate in that the
single argument 'they 2' is coded with an enclitic, *naadá*. The PROX1 suffix in 31
does not impart time reference, but rather specifies that the location of Mokayu's
shelter was near the place of the twins exit. This is consistent with the use of *jásiy*
(and many other suffixes) with predicate nominals and predicate locatives. For
example:

(32)   Ta̯a̯ri-ñiy   jásiy   sa-tuunu-naada.
        long:while-NIY   PROX1   3SG-side-3DL
        'They 2 are there at his side a long while.'

    Not: 'They 2 were (earlier today) at his side a long while.'

(33)   Tá̯á̯ra   sííva   jásiy?
        tá̯á̯ra   sa-íva   jásiy
        what   3SG-DAT   PROX1
        'What does he have there?' (lit.: 'What is to him there?')

    Not: 'What did he have (earlier today)?'

(34)   Ráju-ra   mákindya-jásiy.
        many-INAN   machine-PROX1
        'Lots of machines are there.'

    **Not*: 'Lots of machines were there (earlier today).'

These examples illustrate that verbal predicates with S_o coding have much in common
with predicate nominals. However, on semantic grounds we must say that such
predicates are not nominals. Specifically, there is no sense in which example 29b can
mean 'there is the rushed out one.' The stem *siimyaasíy* can only be interpreted as a
verb in that (1) it cannot fill the role of a noun phrase, e.g., subject or object, in a
clause; and (2) it must take nominalizing suffixes in order to fill such a role. This is
true for all verbs that can occur with S_o coding.

The use of a locative demonstrative (*múúy* in example 29b above) correlates highly, but not absolutely, with the presence of S$_o$ coding. Example 35 illustrates another S$_o$ verb with the locative demonstrative *múúy*:

(35) Múúy   kinchunuveejásiryíy.
      múúy   kinchu-nuvee-jásiy-ríy
      there   light:fire-ARR2-PROX1-3PL
      'There upon arrival they light a fire.' (KT53)

Occasionally, however, verbs occur with S$_o$ coding without a preceding locative demonstrative:

(36) Siiryịịdañíí   koodidyéé.
      siiy-rịị-day-níí   koodiy-dee
      run-in:passing-immediately-3COL   snake-DIM
      'Immediately the little snakes[7] scurried.'

(37) Kuutya-nuvaa-níí . . .
      whisper-ARR2-3SG
      'He whispers on arrival . . .'

In summary, we have seen that enclitics code three general classes of arguments: (1) objects of transitive verbs, (2) subjects of predicate nominals and predicate locatives, and (3) subjects of certain intransitive predicates based on verbal stems, but sharing many features of predicate nominals. Several observations and hypotheses emerge from these data on S$_o$ clauses. These hypotheses will be explored and a quantitative discourse-based study of S$_o$ coding on verbs will be undertaken in Chapter 6.

2.2.2. Post-predicate noun phrase (Post-NP)

A full post-predicate NP may code an O or S$_o$ argument, in which case an enclitic is "optional" from a sentence grammar perspective. The following examples illustrate the simple post-predicate NP device with no coreferential enclitic:

(38) Sạạtú   **buyậậ.**   'S/he drinks manioc beer.' (O)
      sa-jatu   buyạạ
      3SG-drink   manioc:beer

(39) Jiryimimyáá   **raryậậvạtá.**
      jiy-rimiy-maa   ray-rậậvạ-ta
      2SG-spill-PERF   1SG-poison-partitive
      'You spilled part of my poison!' (O)

2.2.3. Enclitic plus noun phrase (E + NP)

However, the enclitic can co-occur with a coreferential NP. This I will term the
E + NP device:

(40) Sa-suutá-**ra**   **sújay**.   'S/he washes the clothes.' (O)
      3SG-wash-INAN   clothes

(41) Maesturu-**níí** **Alcídes**.   'Alcides is a teacher.' (S$_o$)
      teacher-3SG   Alcides

When the E + NP device is used, the NP always immediately follows the enclitic,
and no constituent may intervene between the enclitic and the coreferential NP. These
facts constitute evidence that the enclitic forms a constituent with the following NP,
even though it is phonologically attached (cliticized) to whatever word precedes. I
have suggested in (Payne 1983a) that the difference between the E + NP and NP
constructions has to do with definiteness: the enclitic is used for definite Os and is not
used for indefinite Os. However, there are clear cases where definite Os are coded
without the enclitic and where indefinite Os are coded with the enclitic. For example,
possessed Os occur with or without the enclitic in about the same proportions. This
fact would not be expected if the presence of the enclitic were strictly dependent on
definiteness of the O, since possessed NPs are overwhelmingly definite (see, e.g.,
Du Bois 1980:208). Example 42a illustrates the use of a possessed O nominal without
a preceding enclitic, and 42b illustrates a possessed S$_o$ nominal without the enclitic:

(42) a. Saryey   jíí̧ta-0   **jíchikidíí**.
          sa-ryey   jíí̧ta-0   jíy-sikidii
          3SG-grab JIITA-0 COR-intestines
          'He grabs his own intestines.' (TC519)

      b. Múúñumaatéé-0   **rájaachéy**.
          múúy-numaa-téé-0 rá-jaay-say
          there-now-INTS-0 INAN-heart-CL:tree
          'There now is its (the tree's) heart.' (TC327)

Example 43 illustrates that the E + NP device can be used to code indefinite
participants. In this example, the coca leaves have not been previously mentioned in
the discourse, and the likelihood that they have been implicitly mentioned, or are
perpetually identifiable, is minimal. Therefore we conclude that the leaves are
indefinite in the sense of Du Bois (1980), Chafe (1976), and others. And yet in this
sentence the enclitic is used:

(43) Saruuyéȩrya   **japatíy**.
      sa-ruuy-yȩey-rà   japatiy
      3SG-roast-DIST-INAN coca
      'He is roasting coca.' (TC536)

In Chapter 4, we find a more satisfactory explanation for the use of the E+NP device in the notion of discourse referentiality (Du Bois 1980), persistence (Givón 1983a,b,c), discourse manipulability (Hopper and Thompson 1984), or deployability (Jaggar 1984). Briefly, the simple post-predicate NP device is used for O and S_o arguments that do not persist on the discourse stage, i.e., they are not "destined," as it were, to figure prominently in the immediately ensuing discourse. The E+NP device, on the other hand, is used for participants that will persist for a greater span of text. Quantitative data supporting this claim are presented in Chapter 4, section 4.5.2.2.

2.2.4. Zero

It is difficult in principle to precisely determine whether or not a given construction which might conceivably code an O or S_o argument with a zero is in fact doing so. For example, in every language there are verbs which commonly occur with or without an overtly expressed O argument (e.g., *eat* in English). In many cases, it is difficult to tell whether a given instance of such a verb makes covert mention of some O or not. The same is true for Yagua, though the situation is further complicated by the fact that subjects of predicate nominals are always S_o. Thus nearly any noun can potentially be a predicate nominal with a zero S_o subject. For example:

(44)   Naada-júú-vay   vátanu, vátanu juu-dee-ntiy.
        3DL-hunting:blind-make thick   thick   hunting:blind-DIM-REP
        'They made a thick hunting blind, a little thick one too.'

The second portion of this sentence is either a simple NP meaning 'little thick hunting blind also,' or a predicate nominal with zero subject meaning 'It is a little thick hunting blind also.'

For purposes of this study, I have elected to be as conservative as possible in postulating zero realizations of O and S_o arguments, short of ignoring them altogether. First, I will not consider zero realizations of S_o arguments at all, whether they be subjects of predicate nominals or of S_o verbs. In 44, for example, I interpret the part that follows the comma to be a simple NP interjection.

Second, there are certain sentences in which it is clear that there is a specific referential object that is being acted on, and yet is not coded by any overt coding device. In particular, some verbs allow three core arguments, two of which are coded as Os. Traditionally these two Os would be termed the direct and indirect objects. However, quite often one of the Os, always the patient rather than the recipient, is not coded at all. For example, the following two sentences are a conversational exchange in which speaker A wants speaker B to give him something (a blowgun). The blowgun is coded with the appropriate enclitic in 45a, but receives no overt mention in 45b:

(45)   a. Yạạ   sạạy   rárya.
            yi-ạ   sạạy   ráy-rà
            2SG-IRR   give   1SG-INAN
            'Give it to me!'

b. Néé   rachę́ę́ryų ̧ų ̧jíy-**0**.
   néé   ray-sąąy-rų ̧ų ̧y-jíy-0
   NEG   1SG-give-POT-2SG-INAN
   'I don't want to give (it) to) you.'

I interpret 45b as containing a zero reference to the blowgun.

There are a few other instances in which I determine that it is necessary to postulate a zero reference to an O argument. These are all instances where a specific O argument is clearly implied. Usually, if not always, there are other verbs in the immediate context that describe actions applied to the participant in question, and which do contain overt reference to that participant. For example, the following excerpt describes a very typical Yagua scene. A hunter brings home some game birds to be prepared for supper. In 46a and c, the birds are referenced with the appropriate enclitic. In 46b no overt coding is used, though the semantics of the verb make it clear that the game birds are the O argument of the verb:

(46)   a.   Riryąstya   jį ́įta   samoomusiñíí.
            riy-rąsitya   jį ́įta   sa-moo-mu-siy-níí
            3PL-defeather   JIITA   3SG-face-LOC-from-3
            'They defeather them before his arrival.'

       b.   Riryámutá-**0**.
            riy-ramuta-0
            3PL-eviscerate-0
            'They eviscerate (them).'

       c.   Rimyutiye   jį ́įta   pų ́rijejyą ́ą ́muníí.
            riy-mutiye   jį ́įta   pų ́riy-jay-jąą-mu-níí
            3PL-cook   JIITA   palm:fruit-skin-liquid-LOC-3
            'They cook them in palm-fruit-peel water.'

I consider 46b as containing a zero reference to the birds as a direct object.

2.2.5. Pre-predicate pronoun (PPRO)

As mentioned in section 2.1.5, free pronouns are relatively uncommon in Yagua discourse. The following examples illustrate some O and S_o arguments coded with the pre-predicate pronoun device:

(47)   **Ríñiy**   jį ́įta   vuryąą   ką ́ą ́siy.
        riy-niy   jį ́įta   vurya-ą   ką ́ą ́siy
        3PL:PRO-NIY   JIITA   1PLINC-IRR   finish:off
        'THEM we will finish off!' (O)

(48) Nííniy   Jesu samirya jamikyu vụ́ụ́jyụ.
      níí-niy   Jesu samirya jamikyu vụụy-jụ̀
      3SG:PRO-NIY Jesus good   friend   1PLINC-for
      'JESUS is a good friend for us.' (S$_o$)

Pre-predicate pronouns that code O or S$_o$ arguments are always followed either by
the semantically empty *-niy* (see section 2.1.5) or one of a small set of suffixes that
add certain adverbial and modal shadings to the clause, as in the following:

(49) Níí-numaa   jị́į̣ta   maésturu.
      3SG:PRO-now JIITA   teacher
      'HE is now a teacher.' (S$_o$)

(50) Naada-nta   rimyurá.
      3DL:PRO-seem witch
      'SHE[8] seems to be a witch.' (S$_o$)

2.2.6. Pre-predicate noun phrase (PNP)

O and S$_o$ arguments are sometimes coded with a pre-predicate NP. Examples 51
and 52 illustrate this device used to code O arguments, while 53 illustrates the same
device used to code an S$_o$ argument:

(51) **Ríkya** rạạ   junúúdyíy.
      ríkya   ray-ạ   junúúy-díy
      net   1SG-IRR look:at-priority
      'The net I need to go look at.' (O)

(52) **Suvọ́ọ́**   riivááy,   suvọ́ọ́.
      suvọọ   ri-jivaay   suvọọ
      string:bag   1SG-make   string:bag
      'A string bag I'm making, a string bag.' (O)

(53) **Tomáása** maésturu.   'Tomás is a teacher.' (S$_o$)
      Tomás   teacher

Were example 53 an equational construction (i.e., 'Tomás is the teacher'/'the
teacher is Tomás'), there would be no grounds for calling one member of the equation
the subject and the other the predicate. However, the most natural meaning of this
clause is one of "set membership." That is, Tomás is understood to be a member of
the set defined by 'teacher.' In these constructions, the pre-predicate NP remains part
of the predication, is not set off by an intonational break, and is not recapitulated with
an enclitic within the clause.

2.2.7. Pre-predicate noun phrase plus enclitic (PNP + E)

However, a pre-predicate noun phrase can be recapitulated by a coreferential enclitic if the NP is separated from the predication by an intonational break. The following examples illustrate this PNP + E device for O arguments (examples 54 and 55) and S_O arguments (example 56):

(54) **Váte,**   saruvemaantiñíí.
      váte   sa-ruve-maa-ntiy-níí
      bobwhite   3SG-halve-PERF-REP-3SG
      'Another bobwhite, he halved it.' (O)

(55) **Ratyųųchoonú   muríchiiryá,**
      ray-tųųchu-janú   muríchiiy-ra
      1SG-tell-PART   cost-NOM:INAN
      'My telling price (money to be given in exchange for information),

            yą   sąątyéé   rárya.
            yi-ą   sąąy-téé   ray-rà
            2SG-IRR   give-INTS   lSG-INAN
            you will give me it!'

(56) **Jirya**   **mákina,**   Judeenu   báárya dárya.
      jiy-ra   mákina   Judee-nu   báárya day-rà
      demo-CL:NEUT   machine   create-NOM   thing COP-INAN
      'This machine belongs to God.' (S_O)
      (lit.: 'This machine, God's thing it is.')

2.2.8. Right-dislocated noun phrase (RDNP)

A right-dislocated NP can be used to recapitulate any previous mention of an O or S_O argument in a clause. This marked coding device is commonly used for added detail, as in examples 57 and 58:

(57) Rųatácharaníí   muriñuvį́įta, **pipityú.**
      riy-jųtáy-sara-níí   muriñuvį́įta, pipityú
      3PL-say-HABIT-3COL   mojarra:fish large:mojarra:fish
      'They always call the mojarra fish, the large mojarra fish.' (O) (TC455)

(58) Néé sámirya sa-jáy   váácha,   **vásunuu-jáy.**
      NEG good   3SG-skin huapo:monkey   blue-skin
      'The huapo monkey's skin is no good, blue skin.' (S_O)

2.3. Possessor coding

There are three common coding devices for possessors with respect to their possessed items: head coding (HC), NP, and HC plus NP (HC+NP). The following subsections illustrate these three devices.

2.3.1. Head coding (HC)

The head-coding prefixes are identical to the verb-coding prefixes presented in section 2.1.1, Chart C. The stem classes mentioned in that section are applicable to nouns as well as verbs.

(59) **Vųųjéέy**   'Our father'
vųųy-jáάy   (class I)
1PLINC-father

(60) **Ra**ryooríy   'My house'
ray-rooríy   (class I)
lSG-house

(61) **Sąąnáá**   'His finger'
sa-janaa   (class II)
3SG-finger

(62) **Rą-ąséé**   'My hatchet'
ray-jaséé   (class II)
1SG-hatchet

(63) **Vuryį́ɪ́chantú**   'Our (inc) paternal aunt'
vurya-jį́chantú   (class III)
1PLINC-paternal:aunt

(64) **Rį́ɪ́ryupóó**   'My uncultivated garden'
ray-jį́ryupóó   (class III)
1SG-uncultivated:garden

(65) **Sųųnoodá**   'His/her mother'
sa-jųnooda   (class IV)
3SG-mother

(66) **Naadii**dántá   'Their (2) medicine'
naada-judántá   (class IV)
3DL-medicine

2.3.2. Noun phrases (NP)

Possessors with respect to their heads are analogous to subjects with respect to verbs, in that if the possessor is expressed with a full NP occurring before the head, head coding is disallowed:

(67)   **Tomáása** rooríy   'Tom's house'
       Tom   house

       *Tomáása sarooríy

(68)   Vụụjéẹ́y   ruudasíy   'Our father's blowgun'
       vụụy-jáạ́y   ruudasiy
       1PLINC-father   blowgun

       *Vụụjéẹ́y saruudasíy

2.3.3. Head coding plus noun phrase (HC + NP)

The parallel between subjects and possessors is maintained when the possessor appears after the head. In such a case, head coding co-occurs with the overt expression of the coreferential possessor NP:

(69)   Sa-rooriy   **Tomáása**   'Tom's house'
       3SG-house   Tom

(70)   **Naada**-duuduu **sa-vaturụ́y**   'His wife's flute'
       3DL-flute   3SG-woman

2.4. Oblique coding

Obliques are coded with exactly the same set of coding devices as possessors: HC, NP, and HC + NP. The head of an oblique nominal is the postposition indicating its semantic role. In the following subsections, examples of each of the coding devices used for postpositions are illustrated.

2.4.1. Head coding (HC)

Like nouns, postpositions also fall into the same stem classes as do verbs. The following examples illustrate some simple phrases where the participant is coded with an HC prefix on the postposition:

(71)   **Rá**-tạạsá   'In the middle of it'
       INAN-middle   (class I)

(72) **Sąąríy**   'Underneath him'
sa-jaríy   (class II)
3SG-underneath

(73) **Sųųsíy**   'From/after him'
sa-jųsíy   (class IV)
3SG-from/after

2.4.2. Noun phrases (NP)

Oblique roles may be indicated by postpositions on full NPs:

(74) **Núú tąąsá**   'In the middle of the path'
path   middle

(75) **Tą́ą́ra rudamú sayasíy?**   'On what day did he go?'
tą́ą́ra   ruda-mu   sa-jiya-siy
what   day-LOC   3SG-go-PAST1

2.4.3. Head coding plus noun phrase (HC + NP)

An HC prefix may occur on a postposition, in which case a coreferential full NP may follow:

(76) **Rá-tąąsa   sa-moo-mu-dáy**   'Right on his face'
INAN-middle   3SG-face-LOC-DAY

(77) **Riñeechǫ́   munuñúmiy**   'Toward the savages'
riy-naachǫ   munuñu-mìy
3PL-towards   savage-PL

Though of course the full NP in such constructions is not required (see examples 78 and 79).

The above examples show that postpositional phrases are isomorphic with possessive constructions. In some cases, stems which are clearly nouns are used in postpositional phrases to modify the sense of the relation being expressed. For example, the stem *moo* 'face/forehead' in example 78 is used in combination with postpositions to impart the sense of 'in front of.' Contrast the a and b examples below:

(78) a. Sa-moo-mú   'In front of him'
3SG-face-LOC   (lit.: 'at his face')

b. Siimú   'On him' or 'in his possession'
sa-jimú
3SG-LOC

(79)   a.   Sa-moo-mu-síy   'Away from where he is going'
            3SG-face-LOC-from   (lit.: 'away from his face')

       b.   Siimusíy   'Away from him'
            sa-jimu-siy   (implies he is not moving)
            3SG-LOC-from

2.5. Summary

   In this chapter, I have illustrated the various devices used to code participants in
Yagua. The chapter has been divided into four main sections, each dealing with the
coding devices used for a particular natural class of argument roles. The four classess
considered are A and S_a arguments (section 2.1), O and S_o arguments (section 2.2),
possessors (section 2.3), and obliques (section 2.4). I have classed A with S_a and O
with S_o because these classes each utilize an identical set of coding devices. Were this
criterion applied equally to possessors and obliques, the latter two categories would
also have to be grouped into one larger class, since possessors and obliques also
utilize an identical set of coding devices (HC, NP, and HC+NP). I have chosen to
keep possessors and obliques distinct because of their semantic dissimilarity and in
order to facilitate presentation of the data.
   The HC prefixes for possessors and obliques are identical to the VC prefixes for
verbs. Furthermore, for verbs, possessed nouns and postpositions alike, prefixes can
co-occur with a coreferential NP only if that NP follows the head. Subject, possessor
and oblique NPs occurring in the absense of a coreferential prefix must precede their
heads. Thus, in terms of sets of coding devices, there is a high level of similarity
between the possessor/oblique category and the A/S_a category, as opposed to the O/S_o
category. At this level of generality there are only two classes: (1) the class
represented by A, S_a, possessors and obliques; and (2) the class represented by O and
S_o arguments. The only difference between the set of coding devices used for
possessors/obliques and that used for A/S_a arguments is that the latter arguments can
be coded with PPRO, the right-dislocated devices and zero in addition to the "basic"
devices, whereas possessors and obliques can only be coded with three basic devices,
HC, NP, and HC+NP. This hierarchical pattern of similarities is schematized in
Chart F:

Chart F: Coding Possibilities for Various Classes of Arguments	
Category	Coding devices
A arguments	VC, NP, VC+NP, etc.
S_a arguments	VC, NP, VC+NP, etc.
Possessors	HC, NP, HC+NP
Obliques	HC, NP, HC+NP
O arguments	E, PostPNP, E+PostPNP, etc.
S_o arguments	E, PostPNP, E+PostPNP, etc.

Another observation concerning the coding devices is that the prefixes that code subjects, possessors, and obliques, as well as the enclitics that code O and S_o arguments, are very similar to the free pronouns in form. In fact, the enclitics and the pronouns are virtually identical (see Charts B and C). The prefixes differ from the pronouns most substantially in the third person singular, whereas in the other persons and numbers the difference is only in tone. Because of the formal identity between free pronouns and enclitics, there is a question of whether these two sets of forms are not really better treated as the same. Another argument for lumping enclitics and pronouns in the same class is that it is very uncommon for an enclitic and a distinct post-predicate pronoun to co-index an argument in the same clause. The few examples I do have of this phenomenon may well be due to hesitation on the part of the speaker, or misanalysis of clause boundaries on the part of the analyst. Speakers will not easily produce sentences with an enclitic and a coreferential pronoun in elicitation.

In spite of these facts, I have chosen to treat enclitics and pronouns as distinct because of two characteristics of enclitics: (1) when phonological cliticization is possible (i.e., when the "structural descriptions" for the phonological processes that provide evidence for cliticization are met), enclitics clearly attach to other elements, i.e., they are "bound" morphemes; and (2) an enclitic may occur with a coreferential NP (section 2.2.3), and in fact forms a syntactic constituent with that NP. Neither of these characteristics is expected for the class of devices usually falling under the definition of "pronoun" in linguistic tradition. In particular, both characteristics are usually associated with "agreement" phenomena.

There is no doubt that the pronouns, the prefixes, and the enclitics are etymologically related, as they certainly all share functional as well as formal characteristics. In the process of diachronic change, we see that the enclitics are losing the characteristics of free anaphoric devices and are becoming more like the "bound anaphora" of Givón (1983a), though they have not yet acquired all the characteristics of "grammatical agreement," i.e., they attach to units of any category, not just to verbs, and they are not obligatory, even when a coreferential NP occurs in the clause.

Notes to Chapter 2

1   Forms from the paradigm represented in Chart C will always appear as prefixes. Therefore, in the gloss line of examples, any gloss such as 3SG, 1PLINC, etc. which glosses a prefix refers to a form from this paradigm. On verbs such prefixes always code the subject (A or S), on nouns they code possessors, and on postpositions the same prefixes code the O argument of the postposition. Occasionally a pronoun (see Chart D) will appear with an enclitic attached. In order to distinguish such pronouns from the forms illustrated in Chart C, the gloss PRO will always accompany person and number specification of pronouns, e.g., 3SG:PRO. I will simply rely on linear order to distinguish the forms in Chart C from those in Chart E: forms appearing as prefixes are from Chart C, those appearing as enclitics are from Chart E.

In previous work (T. Payne 1983b), I have presented rules that derive essentially all surface forms of person and number prefixes from the underlying forms represented in Chart C.

2   The form *vurya* for the 1st-person-plural/dual inclusive is the allomorph regularly used for class II, III, and IV stems. The observation that non-third-person-singular prefixes are identical to pronouns except for tone applies only to the class I, or "regular," stems. In the other classes, the prefix forms vary more significantly from the pronominal forms.

3   In Yagua, placentas and uteruses are almost always expressed as possessed noun phrases. Contrary to what may seem natural from an English point of view, the possessors of these items are the children that are born with the placenta, or which come from the uterus. To refer to a person's uterus is to refer to the uterus from which that person was born, even if that person is a full-grown woman, and even if she happens to be pregnant. To refer to the uterus that is located inside a woman's body, one must refer to her child's uterus, even if she has never had a child and/or is not currently pregnant. In the text from which example 7 is taken (another telling of the Non-Identical Twins tale that appears in Appendix 4), the placenta transforms into a human being and becomes a central character. As such, the term *munáá* 'placenta' comes to be used as a proper name, and therefore is not required to be possessed. However, whenever it is possessed, it is possessed by Placenta's elder brother, i.e., the child that was born with the placenta.

4   Full NPs referring to intransitive subjects do occasionally occur postverbally without a coreferential prefix on the verb. However, the use of this coding device has much in common with S_O coding (see section 2.2.). Quite independently from their defining characteristics based on subject-coding devices, clauses which employ S_O coding have many features of nonverbal predications, as demonstrated in section 2.2.1.

5   The verb translated here, 'find,' is the same as that elsewhere translated 'see.' Though the semantic similarity between these two concepts is obvious, in this particular case it seemed more appropriate to use 'find.' This construction has much in common with S_O verbs of locomotion as discussed in Chapter 6. However, it doesn't strictly qualify as such a verb, since there is no overt coding of the subject. Thus it is technically impossible to say whether S_a or S_O coding is involved here. However, since S_a is the unmarked configuration for subjects of single-argument verbs, I have considered this example to illustrate zero as a coding device for the S_a role.

6   The form *-day* is an enclitic that appears at or near the end of a clause, and has various functions. Its function when attached to an NP or pronoun is to indicate contrastive focus, as in example 16. It has several other functions, many of which are probably best described as operating on a discourse level.

7   It is a general principle of Yagua discourse that one avoids the use of fully specified noun phrases as much as possible, allowing the rich participant-coding system to keep participants sorted out. Only in marked contexts, or to avoid ambiguity, are fully specified noun phrases used. One strategy for avoiding the use of fully specified noun phrases is to treat one plural participant as singular when two groups are interacting. In such cases, it is the most topical group that is treated properly in terms of its semantic plurality, while the other group is treated as singular. For example, if adults and children are interacting, the adults will be coded as plural, while the children are singular. If humans are interacting with animals, the humans will be plural and the animals singular. If "good guys" are interacting with "bad guys" (as is

often the case in folkloric history narratives) it is predictably the "good guys" which are treated as plural while the "bad guys" are treated as singular:

(80) Rityęęryá   rumusíy   váriy,
      riy-taarya   rumusiy   váriy
      3PL-return   from:there   then
      'They (good guys) returned from there,

        sasiityatítyiiyanuntiryíy.
        sa-siiy-ta-títyiiy-janu-ntiy-riy
        3SG-run-TRNS-going-PAST3-REP-3PL
        they (savages) chasing them again.'

In this example, the savages are treated as singular in the second clause, even though they are obviously a group of people, and in other examples in the same story are treated as plural. The people being attacked (the clan to which the narrator belongs) are treated as plural. The "good guys" as a group are never treated as singular. This bending of the categories "plural" and "singular" is a very obvious feature of Yagua narrative, and is clearly used in order to avoid the use of fully specified noun phrases.

8

One interesting and apparently unique aspect of the Yagua participant-coding system is the use of second- and third-person-dual forms to code women who have had children:

(81) Naaniitáy   naadííva   jíryeenu   vaturúy,
      naana-jitay   naana-íva   jíy-reenu   vaturuy
      3DL-say   3DL-DAT   COR-kinsman   woman
      'She says to the other woman,

        'Saanííduutyatą́ą́tíyu.'
        saana-jíduutya-tą́ą́ta-yù
        2DL-get:ready-should-REFL
        "You should get yourself ready."'

In this example, the woman who is speaking is coded with third-person-dual forms, and she in turn addresses the other woman with a verb in the second-person-dual form. This use of special forms to code women who have had children is a pervasive aspect of Yagua, being manifested not only in the participant-coding system but also throughout the kinship system, i.e., special terms are used for nieces, aunts, sisters, sisters-in-law, etc. who have had children. In terms of participant coding, however, it could be viewed as another strategy for avoiding the use of fully specified noun phrases, in that the more distinctions that are handled by the participant-coding system, the less a speaker will have to identify his or her referent with a fully specified NP.

Chapter 3

COREFERENCE PHENOMENA

This chapter will deal with the morphological coreference system. The Yagua system is particularly interesting, as it clearly functions within a clause (sections 3.1 and 3.2), between dependent and independent clauses (section 3.3), and even between pairs of fully independent sentences (section 3.4).[1]

3.1. A, S_a, possessor and oblique coreference

There is a special participant-reference category, realized by the prefix *jíy-/yí-*, which indicates that the participant being coded is coreferential with some recently mentioned participant. In most cases the antecedent of *jíy-/yí-* is the A or S_a of the preceding verb, possessor of the preceding possessed noun phrase, or object of the preceding postpositional phrase. However, this constraint is by no means categorical. Except in indirect discourse, verbs with *jíy-/yí-* are grammatically dependent, as discussed briefly below. This prefix is referred to as the COR1 prefix (Payne and Payne 1990). The coreference system of Yagua differs slightly from other coreference systems in that, at least in some dialects, semantic first and second persons may also be coded with the coreference forms. However, in the downriver dialects, coreference forms are restricted to semantic third persons. The coreference prefix is most commonly used with possessed noun phrases:

(1) Núúdyeeyanumáá   **jíry**oorimyújụ.
     Núúdya-jiya-numáá   jíy-rooriy-mu-jụ̀
     1PLEX-go-now   COR1-house-LOC-DIR
     'We are going to our house.' (upriver only)

(2) Sapụ́ụ́chiñíí   Anita   **jíry**oorimyújụ.
     sa-pụ́ụ́chiy-níí   Anita   jíy-rooriy-mu-jụ̀.
     3SG-carry-3SG   Anita   COR1-house-LOC-DIR
     'He$_i$ carries Anita to his$_i$ house.'

In example 1, the prefix *jíy-* on the possessed locative noun phrase meaning 'to our house' indicates that the possessor of *rooriy* 'house' is coreferential with the subject of the preceding verb *jiya* 'go.' Similarly, in the transitive clause in example 2, *jíy-* again indicates that the possessor of *rooriy* is coreferential with the subject of the verb. There is no possibility that the possessor of *rooriy* could be Anita or any other person.

The coreference prefix always follows its antecedent. If a possessed noun phrase occurs before a verb whose third-person subject is the possessor, the noun phrase will receive the normal possessor marking and the verb will receive *jíy-/yí-*:

(3)   Saroorimyújų   **jípyų́ų́chiñíí**   Anita.
      sa-rooriy-mu-jų̀   jíy-pų́ų́chiy-níí
      3SG-house-LOC-DIR   COR1-carry-3SG   Anita
      'In his₁ house he₁ carries Anita.'

(4)   Satááryį́įvasiy   **jíñuvay.**
      sa-tááryį-íva-sìy   jíy-nuvay
      3SG-brother-dat-for   COR1-mourn
      'For his₁ brother he₁ mourns.' (FSQ27)

Also, an object of a postpositional phrase can antecede a coreference prefix:

(5)   Naaniinchájų   **jít**yiryǫ   savïïmú   koodíy.
      naada-jinchajų   jíy-tiryǫ   sa-vïïmu   koodiy
      3DL-upon   COR1-lie   3SG-inside   snake
      'They 2 lie on top of each other inside the snake.' (FSQ64)

Here two animals have been swallowed by a snake. They are coded in the postpositional phrase *naaniinchájų* 'on top of them' and then again with the coreference marker as the subject of the verb.

The general intraclausal constraint on what can antecede a COR1 prefix, then, is that it must be an argument that can be referred to with a prefix, i.e., a subject, a possessor, or the object of a postpositional phrase. The question arises as to whether there is a preference for one or another of these categories when more than one is present in the clause. In cases where both a VC and a HC prefix compete to antecede a given instance of the COR1 prefix, the VC (i.e., the subject rather than the possessor or oblique participant) will normally win out. Such situations are not particularly difficult to find in texts:

(6)   Pariché sarootyatéé   siimusírya   **jíd**yuudúú.
      pariche sa-rooy-ta-téé   sa-jimu-siy-rà   jíy-duuduu
      finally 3SG-break:loose-TRNS-INTS   3SG-LOC-from-INAN   COR1-flute
      'Finally he₁ breaks his₁ flute loose from him₁.' (TC135)
      Not: 'Finally he₁ breaks his₁ flute loose from him₁.'

Here the coreference prefix occurs on the NP *duuduu* 'flute.' An interpretation whereby the possessor of the flute is coreferential with the object of the postposition in *siimusírya* is impossible, even though this was the last prefix that occurred before the coreference marker. The antecedent must instead be the subject of the main verb, as the gloss indicates. It appears, then, that subjects rank higher than objects of postpositions as potential antecedents for coreference prefixes. Since objects of postpositions have the same syntactic status as possessors (e.g., many postpositions are transparently related to nouns; see Payne and Payne 1990) we infer that subjects also outrank possessors as potential antecedents.

Most verbs which take *jíy-/yí-* are dependent, in that they cannot be inflected for time reference. It might be argued, therefore, that such verbal forms with *jíy-/yí-* are nominalizations, since nouns (even predicate nominals) cannot be inflected for time reference. This argument is especially convincing when the stem to which *jíy-/yí-* is attached can be interpreted as a noun:

(7) Sadííñumáá   **jíjeechiy**   jąąnumú.
     sa-dííy-numaa   jíy-jaachiy   jąąnumu
     3SG-die-now   COR1-hunger   because
     'He's dying of hunger.' (or 'He's$_i$ dying because he$_i$
     hungers,' or 'He's$_i$ dying because of his$_i$ hunger.')

However, in indirect discourse, fully inflected verbs can occur with *jíy-/yí-*:

(8) Sųųtéésiy   **yą́**   jiyá.
     sa-jųtay-jásiy   yí-ą   jiya
     3SG-say-PROX1   COR1-IRR   go
     'He$_i$ said that he$_i$ will go.'

(9) Sųųtéésiy   **jíyasiy.**
     sa-jųtay-jásiy   jíy-jiya-sìy
     3SG-say-PROX1   COR1-go-PAST1
     'He$_i$ said (today) that he$_i$ left (a few months ago).'

In both of the above examples, the tense/aspect of the indirect-discourse complement is different from that of the verb of speaking. Indirect discourse is the only environment in which this phenomenon has been observed in our corpus.

3.2. Reflexivity/reciprocity

The enclitic *-yù* codes third-person O participants which are coreferential with a preceding A, S$_a$, or possessor. I will refer to this enclitic as the COR2 enclitic. In the upriver dialects, *-yù* may code first- and second-person dual and plural Os as well. Thus when used in simplex constructions, *-yù* indicates reflexivity or reciprocity:

(10) Suunumívachi**yu.**
     sa-junumívay-sìy-yù
     3SG-paint-PAST1-COR2
     'He painted himself.'

(11) Ruuvañúúyanú**yu.**
     riy-juvay-núúy-janú-yù
     3PL-kill-CONT-PAST3-COR2
     'They were killing each other.'

However, *-yù* can also occur in constructions with possessed nouns to code O participants that are coreferential with the possessor:

(12)   Suumutyǫ   jíịta   naandaanúyu.
        sa-jumutyǫ   jíịta   naana-daa-nú-yù
        3SG-answer   JIITA   3DL-little-person-COR2
        'Her$_i$ son answered her$_i$.'

Example 12 is technically ambiguous since *-yù* can be interpreted as coding either the subject of the clause or the possessor of the subject NP. That is, 12 could mean 'Her son answered himself.' This reading, however, is pragmatically much less likely than the one given above. These data indicate that for the COR2 enclitic, subjects do not outrank possessors as potential antecedents.

Another use of the *-yù* enclitic is with the verb *jutay* 'say' to mean roughly 'say of oneself,' or 'call oneself.' For example:

(13)   Sụụtay   pucájụdáyu.
        sa-jutay   puca-jụ-dáy-yù
        3SG-say   water:turtle-for-DAY-COR2
        'He calls himself a water turtle.' (TC437)

Regardless of the order of the possessed NP with regard to the verb, *-yù*, like the other enclitics, always occurs after the verb, though not necessarily attached to it. In 14 the possessed NP is preposed, yet the enclitic immediately follows the verb:

(14)   Saroorimyú   sụụvásiyu.
        sa-rooriy-mu   sa-jụva-sìy-yù
        3SG-house-LOC   3SG-strike-PAST1-COR2
        'In his$_i$ house he$_j$ struck him$_i$.'

Example 14 could mean 'in his$_i$ house he$_j$ struck himself$_j$.' However, the reading given above is pragmatically more acceptable.

Both *jíy-/yí-* and *-yù* can occur in the same clause to indicate three-way coreference:

(15)   Saroorimyú   jíchụụ́yu.
        sa-rooriy-mu   jíy-sụ́ụ́y-yù
        3SG-house-LOC   COR1-bite-COR2
        'In his$_i$ house he$_i$ bit himself$_i$.'

Like *jíy-/yí-*, *-yù* is not used with first- and second-person singular referents, and in the downriver dialects is not normally used with first- and second-person dual and plural referents either. To indicate reciprocity or reflexivity when first or second persons are involved, the regular enclitics are used:

(16)   Rịịnúúryéy.   'I look at myself.'
        ra-jịnúúy-ráy   (all dialects)
        1SG-look:at-1SG

(17)   Jiryạạ   jụváy   jiryéy.   'You'll kill each other.'
        jiryey-ạ   jụvay   jiryéy   (downriver dialects)
        2PL-IRR   kill   2PL

3.3. Coreference in participial complements

In constructions with participial (nominalized) complements, the subject of the participle may simply be omitted to indicate identity of reference with the subject of the main clause:

(18) Jááseenújụ   núúdyiitọọjásiy.
     jáásiy-janu-jụ̀   núúdya-jitọọ-jásiy
     cut:grass-PART-for   1PL-arrive:there-PROX2
     'We arrived to cut grass.'

(19) Murrạyanú   siitị́ị́ta.
     murrạy-janu   sa-jitị̣i-tà
     sing-PART   3SG-arrive:here-TRNS
     'He arrives here singing.'
     (lit.: 'With singing he arrives.')²

In these examples the subject of the preverbal participial is omitted. If a VC prefix is added to the participle, switch reference is implied:

(20) Samurrạyanú   siitị́ị́ta.
     sa-murrạy-janu   sa-jitị̣i-tà
     3SG-sing-PART   3SG-arrive-TRNS
     'While he$_i$ sings, he$_j$ arrives.'
     (Lit.: 'With his$_i$ singing, he$_j$ arrives.')

When the participle follows the main verb, the coreference marker may be used on the participle to indicate subject coreference:

(21) Riyarọ́ọ́vanumaa   jíyạanumú.
     riy-yarọ́ọ́va-numaa   jíy-jiya-janu-mu
     3PL-make:noise-now   COR1-go-PART-LOC
     'They make noise going.'
     (Lit.: 'They$_i$ make noise in their$_i$ going.')

(22) Sasíímyaa   yímuutyạạnújụníí.
     sa-síly-maa   yí-jumuutya-janu-jụ̀-níí
     3SG-run-PERF   COR1-help-PART-for-3SG
     'He ran to help him.'
     (Lit.: 'He$_i$ ran for his$_i$ helping (of) him$_j$.')

The restriction that *jíy-/yí-* must follow its antecedent holds for constructions with participial complements as well as those with possessed NPs:

(23) Riiyạạnumu   jíyarọ́ọ́va.
     riy-jiya-janu-mu   jíy-yarọ́ọ́va
     3PL-go-PART-LOC   COR1-make:noise
     'They are going making noise.'

In sentences such as 23, the "main" (nonparticipial) verb is very limited in the inflectional information it expresses, e.g., it cannot express time reference directly. The participle is similarly restricted, thus limiting the usefulness of this construction type considerably.

3.4. The pragmatic uses of coreference forms

In this section I will show that the antecedent of either of the coreference markers cannot be strictly predicted in terms of morphosyntactic categories such as subject, A, S, possessor, oblique, etc.

Though there is a clear tendency toward grammaticalization of the restriction on antecedents to a specific morphosyntactically defined category (along the lines of the analysis proposed by Everett 1989), there is still much flexibility in the system. For example, subjects apparently outrank possessors in their ability to antecede a COR1 prefix (example 6), though no such ranking occurs with respect to antecedents for COR2 enclitics. Furthermore, there are situations such as those illustrated in examples 12 and 14 where more than one nominal compete as antecedent for a COR2 enclitic. In such cases, only the pragmatics of the situation determine the appropriate interpretation. Finally, inspection of texts reveals that grammaticalization of a constraint on antecedents is still far from absolute. Coreference prefixes can function as free anaphors whose reference is determined from the extraclausal context.

Two hypotheses regarding possible morphosyntactic constraints on antecedents of these markers follow, and I will show that each is insufficient to account for all the observed data.

The first morphosyntactic constraint is hinted at in section 3.1, and is made explicit in 24:

(24)   The most recently mentioned A, S_a, possessor or head of a postposition will antecede a COR1 or COR2 marker.

This statement accurately describes most of the observed data in texts and elicitation. However, it is violated by sentences such as example 6 where a *subject* (in this case an A) overrides a more recently mentioned head of a postposition for interpretation as the antecedent of *jíy-*. Thus a second possible constraint is suggested:

(25)   The most recently mentioned subject will antecede a COR1 or COR2 marker. If there is no previously mentioned subject in the clause, then the previously mentioned possessor or head of a postposition will be the antecedent.

However, this restriction does not account for all the data either, as the following example from the Twins Cycle shows:

(26)   Níí-niy   sa-tááryi̧-téé   sa-sá̧á̧-**yu**.
       3SG-NIY 3SG-brother-INTS 3SG-give-COR2
       'His$_i$ BROTHER he$_j$ gives to him$_i$.' (TC506)
       (or 'It's him$_i$, his$_i$ BROTHER, he$_j$ gives to him$_i$.')

In this example, the reflexive enclitic codes the recipient of the ditransitive verb *sǫ́y* 'give.' The antecedent of this enclitic may not be the subject of the clause, but must be the possessor of the preverbal patient nominal.

Example 26 uses the preverbal pronoun strategy, with a recapitulating preverbal noun phrase to code the patient. This strategy is used to code contrastiveness, as discussed in Chapter 7. The reference of *táárγi̧* 'brother' in this case is established with respect to the possessor, Elder Brother, who has figured very prominently (or is highly topical; see Chapter 4) in the preceding discourse and who is, of course, a central character of the entire story.

Another example that even more clearly violates the restriction formulated in 25 occurs in another text:

(27) Níí-niy   jí̧í̧ta   sǫǫrǫ   yí-sǫǫ-ju̧.
      3SG-NIY   JIITA   serve/be:sufficient   COR1-COM-for
      'HE will serve as his companion.'
      (Lit.: 'HE$_i$ will serve to be with him$_j$.')

In this example, the subject cannot antecede the coreference prefix, even though there are no competing possessors or heads of postpositions within the clause. Here the antecedent of the coreference prefix lies outside the clause entirely.

Examples such as 27 are not particularly uncommon in oral discourse, though it is difficult for our language consultants to contextualize such examples in elicitation. Another example occurs in a second version of the Twins Cycle, recorded, transcribed and translated by a native speaker. Example 28 is the transcribed version, including the preceding clause, while 29 is the relevant sentence as it actually is uttered. In these examples, A and B refer to two interactants; A is a member of the audience, and B is the storyteller:

(28) A: Naani-idátya?   'Does she suspect?'
          3dl-suspect

      B: Jóó.   Naani-idátya-nikyéé . . .   (as transcribed)
          yes   3DL-suspect-say
          'Yes. She suspects, saying . . .'

(29) B: Jóó.   Yí-dátya-nikyéé . . .   (as uttered)
          yes   COR1-suspect-say
          'Yes. She suspects, saying . . .'

This replacement of the coreference prefix with third-person forms when the morphosyntactic constraint represented by 25 is violated occurs several times in this transcription. It appears that the transcriber, as he works one sentence at a time, loses track of the continuity of the whole narrative and prefers a morphosyntactic rather than discourse/pragmatic condition on coreference. In context, examples such as 29 make perfect sense, but in elicitation it is difficult to construct a context in which they would be acceptable. In my opinion this pragmatic use of the COR1 prefix is too common in discourse to be written off as "performance error."

Everett (1989), working within the Principles and Parameters approach of Government and Binding theory, explains the coreference facts of Yagua on the basis of two independently justified morphosyntactic principles: morphological visibility, and generation of AGR independent of INFL. In brief, this account identifies all nominals that can be referred to with prefixes (i.e., subjects, possessors, and objects of postpositions) as potential antecedents. As far as I can tell, no asymmetry (i.e., ranking) among these three categories is implied, and no allowance is made for pragmatic interpretation when more than one nominal compete to antecede a coreference form. Also, the extraclausal use of the COR1 prefix must be considered performance error or stylistic variation from grammaticality. Finally, this account depends on a notion of "basic word order" that identifies SVO as the syntactically basic constituent order, even though this is an infrequent and pragmatically marked order in discourse (Doris Payne 1990). Nevertheless, within the Principles and Parameters framework, Everett's analysis accounts for the tendency toward grammaticalization of a constraint on antecedents for coreference forms.

Notes to Chapter 3

[1] Everett (1989) insightfully discusses the intraclausal use of this system in terms of the Principles and Parameters approach within Government and Binding theory. Everett's paper is based on data presented in prepublication versions of the present work and others by Doris Payne and myself. The transcription in Everett's paper consists of the underlying morphological structures of sentences prior to the operation of morphophonemic processes. This is equivalent to the second line of transcription in the present work. In a few cases, Everett misanalyzes or misglosses certain forms. Though such problems do not seem to affect the analysis Everett proposes, they do affect the reliability of the data.

[2] The suffix *-tà* in this example increases the valence of the clause by one argument, and hence is glossed as a transitivizer. Doris Payne (1985: Chap. 5) discusses the semantics of *-tà*. In examples 19 and 20, it indicates that the direct object is a semantic comitative. Hence an even more literal translation of 19 might be 'A song, he arrived with.'

Chapter 4

TOPIC CONTINUITY

How do discourse-pragmatic factors affect the choice of participant-coding devices in Yagua discourse? In attempting to answer this question I tentatively adopt the framework set out by Givón (1983a, b, c) for assigning quantitative topicality values to the various coding devices. This approach is a logical first step in that it rests on a well-defined limiting hypothesis, namely, that the use of all coding devices can be explained in terms of "continuity" (as defined below). Once this preliminary hypothesis is tested, deviations from the expected results will point to other factors affecting choice of coding devices, thereby defining areas for further investigation. In Chapter 5 I examine specific examples that violate the general findings of the topic-continuity study, and attempt to isolate additional variables. Chapter 6 shows how the use of S_o coding on verbs is explained in terms of text structure, and the use of pre-predicate pronouns is examined in Chapter 7. In Chapter 8 I step back and take a second, more general look at the topic-continuity figures and summarize the conclusions of this study.

4.1. The contribution of topic continuity to a theory of anaphora

According to Givón (1983b:7) "The *clause* ('sentence') is the basic information processing unit in human discourse." Discourse is made up of chains of clauses, which are in turn combined into larger units called "paragraphs," "sections," "chapters" etc. In order to qualify as a discourse, a chain of clauses must "hang together" in certain demonstrable ways, i.e., it must exhibit CONTINUITY. This particular observation certainly does not originate with Givón, but plays a central role in much previous work in discourse analysis, though under different terminology. For example, Halliday (1967), Haliday and Hasan (1976) and Joseph Grimes (1975) among others use the term "cohesion" for essentially this same concept. Givón's central insight is that discourse is most naturally continuous, i.e., continuity (cohesion, if you will) from one clause to the next in real discourse is the most expected, unsurprising and unmarked situation. Discontinuity is unexpected, surprising and marked. This observation suggests an "iconicity principle" of human communication in general, and of topic continuity in particular:

(1)   "The more disruptive, surprising, discontinuous or hard to process a topic is, the more *coding material* must be assigned to it." (Givón 1983b:18, emphasis in the original.)

This principle is consistent with a more general and obvious behavioral principle: "Expend only as much energy on a task as is required for its performance" (ibid.). Principle 1 is iconic in that it relates a formal coding scale (amount of coding material) to a scalar functional domain (continuity) in a nonarbitrary way, i.e., the less continuity the more coding material. I will have more to say on the subject of functional domains and their formal coding in Chapter 8. Characteristically, then, continuity (of various sorts) is either not marked morphologically, or is encoded with minimal morphological marking. Discontinuity, on the other hand, is encoded with more substantial morphological marking, or with otherwise more "marked" morphosyntactic structures.

There are three types of continuity mentioned in Givón (1983b): Thematic continuity; Action continuity; and Participant, or Topic, continuity. Although he acknowledges that these three kinds of continuity are intimately related to one another, Givón concentrates on topic continuity for purposes of the quantitative analytical procedure he proposes. In Givón's view, "topic" is seen as a scalar category. Participants are more or less topical at any given point in a discourse. It is more continuous (and therefore less surprising, or less marked) for a speaker to refer to (or mention) a more highly topical participant than a less highly topical one.[1] Certainly there are times when a speaker needs to refer to participants that are low in topicality. In particular, participants that have not been brought onto the discourse stage have no topicality whatsoever.[2] Therefore, in order to introduce a participant, or to reintroduce a participant after a significant period of absence, more marked morphosyntactic coding devices are called for. The speaker/writer must "work harder" to signal discontinuity since it is not the most natural state of affairs in human discourse. Givón's quantitative method is a way of determining how topical any participant is at any given point in a text. Once topicality is determined in a rigorous, noncircular, nonimpressionistic way, participant-coding devices can be ranked in terms of the average topicality values of the participants they code.

Certainly an all-inclusive theory of anaphora would have to take into account many factors other than brute number of mentions and number of clauses since previous mention in order to accurately characterize the use of participant-coding devices in discourse. These other factors fall into two categories: (1) factors involving the TOPICWORTHINESS of the participants themselves, and (2) those involving the structure and flow of the discourse. These two factors will be discussed in the following two subsections respectively.

4.1.1. Participant topicworthiness

Participant topicworthiness is here defined as the relative likelihood for a participant to be "talked about" (Reinhart 1982). There are at least two kinds of topicworthiness associated with any potential participant in a discourse: INHERENT topicworthiness and CONTEXT-IMPARTED topicworthiness. These notions are reminiscent of, but not identical to, Du Bois' notions of INTRINSIC SALIENCE and PLOT SALIENCE (Du Bois 1980:248-249). Certain entities are inherently more topicworthy than others, e.g., humans are more likely topics than nonhumans, animates are more likely topics than inanimates, etc. Other entities are likely topics because of the semantics or pragmatics of the particular speech context. The second kind of topicworthiness will be the focus of the rest of this chapter and hence merits some elaboration.

To take an obvious case of context-imparted topicworthiness, the speech-act participants themselves are always highly topicworthy. They are always "available" for reference in any discourse, since interlocutors must always be conscious of one another. This fact explains why speech-act participants can be universally referred to with reduced morphosyntactic coding devices, such as first- and second-person pronouns, regardless of whether or how many times they have been mentioned previously in the discourse. In addition, however, particular speech situations may impart topicworthiness to certain classes of entities. For example, in certain religious circles God is perpetually a highly topicworthy entity. Hence, in the context of a religious gathering of this type, a participant-coding device of the appropriate inflectional category but with no obvious antecedent is taken to be a reference to God. Another, more commonplace example of this phenomenon is the fact that entities can be nonlinguistically or implicitly brought onto the discourse stage, by deixis, inference, body language and shared presuppositions of the speech-act participants. Also, the choice of a particular verb causes the class of participants that are typical for that verb to be more topicworthy. For example, 'to spew' in English implies a liquid participant, 'to speak' a human (or at least rational) participant, etc. Finally, in narrative the central characters of the story are more likely topics than the noncentral characters. In short there are a myriad of factors that affect "degree of topicworthiness" many of which are not accessible to the linguist working from transcribed materials, especially when the linguist does not have native understanding of the language or of the culture of its speakers. Topicality (in the sense of Givón 1983b, as number or density of mentions) is only one kind of context-imparted topicworthiness; i.e., if a participant has already been mentioned repeatedly and/or has recently been mentioned in the current discourse, it is more likely to continue as topic (it is more topicworthy) than are other entities, other factors being equal.

Despite the fact that the topic-continuity methodology is sensitive to only a few of the factors involved in topicworthiness, it does represent a step in the right direction. The value of this methodology is that it is quantitative, rigorous, and nonimpressionistic. If participant-coding in discourse continues to be a topic of interest to linguists, future research will certainly refine the methodology and the theoretical principles that underlie it as more variables are isolated and incorporated into the findings.

In the quantitative study of Yagua presented in this chapter, I have attempted to control for some of the variables outlined above by (1) distinguishing between central, major, and minor characters (section 4.3); (2) by excluding from the general topic-continuity counts references to entities which are clearly perpetually topicworthy due to their universal presence on the discourse stage, e.g., "the sun," "the day" etc.; and (3) by excluding references to speech-act participants. The other factors (e.g., deictic mentions, implicit mention due to semantic subcategorization of verbs) will only be dealt with as they are obviously relevant in particular cases.

4.1.2. Discourse structure

The second major group of factors affecting the choice of coding devices has to do with the structuring of the information contained in a text. Again, there are two subtypes of factors: (1) the hierarchical thematic or episodic structure of the text, and (2) factors of grounding, i.e., foregrounding and backgrounding of information (Hopper and Thompson 1980). The first factor corresponds to Givón's "thematic continuity" and relates to the fact that thematic (or episode) boundaries crucially affect a speaker's choice of coding devices. The second group of factors corresponds to Givón's "action continuity." Neither of these areas is dealt with in great detail in Givón (1983a,c,d), though he does compare continuity, in terms of topicality indices, for participants at thematic junctures with those not at such junctures (1983d:192ff).

Two recent works which incorporate the notion of thematic structure into the question of choice of participant-coding devices are Clancy (1980) and Barbara Fox (1986). As noted in Chapter 1 section 1.5.2.2, Clancy's is the first work in which topicality (though she does not use this term) is measured in terms of distance, in number of clauses since last mention. However, in addition to counting numbers of clauses, Clancy also notices that discourse boundaries tend to elicit stronger coding devices than would be expected, given a strictly linear view of continuity based on number of mentions or distance since last mention. The particular boundaries that Clancy finds relevant are "world shifts," where a narrator shifts between the "real world," i.e., the situation in which the narrative is being recounted, and the "story world," i.e., the world being depicted in the narrative. Clancy also finds "episode" boundaries significant. There are many other factors that Clancy deals with in her article on a case-by-case basis.

Barbara Fox (1986), working primarily in the framework of Rhetorical Structure Analysis (Mann and Thompson 1986) for written texts, and Conversational Analysis (Sacks, Schegloff, and Jefferson 1974) for conversational texts, shows that the choice between use of a pronoun versus a full noun phrase in English is influenced by the hierarchical structure of the content of the text. Fox takes particular examples of what would, from a strictly linear point of view based on number of clauses since previous mention, appear to be excessively strong coding devices (i.e., full NPs) or excessively weak devices (i.e., pronouns), and shows how from a hierarchical point of view such patterning is explainable (Fox 1986:240ff). On the basis of such examples, Fox rejects the "distance" view of topicality in favor of a hierarchical view.

There is no question that hierarchical structure must be taken into account in an all-inclusive theory of anaphora. However, the essential contribution of Givón's work on topic continuity is that it provides a quantitative method of calculating at least some of the factors affecting choice of coding devices. It is not meant to be all-inclusive or predictive, in the sense of being able to provide an algorithm for generating exactly the correct coding choices in a text, and none of the incorrect ones. It simply provides a rigorous, quantitative method of comparing the functions of coding devices according to certain well-defined parameters (Referential Distance, Persistence and Ambiguity, as defined below). Future research on the use of anaphora in discourse must still provide a rigorous, preferably quantitative way of characterizing the effect of thematic continuity on participant-coding choices.

In Chapter 5, sections 5.1.2 and 5.2.5, I will illustrate two respects in which the hierarchical structure of the text affects the choice of coding devices in Yagua, and in Chapter 6 I will examine one specific construction in depth, namely, S_o coding on verbs. The use of this construction is better explained in terms of thematic structure than of strict continuity.

4.2. Technique

Topicality will be measured in terms of two indices: Referential Distance ("look back") and Persistence ("decay"). A third index, Ambiguity ("interference"), will be calculated for a subset of the examples in the corpus, for reasons discussed below.

The index of Referential Distance (RD) is based on the assumption that participants that have not been mentioned recently in the discourse are more difficult to process and are therefore less topical than those mentioned more recently. This index measures the gap between the current mention of a participant and its previous mention in the discourse in terms of number of clauses. Thus an RD of 1 indicates that the participant was last mentioned in the immediately preceding clause and is therefore maximally continuous. In the extreme case of discontinuity, where a participant has not been mentioned at all in the present discourse, the RD index is technically infinite. However, since we cannot deal satisfactorily with infinite values, I will follow Givón (1983a,c,d) in imposing the somewhat arbitrary limit of 20 on the RD index. Thus, participants introduced into the discourse for the first time, or absent from the discourse stage for 20 clauses or longer receive an RD index of 20.

The index of Persistence is based on the notion that some participants are "destined," as it were, to figure more prominently in the ensuing discourse than are others. Those that the speaker plans to continue talking about will be treated as more highly topical than those that will play only a transitory role. Givón (1983a,c,d) and the authors of the specific topic-continuity studies appearing in Givón (1983b) calculate the Persistence index for a particular instance of a coding device by counting the number of subsequent clauses in which the participant coded by that device continues as topic in an unbroken chain. This methodology seems overly artificial to me, in that it is very common for a clause to not mention a participant that in all other respects is highly topical. Under the original counting method, such a clause will immediately terminate a Persistence chain for that participant, even though the participant may be picked up again and referred to continuously for many subsequent clauses. For this reason, I depart from the original methodology in favor of a method that measures the DENSITY of mentions of a participant in a subsequent stretch of text, as follows: count the number of mentions of the participant in question within 10 clauses to the right of the current mention (T. Payne 1987:8, Sun and Givón 1985). The minimal value of this index, then, would be zero for participants that are not mentioned at all in the following 10 clauses. There is in principle no maximal value to this measurement, since participants can be mentioned more than once in a clause. However, the highest Persistence index in the corpus on which this study is based is 14.

Finally, the index of Ambiguity relates to the fact that whenever a participant is mentioned, there may be other participants on stage that compete for interpretation as the referent of the particular coding device employed. In other words, RD and Persistence being equal, a stronger coding device will be necessary to identify a participant if there are other semantically appropriate participants in the immediate discourse context. This index is limited to two values, 1 and 2. If there are no additional semantically appropriate participants on stage at the time of coding, the Ambiguity index is 1. If there are other such participants, the index is 2. A participant is considered to be "on stage" if it has been mentioned within three clauses prior to the mention in question.

In many cases it is quite clear whether or not there are potentially interfering participants on stage. In many other cases in the corpus studied, however, it is not clear. Operationalizing this index in a way that would be rigorous and replicable proved very difficult for several reasons, though the essential problem is that of defining the notion of semantic appropriateness. Any verb in a particular discourse context is usually very restricted as to the participants that might conceivably take part in the action described. Many participants may be on stage, but context, common sense and semantics all interact to determine which participants are acting at any given point. At times it seems rather arbitrary to select out semantics as the one factor determining whether any two participants might compete as referents for a given coding device. For example, in the Twins Cycle there are many cases where several participants are interacting. Technically, in such a circumstance, the use of a third-person-dual coding device could refer to any possible pairing of participants that are on stage; thus Ambiguity would be high. However, the only pair ever referred to *as a pair* in the story are the twins themselves. Thus from a pragmatic point of view the Ambiguity is very low. For this and other reasons, the Ambiguity index was not calculated on the corpus as a whole, but only for examples of strong coding devices used for recently mentioned participants (Chapter 5, section 5.2), and for the PPRO device (Chapter 7).

4.3. Modifications

The major modifications I have introduced into Givón's methodology involve the treatment of quoted material. This is particularly important for this study, since over 30% of the clauses in the corpus are quotes. Participant mentions within quotes have not been given topicality indices, since I judge that their topicality pertains more to the quoted discourse than to the discourse in which the quote appears. However, such mentions are counted for purposes of determining the topicality of other mentions that occur outside the quotes. This decision rests on the assumption that if a participant is mentioned in a quote, that participant is "on stage" and therefore is just as potentially topical as it would be were it mentioned outside of a quote.[3]

A second modification that I have introduced is to count the character that utters the quote as having been mentioned, even if no overt mention of that character is made. This modification is based on the assumption that a participant that has a "speaking part" in the discourse drama must be "on stage," and therefore available as a discourse topic at the point where he or she speaks. It is quite common in Yagua discourse for a series of quotes to occur in which two or more participants are interacting, but where explicit verbs of saying are not indicated for every conversational "turn" in the quoted discourse. It is simply understood by the content of the turn which interactant is speaking. Such situations are considered here to constitute a mention of the speaker for purposes of calculating topicality indices of other mentions; however, such implicit mentions have not themselves been assigned topicality indices.

Other modifications involve the measurement of mentions of participants that are referentially included within mentions of other, nonsingular, participants. Nonsingular mentions are considered to be mentions of each of the individuals contained in the group. Thus the RD of a nonsingular mention would be the distance back to the last mention of any of the included individuals. The Persistence index would be the number of mentions of any of the individuals within 10 clauses to the right. Similarly, nonsingular mentions are considered to be mentions of each of the individuals for purposes of counting RD and P indices of other singular mentions of those individuals.

Finally, I will introduce four CHARACTER STATUSES as follows:

1. Central characters: These are the characters that the text is about, and which are normally present throughout the text. Central characters do not lose their status as central characters, even if they are not mentioned for an entire episode (e.g., the snail episode of the Twins Cycle, TC398 to TC458).

2. Noncentral major characters: those characters mentioned 5 or more times in 20 clauses in a single episode. Characters mentioned only 4 times in 20 clauses are also considered major if in the majority of those mentions (i.e., 3 or 4) the character was a subject, i.e., an A or S participant. For purposes of determining whether a character is major or not, a quote is considered to be a (nonsubject) mention of the character who utters the quote. Major characters may lose this status in a subsequent episode if they do not meet the criterion.

3. Perpetually present: This category encompasses that small number of referents that are automatically present on the discourse stage and therefore do not need to be introduced, e.g., the sun, the day, etc. Also, dummy referents like the subject of 'thunder' in 'It thunders.' Mentions of such participants are not given topicality indices, and therefore do not figure into the counts for the various coding devices.

4. Minor characters: all other participants.

The scope of this study is purposely limited in several respects. I am concerned here only with A, O, S (all types, including subjects of nonverbal predicates),[4] and all Oblique (OBL) participants. I have not calculated topicality values for interjections or possessors, though these categories of mentions are considered in the calculations of topicality values for other mentions. Furthermore, I have not calculated topicality indices for zero or the right-dislocated devices (RDNP and RDPRO), or for the left-dislocated NP device (LDNP) since these occur only very rarely, and then only in combination with some other device. Doris Payne (1990) deals with the pragmatic functions of left-dislocated NPs.

4.4. Data Base of the quantitative study

The data base for this study, summarized in Table 1, consists of four texts, all essentially folkloric narratives:

Table 1. Data Base for the Topic-Continuity Study

Text	Number of clauses			
	Quotes	Nonquotes	Total	
1. Kneebite Twins (KT)	62	131	193	Appendix 1
2. First Squirrel (FSQ)	48	86	134	Appendix 2
3. Twins Cycle (TC)	232	371	603	Appendix 4
4. Hunter Narrative (HN)	72	154	226	Not appended
Totals:	414	742	1156	

The fact that all these texts are folkloric narratives biases the sample, to be sure. However, I have made this choice for several reasons: (1) to eliminate genre as a possible complicating factor as much as possible; (2) folkloric narrative is virtually the only non-first-person genre available in Yagua, and questions of topic continuity are not as relevant when the primary characters are speech-act participants, which are always highly topicworthy; and (3) since little is known about Yagua in general, I judge it appropriate to begin the investigation with straightforward, narrative material.

These texts were all orally composed by unquestionably competent native storytellers, under reasonably natural circumstances. Transcriptions and translations were made either by native speakers or by linguists working closely with the storytellers themselves (all of whom were preliterate at the time of storytelling). Text 1 (Appendix 1) is an episode of a longer Yagua folktale titled "Little Baldy" in Paul Powlison (1969). This particular version was recorded as a self-contained unit, so all continuity is relevant within the span of text examined. The other texts were also recorded by Paul Powlison. Texts 2 (Appendix 2) and 3 have not been published; text 4 is given in Powlison (1969), though in a different orthography from that used in this study, and without clause numbering.

4.5. The Results

The tables and discussion presented here are only a few of the possible ways of displaying the results of the quantitative study. I have tried to provide enough figures so that the reader with interest in a specific issue not discussed here will be able to glean appropriate data from the tables. However, the discussion is limited to a few areas of particular interest to this study. The following abbreviations (see section 4.3) are used in the tables: C = Central character, MA = MAjor character, and MI = MInor character; A, O, S_a, and S_o refer to semantico-syntactic roles, as outlined in Chapter 1, section 1.5.2. T = totals, n = number of instances, and Mn = mean.

Mean values for all indices are shown on the bottom row of each table. Since individual deviations from these values are of particular interest, the total number of instances of each value of each index for each coding device is also indicated. Thus the tables graphically represent the distribution of instances of particular values within the entire range of possible values.

The pre-predicate pronoun device occurred only 9 times in the four texts summarized in Table 1, for all roles. Hence further examples were selected at random from other texts, increasing the total number of examples to 25. All but one of these examples were of central or major characers. Due to the relatively few examples, the three character statuses were not distinguished for the preposed pronoun device.

4.5.1. A and S_a participants (subjects)

4.5.1.1. Referential Distance

Table 2 gives Referential Distance counts for A and S_a participants coded with the VC (verb coding) device:

Table 2. Referential Distance, Verb Coding Device

RD	A				S_a				Total
	C	MA	MI	T	C	MA	MI	T	
1	90	44	2	136	134	67	9	210	346
2	14	14	1	29	27	25		52	81
3	7	5		12	10	8		18	30
4	2	1		3	6	5	1	12	15
5	2			2	1	1		2	4
6		1		1		2		2	3
7									
8					1			1	1
9						1		1	1
10						3		3	3
11		1		1					1
(no instances for RD of 12 to 16)									
17					1			1	1
18									
19									
20	1			1	3			3	4
n =	116	66	3	185	183	112	10	305	490
Mn =	1.53	1.64	1.33	1.56	1.50	2.63	1.3	1.84	1.74

From Table 2 we observe that Referential Distance for the VC device is quite low and roughly equal for all participant categories. The majority of instances (346/490 or 71%) code participants that had been mentioned in the immediately prior clause (RD = 1), and most of the others cluster near the lower end of the scale. These gross facts lead me to classify VC as a SHORT-RANGE coding device. That is, its primary function is to code participants that have been mentioned very recently in the discourse. However, it is occasionally used to code quite distant participants. In fact, 4 times in this corpus the VC device has the maximal RD index of 20. In Chapter 5, section 5.1, I will look at specific examples of VC used to code relatively distant participants (RD > 8) for possible explanations for this patterning.

Table 3 gives Referential Distance counts for A and S_a participants coded with the PVNP device:

Table 3. Referential Distance, Pre-predicate NP Device

RD	A				S_a				Totals
	C	MA	MI	T	C	MA	MI	T	
1		2		2	1		1	2	4
2									
3					1			1	1
4									
5							1	1	1
6						1		1	1
7									
8	1			1					1
(no instances for RD of 10 to 19)									
20			1	1		1	5	6	7
n =	1	2	1	4	2	2	7	11	15
Mn =	8	1	20	7.5	2	13	15.14	12.36	11.07

An obvious and expected finding of the figures in Table 3 is that PVNP is a relatively LONG-RANGE coding device. That is, it typically codes participants that have been absent from the discourse stage for a substantial number of clauses. The mean RD of 11.07 for the PVNP device is significantly higher than that of 1.74 for the VC device. However, the figures in Table 3 do not show nearly as much homogeneity as do those for the VC device. In particular we notice that S_a participants taken as an aggregate exhibit higher Referential Distance than do A participants (RD = a mean of 12.36 for S_a and 7.5 for A). This fact indicates that participants coded in the S_a role (subjects of intransitive verbal predicates) are generally less topical and more discontinuous than those coded in the A role (transitive subjects). This observation is consistent with Du Bois (1985), who observes that intransitive subjects and transitive objects share the characteristic of being the primary roles in which "new" information is introduced, as opposed to transitive subject, which is typically "given" information. And in fact a quick glimpse ahead reveals that the preverbal NP device used to code O participants has an RD more similar to that of the same device used to code S_a rather than A participants (see Table 13).

The individual figures for central, major, and minor participants in Table 3 are not particularly helpful, since the number of examples is so low. However, we may make two general observations: (1) the PVNP device is relatively uncommon, occurring only 15 times in 742 nonquote clauses of text; and (2) when it is used, it tends to code noncentral (12 instances) rather than central characters (3 instances).

Table 4 gives Referential Distance counts for A and S_a participants coded with the verb coding plus (post-verbal) noun phrase (VC + NP) device:

Table 4. Referential Distance, Verb Coding Plus NP Device

RD	A				S_a				Totals
	C	MA	MI	T	C	MA	MI	T	
1	2	6		8	10	12		22	30
2	1	1		2	4	6	1	11	13
3	1			1	3	1	3	7	8
4						3		3	3
5	1			1	1			1	2
6		1		1	1	3		4	5
7		1		1			1	1	2
8									
9					2			2	2
(no instances for RD of 10 to 17)									
18					1	1		2	2
19									
20	1	2	4	7	2	9	9	20	27
n =	6	11	4	21	24	35	14	73	94
Mn =	5.33	5.55	20	8.24	4.75	6.77	14.14	7.77	7.87

The aggregate mean for RD with the VC + NP device (7.87) is not as high as with the PVNP device (11.07). Thus I conclude that participants coded with the PVNP device are less topical than those coded with the VC + NP device. This fact is consistent with the view expressed in Givón (1983c:19) that in flexible-word-order languages, preverbal NPs are universally associated with higher discontinuity than are postverbal NPs.[5] However, these same facts seem counter to the scale of phonological size (Givón 1983c:18), which indicates that the phonologically "larger" device (in this case VC + NP) should be correlated with higher discontinuity than the "smaller" device (PVNP). Clearly there is some other factor involved here. This issue will be taken up in Chapter 8.

Again, the figures in Table 4 exhibit less homogeneity than those for the VC device. Unlike the PVNP device (Table 3), Referential Distance counts for the VC + NP device do not separate out according to semantico-syntactic role, i.e., for the VC + NP device, A and S_a participants as a whole exhibit statistically equivalent RD counts (8.24 and 7.77 respectively). However, what we notice in Table 4 is that the counts do separate out according to character status. Central characters are consistently more topical, in terms of RD, than major characters, which in turn are consistently more topical than minor characters.

Finally, Table 5 gives Referential Distance counts for A and S_a participants coded with the PPRO device:

Table 5. Referential Distance, Preverbal Pronoun Device

RD	A		S_a		Totals
1	3		10		13
2	1				1
3	1				1
n =	5		10		15
Mn =	1.6		1		1.2

From Table 5, I conclude that PPRO is a short-range device. It is interesting that its RD count is actually slightly less for the other short-range device, VC (see Table 2). However, even if we take these figures to be equivalent, we seem to have a violation of the iconicity principle of topic continuity stated in example 1. PPRO is a "larger," more complex, and more marked device than VC, and therefore should code topics that are less continuous. In several previous studies (Clancy 1980, Barbara Fox 1986, Derbyshire 1986, *inter alia*) it has been observed that the functional domain of pronouns, in particular stressed independent pronouns for languages that have more than one type, is quite distinct from straight topicality. In Chapter 7 I look at other factors that account for the use of the PPRO device, and compare the use of pronouns in Yagua to other languages for which comparable data are available. In Chapter 8 I present some ramifications of this kind of anomaly for the topic-continuity framework.

From Table 5, I conclude that PPRO is a short-range device. It is interesting that its RD count is actually slightly less for the other short-range device, VC (see Table 2). However, even if we take these figures to be equivalent, we seem to have a violation of the iconicity principle of topic continuity stated in example 1. PPRO is a "larger," more complex, and more marked device than VC, and therefore should code topics that are less continuous. In several previous studies (Clancy 1980, Barbara Fox 1986, Derbyshire 1986, *inter alia*) it has been observed that the functional domain of pronouns, in particular stressed independent pronouns for languages that have more than one type, is quite distinct from straight topicality. In Chapter 7 I look at other factors that account for the use of the PPRO device, and compare the use of pronouns in Yagua to other languages for which comparable data are available. In Chapter 8 I present some ramifications of this kind of anomaly for the topic-continuity framework.

4.5.1.2. Persistence

In calculating Persistence indices, the categories of major and minor characters were collapsed into one, for the simple reason that minor characters could by definition not have a Persistence index of more than 4 (see section 4.3). Also,

Persistence indices were not recorded for mentions closer than 10 clauses to the end of a text, to assure that all those counted were calculated on full spans of 10 clauses.

Table 6 gives Persistence indices for A and S_a categories coded with the VC device.

P	A			S_a			Totals
	C	NC	T	C	NC	T	
0	1	7	8	1	10	11	19
1	1	8	9	3	14	17	26
2	4	3	7	8	15	23	30
3	8	3	11	15	11	26	37
4	4	6	10	11	20	31	41
5	7	14	21	15	13	28	49
6	15	7	22	22	14	36	58
7	16	9	25	22	10	32	57
8	20	8	28	26	5	31	59
9	19	1	20	19	3	22	42
10	17	1	18	19	2	21	39
11	3	2	5	7		7	12
12	3		3	1		1	4
13	1		1				1
14				1		1	1
n =	119	69	188	170	117	287	475
Mn =	7.39	4.61	6.36	6.54	3.96	5.61	5.88

Table 6. Persistence, VC Device

From Table 6, we see that central characters coded with the VC device are higher in persistence than noncentral characters. This is not particularly surprising, since central characters are almost by definition those that are mentioned most often. Thus for any random stretch of text, we would expect to find more repeated mentions of individual central characters than of any individual noncentral characters. As with the RD index, we find the Persistence index for the VC device to be roughly equal for both A and S_a participants.

Table 7 gives Persistence counts for A and S_a categories coded with the PVNP device:

	Table 7. Persistence, Pre-verbal NP Device							
P	A				S_a			Totals
	C	NC	T		C	NC	T	
0		2	2			5	5	7
1						3	3	3
2						1	1	1
3		1	1					1
4								
5		1	1					1
6								
7					1		1	1
8								
9								
10	1		1		1		1	2
n =	1	4	5		2	9	11	16
Mn =	10	2	3.6		8.5	.56	2	2.5

In Table 7, we notice that the figures for central and noncentral characters separate out even more strongly than they do for the VC device. Central characters coded with the PVNP device are much more strongly persistent than noncentral characters referred to with the same device. Again, however, there seems to be no significant distinction based on semantico-syntactic role.

Table 8 gives Persistence counts for the VC plus (post-verbal) NP device:

Table 8. Persistence, VC plus NP device

P	A				S_a			Totals
	C	NC	T		C	NC	T	
0		4	4			6	6	10
1	1		1			7	7	8
2	1	3	4			7	7	11
3		1	1			4	4	5
4					3	7	10	10
5		1	1		1	5	6	7
6	1	2	3		3	5	8	11
7		1	1		3	2	5	6
8	1	2	3		2	5	7	10
9	1	1	2		4	1	5	7
10					3	1	4	4
11	1		1		5	1	6	7
12						1	1	1
n =	6	15	21		24	52	76	97
Mn =	6.17	3.87	4.52		8.04	4.08	5.33	5.15

The figures in Table 8 are closer to those in Table 6 than to those in Table 7. That is, in terms of topic Persistence as measured according to number of mentions, VC + NP functions more like VC than like PVNP.

Finally, Table 9 gives Persistence counts for A and S_a participants coded with the PPRO device:

Table 9. Persistence, Preverbal Pronoun Device

P	A		S_a		Totals
0	1		3		4
1			3		3
2			1		1
3					
4	1		2		3
5	1		2		3
(no instances for Persistence of 6 to 8)					
9	2				2
n =	5		11		16
Mn =	5.4		2.09		3.13

4.5.2. O and S_o participants

4.5.2.1. Referential Distance

Table 10 gives Referential Distance counts for O and S_o participants coded with the simple E (enclitic) device. A distinction is also drawn between S_o participants of predicate nominals and S_o participants of verbal predicates (see Chapter 6 for a text-based analysis of S_o coding with verbs).

Table 10. Referential Distance, Enclitic Device

RD	O				S_o (pred. nom.)				S_o (verb)				Totals
	C	MA	MI	T	C	MA	MI	T	C	MA	MI	T	
1	18	25	8	51	1	3	1	5	9	3		12	68
2	7	12		19						3		3	22
3	4	4	1	9					1			1	10
4		2		2					1			1	3
5	1	1		2									2
(no instances of RD 6 to 19)													
20		2	2	4					1			1	5
n =	30	46	11	87	1	3	1	5	12	6		18	110
Mn =	1.63	2.48	4.64	2.46	1	1	1	1	3	1.5		2.5	2.43

From Table 10 we can conclude that, like VC and PPRO, the enclitic device is short-range in that most instances cluster toward the low end of the RD scale. Another interesting parallel between the enclitic device and VC is that for both there are some instances of its being used to code quite distant participants, even though there is a significant gap in which none are found. For the enclitic device the gap is from RD 6 to 19, with three instances of its being used to code participants with an RD of 20. One dissimilarity is that, especially for O participants, RD is slightly higher for E than for VC (Table 2). This fact indicates that O participants coded with the E device are slightly less continuous than A and S_a participants coded with the VC device.

There is no clearly significant patterning of RD indices for the E device by semantico-syntactic role or character status. For the O role, central characters exhibit a slightly lower RD than major characters, which in turn exhibit a slightly lower RD than minor characters. This is yet another example of central characters being more topical than noncentral ones, and major characters being more topical than minor ones. However, the overall spread between the RD indices of the various character statuses is not particularly striking, and the overall RD indices for O and S_o participants of verbal predicates are very similar. I judge that there are not enough examples of S_o participants of nonverbal predicates to draw any conclusions from their RD indices, which are consistently 1.

Table 11 gives Referential Distance counts for O and S_o participants coded with the post-predicate NP device:

Table 11. Referential Distance, Post-predicate NP Device

RD	O				S_o (pred. nom.)				S_o (verb)				Totals
	C	MA	MI	T	C	MA	MI	T	C	MA	MI	T	
1		1	3	4									4
2		2	1	3									3
3													
4			1	1									1
5													
6		1		1									1
7		1		1									1
(no instances of RD 8 through 19)													
20		3	7	10			5	5					15
n =		8	12	20			5	5					25
Mn =		9.75	12.42	11.35			20	20					12.8

As Table 11 shows, the simple post-predicate NP device is not used to code central characters at all. However, the generalization that major characters exhibit lower RD (9.75) than minor characters (12.42) still holds. Also, subjects of nonverbal predications (S_o participants) are only used to code participants with the maximum RD (20), though we have so few examples of subjects of nonverbal predications coded with this device that any generalizations must remain tentative.

Table 12 gives Referential Distance counts for O and S_o participants coded with the enclitic plus NP device:

Table 12. Referential Distance, Enclitic Plus NP Device

RD	O				S$_o$ (pred. nom.)				S$_o$ (verbal)				Totals
	C	MA	MI	T	C	MA	MI	T	C	MA	MI	T	T
1	1	6	2	9	4			4					13
2	2	2	1	5	1			1					6
3		1	1	2					1			1	3
4													
5			1	1									1
6		1	1	2									2
7			2	2									2
8			1	1									1
9													
10													
11	1			1									1
(no instances of RD 12 through 19)													
20	2	3	15	20	1			1					21
n =	7	17	19	43	6			6	1			1	50
Mn =	8.43	6.24	16.32	10.8	4.33			4.33	3			3	10.08

In Table 12, we see again that the only substantial number of instances occur in the O columns (n = 43). Central and major characters are similar in RD, while minor characters are substantially higher. However, for the first time the generality that central characters are more topical than major characters is violated; central characters coded with the E+NP device are actually less topical (RD = 8.43) than major characters (RD = 6.24).

Table 13 gives Referential Distance counts for O and S$_o$ participants coded with the PVNP device:

Table 13. Referential Distance, Pre-predicate NP Device

RD	O				S$_o$ (pred. nom.)				Totals
	C	MA	MI	T	C	MA	MI	T	
1	1		1	2		2		2	4
(no instances of RD 2 through 19)									
20			1	7	8			1	1	9
n =	1	1	8	10		2	1	3	13
Mn =	1	20	17.63	16.2		1	20	7.33	14.15

Unfortunately there are so few examples of the PVNP device used to code O and S_O participants that it is very difficult to draw any significant conclusions. However, we do notice that there is only one instance of this device used to code a central character, and in that instance the RD is the minimum. For the other O participants, RD is higher than for any other device (RD = 20 for major characters and 17.63 for minor characters).

Finally, Table 14 gives Referential Distance counts for O and S_O participants coded with the PPRO device:

Table 14. Referential Distance, Pre-predicate Pronoun Device			
RD	O	S_O (pred. nom.)	Totals
1	5	2	7
2	2	1	3
n =	7	3	10
Mn =	1.29	1.33	1.3

Again, the number of examples is so low as to render any generalizations tentative at best. All we can definitively say from these figures is that PPRO is a short-range device (aggregate RD = 1.3).

4.5.2.2. Persistence

The following tables give Persistence counts for O and S_O participants, beginning with the E device:

P	O			S_o (pred. nom.)			S_o (verb)			Totals
	C	NC	T	C	NC	T	C	NC	T	
0		8	8							8
1	1	9	10					1	1	11
2	1	7	8		2	2		2	2	12
3	2	10	12					1	1	13
4	2	4	6		1	1	1		1	8
5	1	2	3				1		1	4
6	2	3	5				2	1	3	8
7	4	3	7				1	1	2	9
8	10	4	14				2		2	16
9	4	1	5				1		1	6
10	3		3				1		1	4
11		1	1				3		3	4
n =	30	52	82		3	3	12	6	18	103
Mn =	6.93	3.27	3.38		2.67	2.67	8	3.5	6.5	4.88

Table 15. Persistence, E device

These figures again show that central characters are more continuous in terms of Persistence than noncentral characters. For both O and S_o (verbal) roles, central characters are substantially more persistent than noncentral characters. In particular, the figures for O participants are roughly equal to, though slightly lower than, those for A and S_a participants coded with the VC device (see Table 6).

Table 16 gives Persistence counts for the simple NP device:

Table 16. Persistence, Post-predicate NP Device

P	O			S_o (pred. nom.)			S_o (verb)	Totals
	C	NC	T	C	NC	T	(none)	
0		7	7		3	3		10
1		5	5		1	1		6
2		1	1		1	1		2
3		2	2					2
4								
5		1	1					1
6		2	2					2
7								
8		1	1					1
9								
10								
11		1	1					1
n =		20	20		5	5		23
Mn =		2.45	2.45		.6	.6		2.08

Table 16 shows that participants coded with the post-predicate NP device exhibit very low Persistence indices, though O participants are slightly more persistent than S_o participants.

Table 17 gives Persistence counts for the E plus NP device:

P	O			S_o (pred. nom.)			S_o (verb)			Totals
	C	NC	T	C	NC	T	C	NC	T	
0		9	9							9
1		7	7		1	1				8
2		6	6		1	1				7
3	1	5	6		1	1				7
4		2	2		1	1				3
5		3	3							3
6	1		1					1	1	2
7	2		2							2
8	1		1		2	2				3
9	2	1	3							3
10										
11					1	1				1
n =	7	33	40		7	7		1	1	48
Mn =	7	2	2.8		5.29	5.29		6	6	3.63

Table 17. Persistence, E plus NP device

Again, central characters are a distinct minority, but when they are coded with the E + NP device their Persistence is somewhat higher than with the other devices (e.g., E and post-predicate NP). It may be significant that S_o participants of nonverbal predicates have a higher mean Persistence index (5.29) than do O participants (2.8 for all statuses, 2.0 for noncentral characters only), even though all examples of S_o participants coded with this device are noncentral characters.

Table 18 gives Persistence counts for O and S_o participants coded with the PVNP device:

Table 18. Persistence, Pre-predicate NP Device

P	O			S_o		Totals
	C	NC		C	NC	
0		4				4
1		1				1
2					1	1
3						
4					1	1
5		1			1	2
n =		6			3	9
Mn =		1			3.67	1.89

Again, the number of examples is very small. Nevertheless, we find that the PVNP device is used primarily for relatively nonpersistent participants.

Finally, Table 19 gives Persistence counts for O and S_o participants coded with the PPRO device:

Table 19. Persistence, Pre-predicate Pronoun Device

P	O	S_o (pred. nom.)	Totals
0	1		1
3		1	1
6	1	1	2
7	2		2
8	1		1
9	1		1
10	1		1
13		1	1
n =	7	3	10
Mn =	6.71	7.33	6.9

4.5.3. Oblique participants

In this section the tables giving Referential Distance and Persistence counts for oblique participants are presented. The only devices ever used to code oblique participants in my corpus are HC, NP, and HC + NP (see Chapter 2, section 2.4).

Topic Continuity

4.5.3.1. Referential Distance

Table 20 gives RD counts for oblique participants codedwith the HC device:

Table 20. Referential Distance, Head-Coding Device

RD	C	MA	MI	Totals
1	32	44	10	86
2	8	11		19
3	3	5	1	9
4		2		2
5		1		1
6				
7	1			1
8				
9		1		1
(no instances of RD 10 through 16)				
17		1		1
n =	44	65	11	120
Mn =	1.45	1.85	1.18	1.64

From Table 20 we observe that the RD indices for the HC device are roughly comparable to those for the VC (Table 2) and E (Table 10) devices, i.e., HC is a short-range device in that instances cluster near the lower end of the scale. However, these counts differ from those for VC and E in that there are no instances of the HC device with the maximum RD of 20. In other words there is no secondary clustering toward the upper end of the scale as there is for VC and E.

Table 21 gives RD counts for the (pre-head) NP device:

RD	C	MA	MI	Totals
Table 21 Referential Distance, NP Device				
1		3		3
2		3	5	8
3		2		2
4			2	2
5		1		1
6		3		3
7			1	1
8		2		2
9		1		1
10			1	1
11				
12			2	2
(no instances of RD 13 through 19)				
20		5	54	59
n =		20	65	85
Mn =		8.2	17.51	15.32

The simple NP device used to code oblique participants is reserved for noncentral characters.

Table 22 gives RD counts for the HC + NP device:

Table 22. Referential Distance, Head Coding Plus NP Device

RD	C	MA	MI	Totals
1	6	2	1	9
2	1	2	1	4
3	3	2	1	6
4	1			1
5				
6		1		1
7	1	1		2
8		1	1	2
(no instances of RD 9 through 12)				
13		2		2
(no instances of RD 14 through 16)				
17		1		1
18		1		1
19				
20	1	6	8	15
n =	13	19	12	44
Mn =	3.69	11.26	14.5	9.91

From Table 22 we see that for obliques, central characters are much more likely to be coded with a head-coding prefix in combination with an NP than with an NP alone (Table 21). This fact, along with similar observations made for the other semantico-syntactic roles, allows us to make the more general observation that for all roles a simple NP is primarily used to code noncentral participants. Central participants are much more likely to be coded with a VC, E, or HC device in addition to the NP.

4.5.3.2. Persistence

Table 23 gives Persistence counts for the HC device:

Table 23. Persistence, HC Device

P	C	NC	Totals
0		9	9
1	1	11	12
2	1	11	12
3	1	8	9
4	1	11	12
5	1	8	9
6	7	3	10
7	8	5	13
8	9	3	12
9	6	3	9
10	8	1	9
11			
12	1		1
13	2		2
n =	46	73	119
Mn =	7.76	3.49	5.14

Table 23 reveals that oblique central characters coded with the HC device are more persistent than noncentral characters. This fact is also consistent with A/S_a participants coded with the VC device, and O/S_o participants coded with the E device.

Table 24 gives Persistence counts for the (pre-head) NP device:

Table 24. Persistence, NP Device

P	NC
0	45
1	12
2	6
3	8
4	7
5	2
6	
7	
8	1
9	1

n	=	82
Mn	=	1.26

Finally, Table 25 gives Persistence counts for the HC + NP device:

Table 25. Persistence, HC Plus NP Device

P	C	NC	Totals
0		9	9
1	1	7	8
2	1	3	4
3		2	2
4	3	2	5
5	2	3	5
6	2	1	3
7	1	3	4
8			
9	3	1	4
10	1		1
11	1		1

n	=	15	31	46
Mn	=	6.13	2.52	3.7

Again, central characters are more persistent than noncentral characters.

4.5.4. Summary of mean values by coding device

Tables 26-28 summarize the aggregate counts from all of the preceding tables. In the first column of these tables, the counts for the three reduced devices, VC, E, and HC, are found. Since VC is only used for A and Sa participants, the first two boxes in the first column give the appropriate counts for that device; The next two boxes give counts for the E device (used only for O and S_o participants), and the last box gives the count for the HC device (used only for oblique participants in these calculations). The same is true for column 3 where the counts for VC + NP, E + NP and HC + NP are listed. In tables 27 and 28 the aggregate means for each set of devices are given.

Table 26. Coding Devices, Frequency Summary

	VC/E/HC	PVNP	VC/E /HC + NP	PPRO	post-NP	Totals
A	188	5	21	5		219
Sa	305	11	76	11		403
O	87	10	43	7	20	167
So	23	3	8	3	5	42
Obl	120	85	46			251
T:	723	114	194	26	25	1082

Table 27. Referential Distance, Aggregate Means

	VC/E/HC	PVNP	VC/E /HC + NP	PPRO	post-NP	Agg.
A	1.56	7.5	8.24	1.6		2.35
Sa	1.84	12.36	7.77	1.0		3.24
O	2.46	16.2	10.8	1.29	11.35	6.84
So	2.17	14.15	4.14	1.33	20	4.92
Obl	1.64	15.32	9.91			7.97
Mn.	1.82	14.62	8.88	1.24	13.08	4.66

Table 28. Persistence, Aggregate Means

	VC/E/HC	PVNP	VC/E /HC+NP	PPRO	post-NP	Agg.
A	6.42	3.6	4.52	5.4		6.13
Sa	5.56	2.0	5.29	2.09		5.28
O	4.72	1.0	2.87	6.71	3.0	3.93
So	6.12	3.67	5.38	7.33	0.6	4.42
Obl	5.09	1.28	3.7			3.51
Mn.	5.48	1.50	4.33	4.58	2.08	4.76

4.6. Discussion

Of the four major A and Sa coding devices investigated in this study, I conclude that VC and PPRO are "short-range" (or "weak") devices (mean RD = 1.68 and 1.2 respectively). This means that these devices are used to code participants that have very recently been mentioned in the discourse, and which therefore are highly topical. NP and VC+NP, on the other hand, are "long-range" (or "strong") devices (mean RD = 11.07 and 7.95 respectively). Of the four major O and So coding devices, E and PPRO are short-range devices (mean RD = 2.18 and 1.3 respectively), while PVNP, NP and E+NP are long-range devices (mean RD = 13.67, 13.22, and 9.98 respectively). Of the three major oblique coding devices, HC is a short-range device (mean RD = 1.67), while NP and HC+NP are long-range devices (mean RD = 15.15 and 9.91 respectively). These facts are consistent with the iconicity principle of topic continuity stated in section 4.1 in that the VC, E, HC, and PPRO devices are the "smallest" (i.e., they are the most attenuated devices, both in phonological size and in semantic features that they represent) of the major coding devices, and therefore are predicted by the iconicity principle to code the most continuous, least surprising topics. Full noun phrases, on the other hand, should be used to code less continuous topics. That is, when a topic is introduced for the first time, or reintroduced after a long absence from the discourse stage, a semantically highly specified and phonologically large coding device such as a full NP will be needed to code that topic. A small device is likely to be insufficient to distinguish the topic from among all other potential topics available to the hearer.

Though the quantitative RD counts for this study generally support the iconicity principle of topic continuity, there are at least two anomalies if we consider RD to be the only relevant factor in our notion of scalar topicality. In order to explicate these anomalies, it will be convenient to classify the major coding devices into two groups: (1) SIMPLE devices and (2) RECAPITULATING devices. The simple devices consist of VC, HC, E, NP, and PPRO. The recapitulating devices are VC+NP, HC+NP and E+NP, i.e., those devices where an NP recapitulates one of the simple devices within the same clause. Occasionally I will refer to a recapitulating device and its corresponding simple device, or vice versa. This notion simply captures the correspondence between a simple device and the same device with a recapitulating noun phrase. NP and PPRO have no corresponding recapitulating devices.

With these definitions in mind, we can outline the two anomalies. Anomaly 1: Recapitulating devices are larger phonologically than simple NP devices, and yet the recapitulating devices consistently show lower RD indices. Anomaly 2: The PPRO devices are larger than simple VC, HC and E devices in that pronouns carry high tone and are in other ways phonologically independent. Yet PPRO consistently shows slightly lower RD indices than the other simple devices. These problems and others are discussed in Chapter 8.

Some additional problems to be considered with respect to these counts are: (1) under what conditions can the short-range devices be used to code more distant participants? (2) Under what conditions can the long-range devices be used to code recently mentioned participants? (3) What are the functional factors that condition the alternation between simple NP and the recapitulating devices for coding long-range participants? And (4) what are the functional factors that condition the use of PPRO versus the other short-range devices? Questions 1, 2, and 3 are dealt with in Chapter 5 section 5.1, 5.2, and 5.3 respectively. Question 4 is considered in more depth in Chapter 7.

Notes to Chapter 4

1   As discussed in Chapter 1, anaphoric zeros, as well as all other participant-coding devices, are considered
    to constitute "mentions" of the participants they code. (The terms "refer to" and "mention" are to be
    taken as equivalent in this study.) Essentially, high topicality for Givón is correlated with many mentions
    within a thematic paragraph, while low topicality is correlated with few mentions. It stands to reason that
    the participants that a text is "about" will be mentioned more often than others. This conception of
    topicality is logically independent of the notion of topicworthiness as discussed in section 4.1.1, though
    the two notions are intimately related.

2   The assumption that participants that have not been mentioned in the discourse have no topicality
    whatsoever is extreme, but is a logical presupposition of the topic-continuity framework. In section 4.1.1 I
    present some of the problems inherent in this notion of topicality as number of mentions. In 4.3, I
    outline some of my crude attempts to deal with these problems in my own topic-continuity study of
    Yagua. The fact is that speakers are more likely to talk about certain entities apart from whether those
    entities have already been mentioned in the current text or not. It would be unfair to suggest that Givón
    does not recognize this fact, as more recent work has shown that he and his students are sensitive to
    other factors affecting topicality (e.g., Givón 1987). However, these factors have not as yet been
    incorporated into a quantitative study, simply because they are so difficult to deal with. The best we have
    been able to do so far is to control for them.

3   Though see Chapter 5, section 5.2.7, for some evidence that this assumption may be mistaken.

4   Throughout this work the term "nonverbal" is used in the sense of "without a lexical verb." A nonverbal
    predicate is a predicate headed by a nominal, adjectival, adverbial, or postpositional expression.

5   Further studies of Papago (Doris Payne 1987) and Cayuga (Mithun 1987) also confirm this fact. This is
    not to say that Yagua is acting "exactly like" Papago or Cayuga, in this regard. In fact there are some
    very significant differences. For example, postverbal subjects in Yagua require the use of a coreferential
    prefix on the verb, whereas preverbal subjects (within the same intonation unit as the verb) preclude the
    prefix. Second, the preverbal NP device in Ute is used much more often than the postverbal NP device
    (39 to 25), whereas in Yagua PVNP is much less common than VC+NP (15 to 93). Finally, the RD
    indices for preverbal and postverbal NPs in Ute differentiate much more strongly (10.84 for preverbal
    NPs and 1.48 for postverbal NPs) than do the RD indices for PVNP and VC+NP in Yagua (11.07 for
    PVNP and 7.95 for VC+NP). Thus I conclude that the fact that the preverbal NP devices in both
    languages are more discontinuous than the postverbal NP devices is a relatively minor similarity. In
    almost every other respect they are different.

6   The terms introduced here in quotes are impressionistically defined cover terms, not technical terms.
    The same is true of several other terms used in this section and elsewhere, such as "recently," "highly
    topical" etc. At this point in the state of the art of topic-continuity, studies there is no standard by which
    we can evaluate in fine detail the differences between various values for the topicality indices. Therefore
    my conclusions regarding the significance of the difference between any two counts are purely
    impressionistic; the difference between an RD of 11.07 and 1.68 "feels" very significant, whereas the
    difference between 1.68 and 1.2 is less clear. I don't claim to have solved all the problems of the
    topic-continuity framework in this study. Hopefully, further research will be able to render the
    methodology more exact.

7   Two coreferential NPs may occur in the same intonation unit in certain discourse environments, such as
    in answers to information questions:

(1)   Speaker A: Tą́ą́ra   yi-vááy?
                              what   2SG-do/make
                              'What are you doing/making?'

Speaker B: Sụvǫ́ǫ́   ri-iváá-rya   sụvǫ́ǫ́.
               string:bag   1SG-do/make-INAN   string:bag
               'A string bag I am making a string bag.'

Though common in conversation, such constructions occurr very rarely in the corpus, and therefore I will leave their explanation for future research. In this work I will be concerned primarily with the major coding devices of the language.

Chapter 5

ADDITIONAL FACTORS AFFECTING CHOICE OF CODING DEVICE

As discussed in section 4.1, the iconicity principle of topic continuity juxtaposes the formal scale of phonological size to the functional scale of topicality. The correlation between these two scales is predicted as follows:

Phonological size: Topicality:

Large   Low   (RD = numerically high)

Small   High   (RD = numerically low)

In other words, the iconicity principle predicts that smaller, less marked coding devices will be used to code highly topical participants, i.e., participants with generally low Referential Distance. Conversely, larger, more marked, coding devices are predicted to code participants with higher Referential Distance.

The general findings of the topic-continuity study in Chapter 4 support these predictions. In the following sections the relatively few examples that appear to violate the general tendency will be examined. Section 5.1 deals with the 17 examples of short-range devices that code participants with RD greater than 8, and section 5.2 treats the 122 examples of long-range devices that code participants with RD less than 4. In section 5.3 functions of the recapitulating vs. nonrecapitulating long-range coding devices are compared.

5.1. Short-range devices used to code distant participants

Tables 2, 10, and 20 (Chapter 4) indicate that there are 17 occurrences of short-range devices VC, E, and HC used to code participants with an RD greater than 8 (PPRO is never used to code a participant more distant than 3 clauses). These constitute apparent counterexamples to the iconicity principle of topic continuity. Of these 17 examples, 6 refer to central characters, 9 to major characters, and 2 to minor characters. Thus among participant mentions in which a weaker device than otherwise expected is used, the ratio of mentions of central or major characters to mentions of minor characters is 8.5 to 1. In the corpus at large, there are 907 mentions of major and central characters and 222 mentions of minor characters: a ratio of 4.09 to 1. Thus status as a central or major character is a possible factor in allowing a participant to be coded with a weaker coding device than would otherwise be expected. In section 5.1.1 I will show that both instances of a minor character coded in this way have obvious explanations in terms of the context of the utterance. Other anomalous uses of short-range devices are best understood in terms of the hierarchical thematic structure of the text and a special constraint on the referents of dual coding devices. These factors will be discussed in sections 5.1.2 and 5.1.3 respectively.

5.1.1. Contextual inference

The Twins Cycle contains one instance of a minor character with RD > 8 coded with a short-range device. It occurs in an episode where the twins are spying on their grandfather to see where he gets water:

(1)   Sa-mutá̧-nuvee-tée   sa-dííya-**ra**,   jpuu, soon.
       3SG-open-ARR2-INTS   3SG-sight-INAN   SW   SW
       'On arrival he opens it in his sight, gush! pour!' (TC297)

The 'it' of this sentence refers to some kind of 'spigot' (as Paul Powlison 1969:115 terms it, though its identity is not explicit) that Grandfather opens to get his water. This spigot is never mentioned again in the story, and is therefore a very minor prop. In this sentence, the simple enclitic device is sufficient to code the spigot, since the verb *muta̧* 'open' combined with sound words that can only be used for rushing water make it clear that the thing being opened must be the source of the water. The actual identity of the item is not important. Rather, it is its function as the source of the water that makes it relevant at this point in the story, and for that purpose the verb and the sound words make the reference as clear as necessary.

The second example of a minor character coded with an unexpectedly weak coding device occurs in clause 130 of the Kneebite Twins tale. After the main character, Mokayu, kills a giant dung beetle, he removes the shells (wing coverings) and places them on his cheeks as adornments. In clause 129 (example 2a), the act of removing the shells is encoded with the verb *jóta*, which means 'to peel' or 'remove covering.' In clause 130 (example 2b), the shells themselves are referenced with the enclitic -ra:

(2)   a.   Sa-jóta-ri̧i̧   jííta-ra   sa-jó.
             3SG-peel-in:passing   JIITA-INAN   3SG-covering
             'He deshells him going along.' (KT129)

       b.   Sa-rúpa-ñiy   jíí   jí-myusi-tya̧a̧sá-**ra**.
             3SG-stick-TRNS   JIITA   COR1-cheek-middle-INAN
             He sticks it on his cheek. (KT130)

No more explicit mention of the beetle shells is needed in clause 130, because the verb *jóta* allows the hearer to infer the discourse presence of beetle shells. Also, after a hunt Yaguas often adorn themselves with parts of the animals killed (claws, teeth, etc.). Therefore, it is perfectly reasonable for Mokayu to stick the beetle shells on his cheeks after having triumphed over the beetle. These contextual factors render it appropriate to use a very weak device to code the beetle shells, even though they had never been mentioned before in the text.

5.1.2. Levels of Topicality

Central characters are topical throughout a discourse, and therefore are highly topicworthy at any point. Major characters are highly topicworthy throughout particular sections of a discourse. Minor characters, on the other hand, come and go and are, in general, unlikely topics throughout. This inherent topicworthiness of central and major characters is enough in many cases to overcome a high distance index. Ten of the remaining 15 instances of short-range devices coding high RD topics are explainable in terms of this notion of "levels" of topicality.

In the Twins Cycle (Appendix 4), the following sentence occurs with the simple enclitic device used to refer to the object, the spirit father's magic flute, even though it had not been mentioned for 60 clauses:

(3)   Santya   jíȋta   váriy   riinírya.
       sa-ntya   jíȋta   váriy   riy-jiniy-rà
       3SG-test   JIITA   then   3PL-in:presence-INAN
       'Then he tested it in their presence.' (TC213)

The flute is then mentioned three more times in succession, but never with a full NP. Its last previous mention is in clause 153, where the twins test it on their grandmother. Between these two events, however, there is an episode (containing two "scenes"; see Appendix 4) dealing with the creation of the Yagua clans. Thus the flute episode can be analyzed as having the clan-creation sequence *embedded* within it:

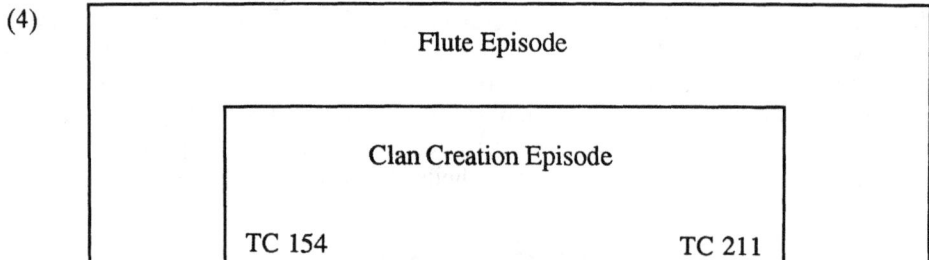

(4)

```
┌─────────────────────────────────────────────────────────┐
│                                                           │
│                       Flute Episode                       │
│                                                           │
│        ┌─────────────────────────────────────┐           │
│        │                                       │           │
│        │         Clan Creation Episode         │           │
│        │                                       │           │
│        │  TC 154                      TC 211   │           │
└────────┴───────────────────────────────────────┴──────────┘
```

In TC153 there is a problem to be solved, namely, how to avenge the death of the twins' father. Clauses 154 to 211 tell how the twins go about solving this problem. In clause 213 (212 is a transition marker) the problem is solved, and the action can continue where it left off in clause 153. The flute resumes as topic because its topicality spans the creation of the clans episode.

Two other cases of unexpectedly weak coding devices constitute examples of high-level topics being topicworthy, even though their RD is quite high. Each of these happens to be where one of the twins in the Twins Cycle is introduced:

(5)   Naanutuvą̄achu   jíȋta   sųųnáȃy   ruudiimú.
       naada-tuvą̄achu   jíȋta   sa-junáȃy   ruudii-mú
       3DL-hear   JIITA   3SG-cry   trash:heap-LOC
       'She hears him crying in the trash heap.' (TC22)

(6)   Naanutuvąąchuntíy   sųųnaantíy.
        naada-tuvąąchu-ntíy   sa-jųnááy-ntíy
        3DL-hear-REP   3SG-cry-REP
        'She again hears him crying.' (TC30)

In TC22 Elder Brother is introduced, and in TC30 Placenta is introduced. We might speculate that even though the twins have not been mentioned prior to this point in the text, they are still highly topicworthy because presumably the hearers know the story well and understand that the Twins Epic is being recounted, even though the twins themselves have not yet been mentioned. Thus we can consider these clauses to be examples of higher-level topics that are topicworthy at any point in the text. At this point, however, the level of topicality rises to the cultural and social setting of the story itself, with all the activities of the group that had taken place since the last telling of the story constituting an "embedded episode" in the ongoing collective awareness of the Twins Cycle.

5.1.3. The "natural pair constraint" on dual coding devices

Participants coded with devices that are "dual" in number tend to be natural pairs, e.g., twins a or a husband and wife. This is in addition to the idiomatic use of dual coding devices to refer to women who have had children. For example, if three characters are on stage, and two of them are a set of twins, any dual coding device will certainly refer to the twins rather than to one of the possible pairings of a twin with the third participant. Though three of the four texts that comprise the corpus for this study (including the longest text) involve a natural pair of central characters (the Kneebite Twins, the Non-Identical Twins, and the Hunters), there are no clear examples in this corpus of one member of a pair acting in concert with anyone other than the other twin (e.g., Elder Brother and Grandfather never act together apart from Placenta, or Mokayu and one wasp twin never act together apart from the other wasp twin). Therefore, I simply do not know if it is even possible to code a "non-natural" pairing with a dual coding device. In any case, it never happens in this corpus. I will term this tendency or requirement for dual coding devices to refer to naturally paired participants the "natural pair constraint" (NPC).

The NPC renders dual coding devices "stronger" in their ability to distinguish their referents than singular or plural coding devices. For example, in the hypothetical case cited above where there are three participants on stage, two of which constitute a natural pair, apart from the NPC any use of a dual coding device could logically refer to any random pairing of participants. A stronger coding device would be necessary to make explicit reference to the twins. However, with the NPC, the dual coding device would be perfectly adequate.

In fact, the NPC in Yagua renders dual coding devices as powerful as full noun phrases in designating referents in those texts that have natural pairs as central characters. For example, three times in the Kneebite Twins tale a dual short-range coding device refers to the twins at the maximum RD of 20 clauses. All three of these instances are at points where Mokayu meets the twins after having escaped their devious plots to destroy him:

(7)   Juuun, múúy   sarye-ñuvee-já-ásiy   **naada**-ntíy.
      SW   there   meet-ARR2-o'land-PROX1   3DL-REP
      'Oops! There the two meet (him) on arrival again.' (KT104)

      (KT160 is identical to KT104 except for the sound word.)

(8)   Múú-ñumaa   jumúsa-jo-mú   **naada**-maasá sa-ají́-ju-dáy.
      there-now   descend-NOM-LOC   3DL-sit   3SG-in:front-for-DAY
      'There in the port the two sit waiting for him.' (KT189)

'The two of them' in this text only refers to the twins. Therefore, no more explicit coding device other than the dual short-range device is needed. The only other dual short-range devices that occur in this text refer to "the vicious woman" of scene 13 (clauses 173-188). In that scene, the context also makes identification of the referent unambiguous.

Another example of the NPC in action occurs in TC459. Here the twins, though the central characters of the entire narrative, have not been on stage for 62 clauses, and have not been mentioned at all for 65 clauses. Yet in TC459 they are coded with simple verb coding:

(9)   Jáschiy   jį́į́tantíy   **naaniiniy**   ránaacho   púúriy.
      jásiy-siy   jį́į́ta-ntíy   naada-jiniy   rá-naacho   púúriy
      there-from JIITA-REP   3DL-come   INAN-after   pifayo[1]
      'From there they (2) came after pifayo.' (TC459)

5.2. Long-range devices used to code recently mentioned participants

In this section we will examine specific instances of long-range devices (all those involving NPs) used to code recently mentioned participants. The long-range devices distribute much more evenly within the possible range of RD variation than the short-range devices, i.e., there are many NPs (122) used to code participants with RD less than 4 (see tables 3, 4, 11, 12, 13, 21 and 22), whereas there arerelatively few short-range devices (17 to be exact) used to code long distance participants (RD > 8). In the following sections I describe seven conditions under which long-range devices are used to code recently mentioned participants, with examples of each one. In section 5.2.8 I give examples that do not seem to fit any of these categories. The examples presented were chosen primarily for their brevity. All but one involve long-range devices used to code participants whose RD is 1, thus allowing most passages cited to be limited to two clauses in length.

5.2.1. Ambiguity

Of course a very likely reason for using a strong coding device where RD is low is where AMBIGUITY (as defined in section 4.2) is high. Of the 122 examples of strong (long-range) coding devices used for participants with RD less than 4, Ambiguity was clearly high (i.e., A = 2) in 64.[2] The following excerpt illustrates this phenomenon in the First Squirrel text:

(10)   a.   Naada-ráąy   jíįta   jás-chiy.
           3DL-jump   JIITA   there-from
           'They jump from there.' (FSQ8)

        b.   Sa-ráąy   jíįta   **múcatyu**   munátyį-į   sa-jïïsíy.
           3SG-jump   JIITA   squirrel   first-NOM   3SG-before
           'The first squirrel jumps before him.' (FSQ9)

In 10a, the squirrel and the deer are collectively referred to with the dual VC form *naada-*, and so in 10b the RD for both is 1. In 10b, the squirrel is singled out from the deer by the use of a full NP in addition to a VC prefix. Without the NP múcatyu, 10b would be ambiguous as to who jumped first, and the point of the sentence would be lost.

The next example is from the Twins Cycle:

(11)   a.   Sa-jíį   jíįta   sụ-ụsíy.
           3SG-fly   JIITA   3SG-after
           'He (Placenta) flies after him (Grandfather).' (TC296)

        b.   Sa-múta-nuvee-téé   sa-dííya-ra,   jpuu,   soon.
           3SG-open-ARR2-INTS   3SG-sight-INAN   SW   SW
           'He (G) opens it in his (P) sight, gush! pour!' (TC297)

        c.   Sa-ráni   jíįta   naada-jáąpa   rá-áriy.
           3SG-stand   JIITA   3DL-grandfather   INAN-under
           'Their grandfather stands under it.' (TC298)

In 11a (TC296), the identities of the two participants are clear from the context: Grandfather has just left to bathe, and Placenta has transformed himself into a hummingbird in order to follow Grandfather and find out where he gets water. Again in 11b, the identities of the participants are clear from the context: the one who has gone to bathe is the only one likely to engage in an act involving gushing and pouring, while the other, the spy, looks on. In 11c, however, the context alone would not help the hearer identify the single participant. Though the bather is the only one likely to stand under the flow of water, the coding device used to refer to the water here is not explicit. Without the full NP reference to the bather, Grandfather, it would not be clear that the thing being stood under is the water flow.

5.2.2. Elaboration

Eleven of the 122 examples of strong coding devices used for recently mentioned participants are what I call ELABORATIONS, where a participant is mentioned in one clause and then further specified, either by noun-phrase modifiers or by a predicate that attributes additional qualities. One example of this phenomenon is found in KT18:

(12)   a.   Naada-supáta-y   jį́ʃ-ra   váriy.
           3DL-emerge-DETRNS JIITA-?   then
           'So they (2) emerge.' (KT17)

       b.   Naada-supáta-myáá-jį́ʃta   da-nu-jųy   vánu-jų-dyéé-rų.
           3DL-emerge-PERF-JIITA   two-CF:ANIM-two   male-two-little-NOM
           'Two emerged, two male children.' (KT18)

In 12b, it is fairly obvious that a full NP is used because the subject is being quantified and specified as to gender. This consideration overrides the fact that the two males had been mentioned in the previous clause.

A similar example occurs in the Hunter's Narrative:

(13)   a.   Sų-ųnúú-ntyíy   rá-tiryǫǫ   sų-ųnóó.
           3SG-see-REP   INAN-lie   3SG-head
           'He also sees his head lying there.'

       b.   Jánariy   junoo   tiryǫ́ǫ́.
           deer   head   lie
           'A deer's head lies there.'

Again, it is clear that the head in 13b is being specified as a *deer's* head, as opposed to any other possible head. For this purpose a full NP is required, even though the head had been mentioned in the previous clause.

5.2.3. Discourse promotion

Twelve of the 122 instances of strong coding devices used to code recently mentioned participants are instances of what Du Bois (pers. comm.) calls DISCOURSE PROMOTION. This is the phenomenon whereby a participant is first mentioned as an oblique or possessor, using an explicit coding device such as a full NP. Then in the immediately following clause this participant is again mentioned with a strong coding device, but "promoted" to a more central semantico-syntactic role, i.e., A, O, or S. For example:

(14)   a.   Naan-dííy   rí-íva   jánariy   múdii   dárajúy.
           3DL-see   INAN-DAT   deer   jawbone   two
           'They see two deer jawbones.'

b. Rá-raníy   jánariy   múdii   naana-ajííjy.
INAN-stand   deer   jawbone 3DL-in:front
'The deer jawbones stood in front of them.'

In 14a, the jawbones are first mentioned as a full NP in the dative case (the verb *dííy* meaning 'see' requires that the entity seen appear in the dative case). Then in 14b the jawbones are repeated as a full NP but this time "promoted" to the S role.

A similar example occurs in the Twins Cycle:

(15)   a. Si-itǫ́ǫ́-ta   jíí   naadi-imú   jí-tyęęyadá-ra.
3SG-arrive-TRNS   JIITA   3DL-LOC   COR1-grandma-INAN
'He takes it to his own grandmother.' (TC69)

     b. Naada-díryey   jíí   sį-įtyę́ę́yadá-yu.[3]
3DL-welcome   JIITA   3SG-grandmother-REFL.
'His own grandmother welcomes him.' (TC70)

Here the grandmother is mentioned with a full NP in 15a in an oblique role, and again in 15b as an S participant.

The phenomenon of discourse promotion illustrates that not all mentions are created equal in terms of activation of participants in memory (Chafe 1987). In particular, mentions of participants in noncore roles such as obliques do not necessarily suffice to activate such participants to the point where they can subsequently be coded with less explicit devices.

5.2.4. Dative objects

In the Hunter's Narrative and in the Twins Cycle, there is a pair of central characters that interact throughout the text (the Kneebite Twins are never distinguished from one another, and so they never interact). When one member of a pair speaks to the other, there is a clear tendency for the addressee to be coded with a full NP, even though that participant may have been very recently mentioned, and even though the NP apparently does nothing to disambiguate between the two members of the pair. For example:

(16)   a. Jutǫǫ-já-ásiy   si-imú   jí-tyeerį-nti-ñíí.
arrive-o'land-PROX:1   3SG-LOC   COR1-brother-REP-3SG
'He arrives there to where his brother is again.' (TC304)

     b. Sa-tų́ų́chu-nuvee   jíí   sí-íva   jí-tyeerį.
3SG-speak-ARR2   JIITA   3SG-DAT   COR1-brother
'He speaks on arrival to his own brother.' (TC305)

In 16a, one participant is coded explicitly with the NP meaning 'his own brother.' In 16b, the same NP is used as a dative complement of the verb *tų́ų́chu* 'to speak.' Ambiguity is technically high at the point of 16b, since both brothers are on stage. However, the NP in 16b does nothing to relieve this ambiguity. Since both participants are brothers to each other, the NP could refer to either one. In fact, we know from the context that the brother who arrives in 16a is the one that speaks in 16b, but we could just as easily have come to this conclusion were the brother spoken to in 16b coded with a less explicit device.

Similar examples occur in the Hunter's Narrative:

(17)   a.   Sį-įmyí-rya   ríchanú   naanu-moo-mú.
            3SG-eat-INAN   shiringara 3DL-face-LOC
            'He eats shiringara fruit in front of them.'

       b.   Sų-ųta-chí-íva   yí-sąą   vichį́-į́ . . .
            3SG-say-3SG-DAT   COR1-COM   be-NOM:ANIM
            'He says to his own companion . . .'

In 17b, the NP meaning 'his companion' (literally: 'his own being-with one'; i.e., 'the one who is with him') does nothing to disambiguate the reference of the addressee. Both hunters are companions to each other, and in this case it could be either one that is speaking. The two hunters are simply not differentiated at this point in the story.

There are eleven examples of this use of full NP for recently mentioned participants in the corpus. The only explanation I have for this phenomenon at present is purely speculative. Since in every case there is a "semantically appropriate" referent in the immediate context, perhaps the speaker feels constrained to use a device normally used in situations of high ambiguity, even though in these particular cases a full NP does not accomplish the task of disambiguation. Under this analysis, these examples would be additional examples of the use of full NP in situations of high ambiguity (section 5.2.1).

5.2.5. Thematic structure

Clancy (1980) shows how coding choices in English and Japanese narratives are at least partially influenced by the thematic structure of the text. In particular, NPs tend to be used at thematic junctures, even though RD may be low. The particular thematic boundaries that Clancy considers are "world shifts," i.e., shifts between the "real world" where the narrator and an interviewer are the participants, and the "story world." Clancy also considers "episode boundaries." Barbara Fox (1986), working primarily in the framework of "story grammar" (Rumelhart 1975), makes similar observations for English.

The general observation that thematic junctures are sometimes accompanied by coding devices stronger than otherwise necessary is also relevant for Yagua, though the nature of the units and boundaries that are especially relevant to Yagua is still a matter for further investigation. In the following excerpt, Squirrel is referred to in 18b with a modified NP 'the one who makes him jump,' even though he is mentioned in each of the 8 previous clauses, and is therefore a highly topicworthy participant:

(18) a. Squirrel: Yi-núúy ra̱-a̱   rá̱a̱-kyu.
                     2SG-see 1SG-IRR jump-potential
                     'You see, I can jump!' (FSQ11)

   b. Sa-niy   suvú̱-tyéé jiñu   munátya
       3SG-MALF   fear-INTS this   ancestor

       su̱-u̱muta̱a̱sá   játiy   sa-ra̱a̱-ñíí.
       3SG-behind   REL   3SG-jump-3SG

       'This ancestor (the deer) is really afraid behind the one that
       makes him jump.' (FSQ12, 13)

   c. Deer: Ra̱-a̱   jú̱ú̱-charatá jiyu-dáy   koodí-vyiimú.
              1SG-IRR fall-might   here-DAY   snake-inside
              'I might fall here inside a snake.' (FSQ14)

However, when we look at the story structure of the text, we notice that FSQ12 (18b)
occurs at a fairly major thematic boundary. Up to FSQ11 (18a), the theme is "the
squirrel tries to trick the deer into crossing the stream on the back of the boa." The
theme beginning in FSQ12, however, is "the deer debates within himself." There is an
obvious shift from the external actions of the squirrel to the internal state of the deer.
In Rumelhart's (1975) terms, this shift corresponds to an "event" boundary, where the
sequence beginning in FSQ12 (and continuing for several clauses) is a "reaction" to
the sequence ending in FSQ11. Of the 122 examples of long-range coding devices used
for recently mentioned participants, 5 are explainable in terms of thematic boundaries,
though not all are as clearly related to story structure as example 18 is.

5.2.6. Crucial inanimate participants

In the Twins Cycle, there are 3 examples of inanimate participants introduced into
the discourse with multiple full NP mentions in succession. In each case, the
inanimate participant is particularly salient in the subsequent episode. Each of these
instances is at the beginning of a major episode of the Twins Cycle: (1) how the twins
obtain water, (2) how the twins obtain pifayo, and (3) how the twins obtain corn. As
might be expected, water, pifayo, and corn are the salient inanimate participants
involved:

(19) a. Sa-tada-chu-muu-myáá   jí̱íta Rísu
          3SG-recede-cause-COMPL-PERF   JIITA God

          naana-jisi-ntí-rya   já̱á̱-ntíy.
          3DL-from-REP-INAN   water-REP

       'God had also caused the water to recede from them.' (TC272)

b. Néé   ją́ą́-dana-ñuudáy.
    NEG   water-not:exist-any:more
    'There is no more water.' (TC273)

c. Múú-chi-ñumaa   naada-ją́ą́pa-mu-síy   jí-ryi-yaa-ra   ją́ą́.
    there-AL-now   3DL-g'father-LOC-AL   COR1-get-DIST-INAN   water
    'Now they repeatedly get water from their grandfather.' (TC274)

According to the definition of the various character statuses (Chapter 4, section 4.3), water is a minor character, since it is never mentioned more than 4 times in any stretch of 20 clauses. However, it is clearly a major element here, since the whole episode is about how the twins obtain water. The use of 3 full NPs in a row to code the water iconically represents the importance of water to the episode.

It is interesting that crucial animate participants are not introduced in this way. In fact, the twins themselves, in the same version of the same story, are first mentioned with simple verb coding (TC22 and TC30; see example 5 in section 5.1.2). This is understandable in view of the fact that inanimates are less likely to be important participants. Whereas mention with a single NP may suffice to activate an animate participant for future deployment, inanimates, by virtue of the fact that they don't characteristically persist as important participants, need the reinforcement of several full NP mentions in order to be sufficiently activated in the hearer's memory.

The following sentences introduce the episode in which the twins obtain pifayo from their stingy grandfather:

(20) a. Jás-chiy   jííta-ntíy   naani-iníy   rá-naachǫ   púúriy.
         there-from   JIITA-REP   3DL-come   INAN-towards pifayo.
         'From there they come after pifayo.' (TC459)

     b. Púúri-vya-numaa   jííta   naada-yasanta-ntí-ñíí.
         pifayo-DAT-now   JIITA   3DL-pester-REP-3SG
         'They now pester him for pifayo.' (TC460)

Here pifayo is mentioned twice in a row with a full NP. This is not technically speaking an instance of discourse promotion, since both mentions of pifayo are in oblique roles. Also, it is not elaboration, since there is no modification of the reference to pifayo in the second sentence. Like water in the previous set of examples, pifayo in 20a and 20b goes on to be a significant element in the subsequent development of the episode introduced in 20a. Of the 122 examples of long-range devices used to code recently mentioned participants, 5 are explained by this notion of "introduction of crucial inanimate participant."

5.2.7. After mention in quotes

There are 4 examples of full NPs used to code participants that had been mentioned in a quote in the immediately preceding clause. Because of my method of counting mentions of participants within quotes as full mentions, the RD for these instances is 1. For example:

(21)   a.   "Ra-chikidi-naachǫ́ǫ́   vuryą-ą   junúú-yąą-téé-kii."
             1SG-intestines-towards   1PLINC-IRR   look-DIST-INTS-must
             "'We must look all around for my intestines!'" (TC517)

        b.   "Díy   ri-jyetyą́-ą́siy   ri-inúú-rya."
             there   3PL-throw-PROX1   3SG-see-INAN
             "'There I saw them throw them.'" (TC518)

        c.   Sa-ryiy   jį́įta   jí-chikidi.
             3SG-get   JIITA   COR1-intestines
             'He gets his own intestines.' (TC519)

In 21c, the intestines are referred to with with a full NP even though they were mentioned in the preceding 2 clauses and there are no other inanimate participants cluttering the discourse stage at this point. It seems from examples such as this that mentions of participants within quotes, like mentions in oblique phrases, are not as salient as mentions in core semantico-syntactic roles in straight nonquote clauses.

5.2.8. Residue

Finally, there are 10 examples of long-range devices used to code recently mentioned participants that do not seem to fall into any of the above categories, and which don't have any obvious idiosyncratic motivation. For example:

(22)   a.   Sa-deenu-dee-rá   yí-náá-tyéniy   váácha   jii-tąąsá.
             3SG-child-DIM-NOM:NEUT   COR1-cry-cause   sp.:monkey   branch-on
             'The huapo monkey makes his own child cry right on the branch.'

        b.   Są-ąta-tyén-níí   tápi   raatya-déé   **jíí**-va.
             3SG-jump-cause-3SG   slow   careful   branch-DAT
             'He makes him jump slowly, carefully, along the branch.'

In 22b, there is no obvious reason why the branch is coded with a full NP. This example is somewhat akin to discourse promotion (see section 5.2.3), in that the reference to the branch in 22a is in an oblique role. However, there is no "promotion" involved, since the reference to the branch in 22b is also in an oblique role. Nevertheless, the explanation of discourse promotion in terms of less salience being ascribed to mentions of participants in oblique roles would still potentially be relevant here, i.e., the branch is referred to with a full NP in 22b because the speaker judged that the mention in 22a insufficiently activated that participant for further nonexplicit mention.

Another unexplained example of use of a full NP occurs in the Kneebite Twins Tale:

(23)   Rá-juu-yaa-múúy   naada-suutá.
        INAN-fall-DIST-COMPL   3DL-shelter
        'Their shelter fell to pieces.' (KT45)

At this point in the story the shelter has an RD of 3, where its last mention was in the O role. There are no potentially interfering inanimate participants on stage, and there is no other obvious reason why the speaker did not use a less explicit coding device. Hence this is an "unexplained" example. It may be that since the shelter is an inanimate participant, and not a very salient one at that, an RD of 3 is sufficient for it to decay from active memory, whereas animate and otherwise more salient participants decay more slowly.

5.3. Alternative long-range devices

In this section I will investigate the use of the simple NP device versus the corresponding recapitulating device, as defined in Chapter 4, section 4.6. Table 29 illustrates the distribution of simple NP and recapitulating NP devices by the central/noncentral distinction:

Table 29: Distribution of Alternative Long-Range Coding Devices[4]		
	Central	Noncentral
NP alone	3	127
NP recapitulating short form (VC, E, or HC)	50	142
Total	53	269

Table 29 reveals that central characters are much more likely to be coded with a recapitulating NP than with a simple NP, whereas for noncentral characters the choice is about equal. The probability factor of .00001 indicates that there is only one chance in 100,000 that the choice of coding device is random, i.e., uninfluenced by the central/noncentral distinction. This observation is formalized as follows:

(24)   Central characters tend to be coded with recapitulating devices rather than simple NP devices, all other factors being equal.

Needless to say, however, we must still look elsewhere for an explanation of the choice with noncentral characters. Table 30 gives the average Persistence for simple and recapitulating NP devices:

Table 30: Mean Persistence, Alternative Long-Range Coding Devices

	Central	Noncentral	All
NP alone	9	1.26	1.46
NP recapitulating short form (VC, E, or HC)	7.13	3.26	4.32
Combined	7.24	2.35	

Table 30 illustrates two facts. First, central characters are more persistent than noncentral characters. This fact is not particularly interesting, since the definition of minor character (one subclass of noncentral characters) is based on few mentions (5 or less) in a particular span of text. Therefore, mention of a minor character can never have a P index of more than 4. Also, it is simply intuitive that the central characters of a story will, in general, persist as topic to a greater extent than noncentral characters, if for no other reason than that they are mentioned more often. For any randomly selected span of text, there will probably be more mentions of central characters than of other characters.

The second fact that table 30 reveals, however, is more interesting. The P index of noncentral characters mentioned with the recapitulating devices averages over twice that of mentions with the simple NP devices. Thus for noncentral characters, Persistence is a crucial factor in determining whether a simple or recapitulating device will be used. Noncentral characters that are "destined" to figure prominently in the ensuing discourse are more likely to be coded with a recapitulating device than with a simple NP device. Conversely, noncentral characters coded with a recapitulating device are destined to figure more than twice as prominently in the ensuing discourse as those that are coded with the simple NP device. This observation is formalized in 25:

(25)   For noncentral characters, all other factors being equal, recapitulating devices are used for more persistent participants.

Table 31 reveals that this generalization distributes unequally among the three general semantico-syntactic roles:

Table 31: Mean Persistence, Noncentral Characters, Simple NP vs. Recapitulating Devices

	A/S_a	O/S_o	Obl	All roles
Simple NP	1	2.08	1.26	1.4
Recap NP	4.03	2.66	2.52	3.29

Table 31 shows that most of the difference in P indices between NP and recap NP devices stems from the categories of A and S_a participants and obliques. The P index for O and S_o devices is not substantially higher than for the corresponding simple NP device. Table 32 summarizes the P indices for noncentral characters in the O/S_o category, broken down into its three logically distinct subcategories:

Table 32: Mean Persistence, Noncentral Characters, Long-Range Devices

	O	S_o (pred nom)	S_o (verbal)
Simple NP:	2.45 (n = 20)	.6 (n = 5)	(none)
E + NP:	2 (n = 33)	5.29 (n = 7)	6 (n = 1)

Although the number of examples is in many cases too small to make strong claims, it is clear from table 32 that the O category violates the general observation made in example 25. The S_o categories, both verbal and predicate nominal, are consistent with 25, although more examples would be needed in order to draw firm conclusions.

Up to this point I have been considering the simple NP devices as a group, without distinguishing them from one another, except insofar as they code different semantico-syntactic roles. However, there is a logical and potentially significant division within them, namely, the distinction between PREHEAD simple NPs (for A/S_a and Obl categories) and POSTHEAD simple NPs (for O/S_o categories). In particular, we might hypothesize that a preverbal NP would have a discourse-pragmatic status that contrasts with a postverbal NP, independent of its semantico-syntactic role (see D. Payne 1987). Table 33 gives P and RD indices for preverbal and postverbal simple NPs:

Table 33: Summary of RD and P for Noncentral Characters,
Simple NP Coding Devices.

	Preverbal (A/S$_a$)	Post-verbal(O)
RD index:	12.83 (n = 12)	12.8 (n = 25)
Persistence:	1 (n = 13)	2.45 (n = 20)

Table 33 reveals that the preverbal NP device does not significantly contrast with the postverbal device in terms of Referential Distance. However, it does contrast somewhat in Persistence. Translated into semantico-syntactic roles, this observation tells us that noncentral characters that are not going to persist in the discourse are more likely to be coded as A or S$_a$ than O. Conversely, noncentral characters that are destined to be mentioned more often (in relation to other noncentral characters) are more likely to be coded as O. This fact accounts for the apparent anomaly observed in Table 32 that the relatively large Persistence figure for simple NP coding an O participant is seen as contrasting with simple NP coding A and S$_a$ participants rather than with E + NP coding other O participants. Table 34 shows that the recap strategies similarly contrast significantly only for Persistence:

Table 34: Summary of RD and Persistence for Recap Devices,
Noncentral Characters

VC + NP	(A/S$_a$)	E + NP (O)
RD index	9 (n = 64)	11.56 (n = 36)
P index	4.03 (n = 67)	2 (n = 33)

Table 35 compares just the Persistence indices for simple and recap devices:

Table 35: Mean Persistence, Noncentral Characters

	A/S$_a$	O
Simple NP	1 (n = 13) (preverb)	2.45 (n = 20) (postverb)
Recap devices	4.03 (n = 67)	2 (n = 33)

Table 35 suggests that the distinction between the P indices of the simple NP devices is due to the difference in ordering of the NP with respect to the verb, and not with the difference in semantico-syntactic role. That is, for the other long-range devices - namely, the recap devices - no such distinction holds. In fact the opposite is true: A/S_a participants coded with the $VC + NP$ device are more persistent than O participants coded with the $E + NP$ device, though this correlation is not as strong (about 2 to 1) as the reverse correlation for the simple NP devices (2.45 to 1). If semantico-syntactic role were what was sensitive to the P index, we would expect a roughly equivalent ratio between P indices of simple NPs and recap devices coding A/S_a and O participants.

5.4. Summary

In sections 5.1 and 5.2, I looked at various "anomalies" to the general patterning of coding devices in terms of Referential Distance. These anomalies fall into two general classes: (1) short-range devices used to code relatively distant participants, and (2) long-range devices (i.e., all those involving full NPs) used to code recently mentioned participants. In the first class, most examples are explained in terms of the hierarchical nature of topicality, i.e., participants are highly topicworthy (and therefore codable with reduced coding devices) throughout the span of text in which they figure prominently, even though they may cease to be mentioned for long stretches. In the second class, most examples are explained in terms of Ambiguity, i.e., the presence of other semantically appropriate participants in the immediate context. Several other classes of examples of long-range devices used to code recently mentioned participants were discussed in sections 5.2.2 through 5.2.7, with tentative, sometimes speculative, explanations. Finally in section 5.2.8, some examples of unexplained uses of long-range devices were presented.

In section 5.3, I examined the alternative long-range coding devices (simple versus recapitulating) for each of the various semantico-syntactic roles. The findings with respect to the functional differences between these alternative long-range coding devices are:

1. All other factors being equal (i.e., character status and semantico-syntactic role), the recap devices code more persistent participants than do the simple NP devices.

2. Postverbal simple NP (i.e., O and S_o roles) is used to code more persistent participants than preverbal simple NP.

The general conclusion of section 5.3, then, is that while Referential Distance distinguishes long-range from short-range devices in a general way, other factors must be considered in order to sort out the specific functions of the various coding devices. The index of Persistence proves particularly useful in sorting out the functions of devices that fall into the "long-range" category, as defined by the RD index. I will have more to say concerning this observation in Chapter 8.

Notes to Chapter 5

[1] *Pifayo* is Peruvian Spanish name for the ripe fruit of a Bactris sp. palm. The Portuguese name is *Pupunha* (Al Jensen, pers. comm.). No English equivalent for the species has been found. It is a bright red fruit that ripens suddenly and abundantly in February, just as the high waters of the rainy season are beginning to recede. It thus correlates with the end of an agriculturally and socially depressed season, and the beginning of a new and potentially prosperous agricultural year. As such it has become somewhat a symbol of regeneration, and figures prominently in folklore and mythology throughout the Amazon region.

[2] As mentioned in Chapter 4, section 4.2, Ambiguity proved to be a very difficult measure to calculate, due to the slipperiness of the notion of "semantic appropriateness." In calculating Ambiguity for the 122 long-range devices used to code recently mentioned participants, I have tried to be as conservative as possible in positing the presence of a semantically appropriate referent on the discourse stage, precisely because I was interested in what factors other than strict ambiguity might be triggering the use of a stronger coding device. That is to say, some of the other six conditions I found for using extra-strong coding devices might well be subsumed under Ambiguity, in a framework that only recognized Ambiguity as a possible reason for using a stronger-than-expected coding device.

[3] See Chapter 3, section 3.2, for an explanation of the use of the reflexive suffix to express coreference with a previous possessor rather than subject.

[4] X^2 with Yates' correction for a four-celled matrix in which one cell contains a value < 5: 28.8. p = < .00001

Chapter 6

DISCOURSE MOTIVATIONS
FOR S$_O$ CODING

As noted briefly in Chapter 2 (section 2.2.1), certain single-argument predicates in Yagua may employ S$_a$ or S$_o$ coding for their subjects. Contrary, however, to observations made for other languages by Klimov (1977), Dixon (1979), Comrie (1978) and others, the difference between S$_a$ and S$_o$ coding on Yagua verbs does not correlate with a difference in semantic role. Thus we must look elsewhere for an explanation for this morphosyntactic distinction. Preliminary work on another Amazonian language, Pajonal Campa (Heitzman 1982), suggests that the discourse notions "change in scene" and "episode climax" may condition the use of S$_o$ coding. In this chapter, this suggestion is formulated as a hypothesis and tested for Yagua by means of a quantitative text study.

6.1. S$_o$ coding and locomotion

Many languages make a formal distinction between two classes of intransitive predicates based loosely on the semantic role of the core argument. In this study I follow Dixon 1979 in using the terms S$_a$ and S$_o$. Merlan 1985 uses the terms SUBJECTIVE and OBJECTIVE predicates to refer to exactly the same distinction.[1] S$_a$ (or subjective) predicates are those in which the core argument is treated morphosyntactically like the most agentive argument in basic transitive clauses. S$_o$ (or objective) predicates are those in which the core argument is treated morphosyntactically like the nonagentive argument of basic transitive clauses.

Most previous discussions of S$_a$ and S$_o$ predicates present some form of the following semantic generalization as a motivation for this formal distinction:

(1)   Intransitive predicates in which the core argument is a semantic AGENT (i.e., the conscious initiator) are assigned to the S$_a$ class, while predicates in which the core argument is not a semantic AGENT are assigned to the S$_o$ class (see, e.g., Fillmore 1968:31, Chafe 1970:98ff, Comrie 1978a:366, Dixon 1979:80, *inter alia*)

All languages which exhibit any kind of S$_a$/S$_o$ distinction conform more or less to this generalization, though no language is completely consistent in this respect. For some linguists (e.g., Rosen 1983), the numerous exceptions to this generalization warrant rejection of the semantic basis of these classes altogether in favor of a strictly autonomous syntactic explanation. For others, the exceptions do not invalidate the intuitive appeal of the obvious, though inexact, semantic basis of these formal classes.

The first objective of this chapter is to show that Yagua, like many other languages around the world, exhibits one major class of exceptions to the generalization expressed in 1. Namely, certain predicates of LOCOMOTION (i.e., change of place) in which the subject is clearly agentive counterintuitively pattern with the S$_o$ group.

The second objective of this chapter is to provide a motivation, in the sense of Lakoff 1987, for this phenomenon. The account that I will propose derives from a quantitative study of Yagua narrative discourse. Yagua is a language for which S_o marking of predicates of locomotion is "optional" according to sentence-based syntactic and semantic theories: no verb is required to take S_o marking in all contexts, and for no verb is the alternation between S_a and S_o marking directly related to an alternation between agentive and nonagentive (or nonpatientive and patientive, volitional and nonvolitional, etc.) interpretations. The circumstances which affect the use of S_o marking on verbs of locomotion in Yagua can only be understood in terms of the structure of the discourse. Specifically, S_o marking is highly favored at discourse junctures termed change in LOCATIONAL SCENE, and EPISODIC CLIMAX, with a few strings attached. These facts are motivated by two semantic/pragmatic principles: (1) Change in scene is a metaphorical extension of change in physical state. This claim is supported by recent work by Keenan 1984 and DeLancey 1982. (2) The morphosyntactic correlates of subjects of S_o predicates in Yagua are normally reserved for more discontinuous participants in discourse (participant discontinuity). Climax and change in scene are both instances of thematic discontinuity. Morphosyntactic correlates of participant discontinuity are often associated with other types of discontinuity in discourse. This claim is supported by work such as that of Clancy 1980, Givón 1983b, and Barbara Fox 1986.

6.2. Definitions

In the following discussion of S_o coding in Pajonal Campa and Yagua, the notions of locational scene and climax will figure prominently.

6.2.1. Locational scenes

Locational scenes are spatially defined areas of attention, parallel to scenes in drama, i.e., the subunits of a play bounded by a lowering and subsequent raising of the curtain. In spoken discourse, of course, visual representation per se is not strictly relevant. Nevertheless, the storytelling process does involve the mental elaboration of a "world" within which the story being told is enacted. Storytellers manipulate that world in various ways in order to achieve the particular communicative effect they desire. One way in which that world might be manipulated is through the use of scenes and scene changes. When Xenophon says of Cyrus in the *Anabasis*, "from there he marched on," he moves the Greek army from one locationally defined scene to another. The reader or hearer of this passage knows that many presuppositions that might have existed in the world of the discourse before this point are now erased, and new ones are likely to be introduced. The audience's attention moves with the Greek army away from a particular scene into another (example from Joseph Grimes 1975:218).

It stands to reason that locational scenes and scene changes will play a more prominent role in certain discourse genres than in others. For example, a recipe will probably not have much use for multiple scenes or scene changes. We would expect such relience on locational scenes to be most prominent in stories, since these are the kinds of discourses in which the elaboration of a locationally well-defined world is the most useful. Even individual stories, however, may vary in the degree to which locational orientation is significant. For example, highly metaphysical stories in which there is a great deal of emphasis on the internal struggles of the participants, such as Djuna Barnes' *Nightwood*, do not, in general, rely heavily on locational orientation. However, in a story like Homer's *Odyssey*, locational orientation is very useful and highly structured. In the *Odyssey*, high-level locational scenes delimit the various episodes in the hero's journey. We also might expect individual authors to vary in "style" and the degree of expertise they bring to bear on the telling of any given story. Therefore, different authors might employ location as a discourse-structuring device to varying degrees, all other factors being equal. Finally, we might expect cultures to vary in the degree to which locational orientation is a significant aspect of their storytelling strategies. In Yagua, it is particularly clear that locational orientation is of great importance in the telling of folkloric narratives (see also T. Payne 1984b).

6.2.2. Climax

An episode in a story typically consists of the building and subsequent release of tension. The point at which that tension is released I am calling the climax. Some episodes may not have climaxes; others may have multiple or multileveled climaxes. The notion of RELEASE OF TENSION, though still impressionistic, is a step toward a concise characterization of what constitutes a climax. Hopefully, it will be clear from the following discussion and the appended texts how this notion influences coding choices in Yagua narrative discourse.

6.3. S_0 coding in Pajonal Campa

Pajonal Campa is a Pre-Andine Arawakan language spoken by about 2,000 people in the Gran Pajonal region of the south-central foothills of Perú. The following Pajonal Campa data come from Heitzman (1982). Abbreviations used are: SAR, subject arriving; SLV, subject leaving; PER, perfective; NF, nonfuture; F, future; E, empty morph; REG, regressive; A, prefix indicating A or S_a participants; O, suffix indicating O or S_o participants.

Campa transitive verbs code As and Os with prefixes and suffixes respectively, e.g.:

(2)   a.   **A-ñ-aapa-aqu-i-ro**   avyoo.
            1PL:A-see-SAR-PERF-NF-INAN:O   airplane
            'On arrival we saw the airplane.'

       b.   **N-aree-tz-i-mi.**
            1:A-visit-E-NF-2:O
            'I visit you.'

Most intransitive verbs always occur with S$_a$ coding, i.e., their only argument is referred to with a prefix rather than a suffix. Throughout the Campa language family, however, there are certain intransitive verbs that can occur with either S$_a$ or S$_o$ coding. For example the Pajonal Campa verb *cam* 'to die' appears in 3a with a subject prefix and in 3b with a zero subject suffix (zero is the normal form for objective third-person-singular arguments):

(3)   a.   **I**-cam-i.   'He dies.' (S$_a$)
                3SG:A-die-NF

       b.   Cam-aqu-i-**0**.   'He died.' (S$_o$)
                die-PER-NF-3SG:O

A few verbs must occur with S$_o$ coding, e.g.:

(4)   Ja-t-a-a-**na**.   'I'm going back.'
        go-E-REG-NF-1:O

There is another stem, *iyaa*, meaning 'go,' that always occurs with S$_a$ coding:

(5)   **P**-iyaa-t-e.   'You will go.'
        2:A-go-E-F

Heitzman lists four environments in which S$_o$ coding is used in Pajonal Campa: (1) when the S undergoes a change of state (as in example 3b), though it is not clear from the translations how 3a differs from 3b in this semantic respect; (2) to indicate a change of location; (3) to indicate the climax of a narrative; and (4) in greetings. The first environment is comparable to the semantics of S$_o$ verbs in classic stative-active languages. The other three environments, however, represent hitherto unrecognized factors. In the following discussion I will be primarily concerned with environments 2 and 3.

The following excerpt illustrates two S$_o$ verbs (italicized in the English translations) signaling changes in location:

(6)   a.   A-poc-aqu-i   irova-qui Oventeni-qui.
                1PL:A-come-PER-NF it-LOC   (place name)-LOC

       b.   A-poñ-aan-ac-a   irova-qui Tsireentsishavo-qui.
                1PL:A-some:from-SLV-PER-NF it-LOC   (place name)-LOC

       c.   A-poc-aqu-i   a-cant-apa-ac-a   'shoc, shoc, shoc.'
                1PL:A-come-PER-NF   1PL:A-do-SAR-PER-NF (sound words)

       d.   **Yov-ac-ae**   **Mencoryaa-qui.**
                exit-PER-1PL:O (place name)-LOC

       e.   **Oerinc-apa-ac-ae,**
                descend-SAR-PER-1PL:O

    f.   A-ñ-aapa-aqu-i-ro   avyoo   o-jeequ-i.
        1PL:A-see-SAR-PER-NF-INAN   airplane   INAN-sit-NF

a. We came to Obenteni.
b. We left from Tsireentsishavo and came.
c. We came doing 'shoc shoc shoc.'
d. *We came out* (of the jungle) at Mencoryaana.
e. *We descended.*
f. We saw the airplane sitting.

Example 6 is a very location-oriented excerpt in which a trajectory of movement is described. The locomotion verbs in 6a and 6b employ S_a coding and simply summarize the entire trajectory. The S_a verb in 6c describes an action that occurs within a certain locationally defined scene, namely, the jungle path out of Tsireentsishavo. Then in 6d the scene shifts, as the travelers exit the jungle and enter a populated area. In 6e the scene shifts again, this time to the field on which the airplane is located. In each case, S_o coding is used where there is a distinct shift in scene.[2]

The following example illustrates several S_o verbs at the climax of a folkloric narrative. In this excerpt, all S_o verbs imply transition of some kind and all but one (6d) are formally marked by either the choice of verb stem or the use of derivational suffixation as involving locomotion. This excerpt is from a story about the origin of the deer. Long ago, the deer was a man who would go to the woods telling his wife that he was hunting for game. However, rather than hunt he would cut the flesh from his own body and smoke it. His body would regenerate, and he would take the smoked meat back to his family. Finally his wife becomes suspicious and follows him out to the jungle. She watches him cut the flesh from his body and smoke it. Then she comes out of hiding and says, 'You just called it game; it was your flesh. I'll never eat your flesh again.' The story continues:

(7)   a.   Oo!   **Pey-an-ac-a-0**   maniro.   Tecatsi.
            oh!   change:to-SLV-PER-NF-3SG:O   deer   not:exist

    b.   Tecatsi-t-a-ni   atziri.
         not:exist-E-NF-F   person

    c.   O-ov-añ-aaqu-i-ri.
         3SG:A-cause-live-PER-NF-3SG:O

    d.   **Caanit-an-aqu-i-0.**
         stay:away-SLV-PER-NF-3SG:O

    e.   **Pey-ac-a-0**   maniro.
         change:to-PER-NF-3SG:O   deer

f. **Shiy-an-ac-a-0.**
run-SLV-PER-NF-3SG:O

g. **Ja-t-aqu-i-0**   r-ov-a   i-votoo-qui-te.
go-E-PER-NF-3SG:O   3SG:A-eat-NF   3SG-fig-fruit-poss

h. Oo! Tecatsi maavoeni pancotsi-qui-nta.   Tecatsi.
oh! not:exist all   house-LOC-distant   not:exist

i. **Pey-an-ac-a-0**   maavoeni.
change-SLV-PER-NF-3SG:O all

j. Tecatsi   i-vatha   janta   pancotsi-qui-nta
not:exist 3SG-flesh there   house-LOC-distant

k. **Pey-an-ac-a-0**   maavoeni.
change-SLV-PER-NF-3SG:O all

a. Oh! *He changed into a deer.* Nothing.
b. He no longer is a person.
c. She caused him to live like that.
d. *He left staying away.*
e. *He changed into a deer.*
f. *He ran away.*
g. *He went* and ate figs.
h. Oh! None of those houses exist anymore. None.
i. *Upon leaving he changed completely.*
j. There isn't any meat there in the house.
k. *Upon leaving he changed completely.*

S_o coding in clauses a, e, i, and k can be accounted for on the basis of change in state, as these clauses embody the change from man to deer. S_o coding in clauses d, f, and g, however, is not so easily explainable in these terms. The man in d, f, and g is not a patient, and does not undergo a physical change in state in the usual sense. What examples d, f, and g have in common with examples 6d and e is a change in location that culminates (brings closure to) a discourse unit. In example 7 that unit is the discourse itself, but in example 6 the relevant units are locational scenes.

6.4. S_o coding in Yagua

Although Yagua and Pajonal Campa share many areal features, there is little evidence for a genetic relationship. There has never been a detailed comparative study of the lowland languages of Perú. Such a study may, in fact, reveal a distant relationship between Yagua and the Arawakan languages. Until then, however, we must consider similarities between these languages to be either areal features or features shared by sheer chance.

As illustrated briefly in Chapter 2 (section 2.2.1) certain verbs in Yagua can occur with either S$_a$ or S$_o$ coding. Some further examples follow:

(8)   a.   Múúy   siimyaasíñaadá.
                múúy   siiy-maasiy-naadá
                there   run-exit-3DL
                'There they rush out.' (S$_o$)

        b.   Sasiimyaasiy   jííta   suusíy.
                sa-siiy-maasiy   jííta   sa-jusíy
                3SG-run-exit   JIITA   3SG-from
                'He rushes out away from him.' (S$_a$)

(9)   a.   Múúy   supatéésiy   tájichintiñíí.
                múúy   supata-y-jásiy   tá-jiy-siy-ntiy-níí
                there   extract-DETRNS-PROX1   other-place-from-REP-3SG
                'There he emerges from another place again.' (KT91) (S$_o$)

        b.   Sasupátamyaantíy.
                sa-supáta-y-maa-ntiy
                3SG-extract-DETRNS-PERF-REP
                'He emerged again.' (KT125) (S$_a$)

Here there is no less control, volition, and/or action ascribed to the subject in the a examples than in the b examples. Both 8a and 9a occur in texts where it is obvious that the participants coded with S$_o$ coding are the active, volitional subjects of the verb. The crucial question, then, is what determines the choice between S$_a$ and S$_o$ coding for the verbs that admit that choice?

In this section I will distinguish several characteristics of intransitive verbs with S$_o$ coding in a corpus of Yagua texts. Some of these characteristics are 100% generalizations, while others are only statistical tendencies. The first two characteristics are 100% generalizations in that counterexamples do not occur in the corpus of this study and are extremely difficult for native speakers to produce, even in elicitation. There is some sense, therefore, in which these first two characteristics are "grammaticalized":

> 1: S$_o$ verbs always imply locomotion, either inherently (examples 8a, 9a) or as a result of the addition of one of several derivational suffixes such as *-nuvaa* 'upon arrival on a new scene' (KT53).

> 2: S$_o$ subjects are always animates. This would be a curious characteristic of S$_o$ subjects were we tied to the notion that S$_o$ coding is strictly, or even typically, associated with patientivity, since animate entities are much less typical patients than are inanimate entities.

The third characteristic is also a 100% generalization, though I would not want to call it "grammaticalized" since it could easily be a feature of the particular corpus used for this study:

3: S_o coding on verbs only occurs in folkloric narrative.

Table 36 illustrates the frequency counts of S_o coding on verbs in almost 1800 clauses of texts from three genres:

Table 36: Frequency of Verbs with S_o Coding in 3 Discourse Genres			
	No. of Texts	No. of Clauses	No. of S_o
Procedural	2	306 (240 + 66)	0
Persexperience narrative	4	421 (100 + 75 + 96 + 150)	0
Folkloric narrative	3	1066 (193 + 720 + 153)	27

The 27 occurrences of S_o coding on verbs in this corpus constitute the data base for this study. Since none of these occur in procedural or personal-experience texts, I will not be considering these genres. The three folkloric texts to be considered are the Kneebite Twins (KT), Appendix 1; Little Baldy (described in Paul Powlison 1969; Appendix 3 is an English translation of the first 336 clauses of this tale); and the first 153 clauses of the Non-Identical Twins Cycle (Appendix 4).

Given an environment, then, where S_o coding is not precluded due to any of the above 100% generalizations (i.e., given a folkloric narrative, a locomotion verb, and an animate subject), the question still remains: What principles influence or determine the choice of S_o over S_a coding? In order to answer this question, I began with the preliminary hypothesis that Heitzman's environments for S_o coding in Pajonal Campa were also relevant for Yagua. I refined the definitions of Heitzman's environments number 2 (change in location) and 3 (climax) to SWITCH IN LOCATIONAL SCENE and EPISODIC CLIMAX, as outlined in section 6.2.

A good translation is an expression of the *content* of a text in the morphosyntactic form of another language. Since locational scenes and climaxes are elements of the content of a narrative, it is possible to identify these environments on the basis of translations. Doing so has the methodological advantage of distancing the analyst from the morphosyntactic forms of the language under study, thus rendering the identification of the discourse environments more genuinely *independent* of the morphosyntactic devices that are hypothesized to be determined by those environments. Working from a translation does not, of course, guarantee independent identification of conditioning environments: morphosyntactic features of the translation may directly map the relevant morphosyntactic features of the source language. But, in this case, I found it easier to be truly objective in my identification of scene changes and climaxes if I did so on the basis of the Spanish translations than if I worked directly from the Yagua. Though verbs of motion in Spanish usually translated verbs of motion in Yagua, there were no more specific Spanish morphosyntactic devices that distinguished translations of verbs of motion with S$_O$ coding from verbs of motion with S$_a$ coding.

After all changes in scene and points of episodic climax were identified on the basis of the Spanish translations, I went back to the Yagua and drew correlations between each environment and the occurrence of S$_O$ coding. The following sections present the results of these correlations.

6.4.1. Episodic climax

Table 37 gives the counts of S$_a$ and S$_O$ coding for verbs of locomotion at points of episodic climax:

Table 37: Verbs of Locomotion Occurring at Episodic Climax		
S$_a$	1	6.25%
S$_O$	15	93.75%
Total	16	

Table 37 indicates that of 16 examples of verbs of locomotion occurring at episodic climax, 15 received S$_O$ coding and 1 received S$_a$ coding. In these figures we observe a fourth characteristic of S$_O$ coding:

> 4: Verbs of locomotion occurring at episodic climax strongly tend to employ S$_O$ coding.

Some examples of this use of S$_O$ coding are KT67, 121, and 122 (see Appendix 1 for the full contexts of these examples):

(10)   Múúy   júú-ñíí,   puu.
         there   fall-3SG   SW
         'There he falls down, thump!' (KT67)

(11)   Jásiy   jaatyo-rii   sa-nyi-ñíí,   tyéé.
         there   hit-in:passing 3SG-at-3SG   SW
         'There he hits in passing at him, pow!.' (KT121)

(12)   Múúy   ráá̧-ñíí,   pu̧u̧.
        there   fall:over-3SG SW
        'There he falls over, thump!.' (KT122)

Most examples of S_o coding at point of episodic climax involve the verbs *ju̧ú̧y* 'fall down' and *ráá̧y* 'fall over.' Both of these concepts can be understood as having agentive or nonagentive subjects, i.e., one can fall volitionally or nonvolitionally. Therefore, one could argue that the use of S_o coding with these verbs is explainable on the basis of the semantic principle presented in 1. However, there are instances of both of these verbs in other discourse contexts where S_a coding is used, even though they seem just as nonvolitional as they do in the environment of episodic climax (see section 1.4.3, example 17, for an illustration of *ju̧ú̧y* used with S_a coding). Furthermore, example 11 shows that clearly agentive subjects can be coded with S_o coding at points of episodic climax. Hence I conclude that even though most instances of S_o coding occurring at episodic climax also involve potentially nonagentive subjects, nonagentive subjects are not automatically encoded via S_o coding. The context of episodic climax more directly predicts the use of S_o coding than does nonagentivity. Outside of situations of episodic climax and scene switch, locomotion verbs virtually always occur with S_a coding, regardless of the question of volitionality (see section 1.1).

6.4.2. Switch in locational scene

The initial investigation of the corpus revealed that the environment termed "switch in locational scene" proved less significant in predicting the use of S_o coding than did episodic climax. Many scene switches were accomplished with the verb *jiya* 'go.' This verb never occurs with S_o coding in the corpus,[3] and it so happens that it is extremely difficult even to elicit a sentence with *jiyá* and S_o coding. This fact is expressed as characteristic number 5 of S_o coding on verbs:

5: S_o coding is precluded for the verb *jiya* 'go.'

Whenever any other verb of locomotion, such as *siiy* 'run,' *rabee* 'to circle' or any verb suffixed with one of the locomotion suffixes, such as *nuvaa* 'on arrival,' accomplished a scene switch, S_o coding was much more likely. So the definition of scene switch was modified to "scene switch plus *unexpected action*," where unexpected action is construed to mean any locomotive action other than the unmarked, neutral, inexplicit action coded by the verb *jiya*. Table 38 summarizes the uses of S_a and S_o coding in this environment:

Table 38: Verbs of Locomotion Coding Scene Switch Plus Unexpected Action

---

S$_a$	2	15.4%	
S$_o$	11	84.6%	(mutually exclusive of S$_o$ coding occuring at "climax," i.e., all are among the 12 S$_o$-coded verbs still unaccounted for)
Total	13		

Table 38 indicates that of 13 verbs of locomotion occurring at points of scene switch plus unexpected action, 11 received S$_o$ coding and 2 S$_a$ coding. From these figures we can infer the sixth characteristic of S$_o$ verbs:

> 6: S$_o$ verbs tend to code scene switch plus unexpected action.

Some examples of this use of S$_o$ coding are found in KT24, 44, and 53:

(13)   Múúy   jíñuva-yási-ryíy.
        there   arrive:late-PROX1-3PL
        'There they arrive late.' (KT24)

(14)   Sii-jéé-ñuvee-já-ásiy   Mokáyu   súta-jyari-ñaadá.
        run-enter-ARR2-o'land-PROX1   Mokayu   shelter-into-3DL
        'They force themselves into Mokayu's shelter on arrival.' (KT44)

(15)   Múúy   kíínchu-nuvee-já-ási-ryíy.
        there   light:fire-ARR2-o'land-PROX1-3PL
        'There they light their fires upon arrival.' (KT53)

In contrast to the examples of S$_o$ coding used with verbs of locomotion at episodic climax, those occurring at scene switches always describe volitional acts.

6.4.3. Summary of S$_a$ and S$_o$ coding with verbs of locomotion

In summary, 26 out of 27 (96.3%) instances of S$_o$ coding on verbs occur in the two environments termed climax and scene switch plus unexpected action. Verbs of motion that do *not* employ S$_o$ coding indicate either arrival on the current locational scene, movement within the current locational scene, or departure from the current and continuing scene. In none of these cases is there transition from one scene to another. One or two examples of each of these environments will be given here for illustrative purposes.

The following excerpt from the Twins Cycle (Appendix 4) nicely illustrates the contrast between two verbs of locomotion employing S$_a$ coding and one verb of locomotion employing S$_o$ coding. The scene is the area around the ruins of the twins' parents' house, where the twins are lying in wait for the spirits of their deceased parents to arrive. The twins are hoping to surprise their parents in order to snatch a magic flute from them. The scene is established in TC111 (see Appendix 4), and continues for 10 clauses in which the twins discuss how they are going to grab the flute. Then in clause 122 the spirit parents arrive, and the story continues as follows:

(16)   a.   Naadí-ítįį-mu   jį́į́-téé-ntíy.
             3DL-arrive-down   JIITA-INTS-REP
             'They two arrive descending again.' (S$_a$) (TC122)

       b.   Naani-ipeñi-yą́ą́-nuvïï.
             3DL-file:dance-DIST-ARR1
             'They dance around on arrival.' (S$_a$) (TC123)

       c.   Pųų, naada-niratúúy.
             SW   3DL-dance
             'Thump, they dance.' (S$_a$) (TC124)

       d.   Jásiy   radé-ésumiy-nt-tyéé   naadí-íva-téé-níí,
             there   stand-rising-REP-INTS   3DL-DAT-INTS-3SG
             'There he jumps up at them.' (S$_o$) (TC125)

Example 16a illustrates a verb of locomotion employing S$_a$ coding to describe the arrival of the spirit parents onto the already established locational scene; 16b indicates locomotive action (file dancing) on arrival, but no transition from one scene to another; 16c also indicates motion, but completely within the confines of the current scene (*niratúúy* refers to circle dancing, i.e., where the participants follow one another around in a circle). Finally, 16d is a verb of locomotion describing how one of the twins jumps out of hiding and surprises the spirit parents. Clauses 122 through 124 clearly involve a build-up of tension as the audience knows the twins' plan to spring out of hiding and grab the flute (up to clause 122, the twins discuss their plans and prepare their hiding place). This tension is released when the first twin (it is not explicit which of the two) jumps out of hiding. As predicted by the hypothesis, S$_o$ coding occurs at exactly this climactic point.

S$_a$ coding on verbs of locomotion can also describe the departure of a participant from the current scene. In the One-Eyed Warriors text (Appendix 3), scene XI is the beach on which the deer and the toucan's brother escape from the belly of the water boa. In OW332, the snake departs from the scene:

(17)   Sa-júúy   jį́įta   koodíy   váriy   naadi-íva-siy,
        3SG-fall   JIITA   boa   then   3DL-DAT-from
        'The boa then fell back away from them.' (OW332)

Following this clause, the beach scene continues with the deer and the toucan's brother as topics, and the snake is never mentioned again. Thus this verb of motion takes S$_a$ coding when there is no transition from one scene to another.

Figure 2 schematically represents the distribution of S$_o$ and S$_a$ coding on verbs in relation to these two significant environments:

Figure 2. Summary of Distribution of Verbs Employing S_o Coding

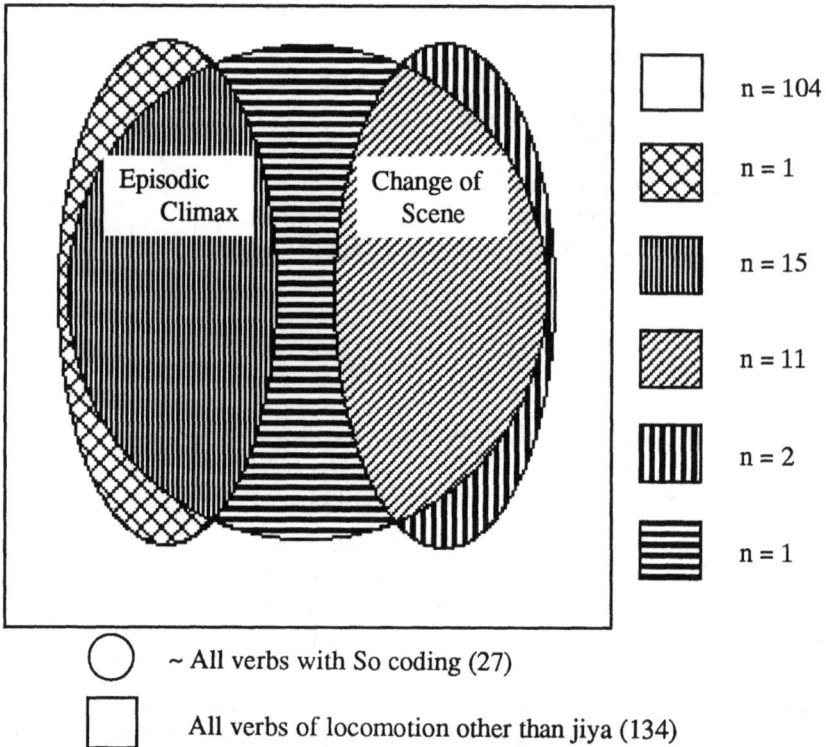

Episodic Climax

Change of Scene

n = 104
n = 1
n = 15
n = 11
n = 2
n = 1

~ All verbs with So coding (27)

All verbs of locomotion other than jiya (134)

The large square in Figure 2 represents the set of all intransitive locomotion verbs other than *jiya* 'go' in the corpus (n = 134). In other words, this square represents all the verbs for which S_o coding would be technically possible according to all the characteristics of S_o coding listed in this section.[4] The central circle represents those locomotion verbs which employ S_o coding for their subjects. The ovals represent the sets of verbs occurring in the two environments termed "change in locational scene" and "episodic climax."

Figure 2 shows that there are 4 examples that seem to contradict the initial hypotheses of the study. The horizontally barred area in the center represents one example of an S_o-coded verb outside of the two significant environments, the cross-hatched area represents one example of an S_a-coded verb of locomotion at episodic climax, and the vertical lined area represents two examples of S_a-coded verbs of locomotion describing scene switch plus unexpected action. In the following section I examine these specific examples and offer some speculative explanations for their occurrence.

6.5. Exceptions to the general pattern

The one instance of S_o coding on a verb of locomotion outside of the two major environments occurs in clause 113 of the Kneebite Twins story (Appendix 1):

(18) Tyen, múúy ráá̰-jíy.
      SW   there fall:over-2SG
      'Plop! There you fall over.' (KT113)

In this clause one of the Kneebite twins warns Mokayu of possible upcoming events. The clause does not refer to an actual event in the episode in which it occurs, therefore it cannot technically be coding the climax of that episode. A possible explanation of this use of S_o coding is that clause 113 is a prediction of the climax of the following episode, which occurs in clause 122. Clause 122 does employ S_o coding, and I speculate that the speaker used S_o coding in clause 113 to create stylistic parallelism between the warning and the actual event. Also, since KT113 is a quote, its discourse function may depend more on the structure of the quoted discourse than on that of the tale as a whole, i.e., the narrator may have structured a "climax" into the discourse of the twins by using S_o coding within a direct quote.

Now we are left with three instances of S_a coding where S_o coding would be expected, one in a context of episodic climax and two others coding a change in locational scene. The one instance of a nonS_o verb of locomotion occurring at episodic climax occurs in clause 286 of the One-Eyed Warriors text (Appendix 3). This nonuse of S_o coding is truly anomalous, and in fact in another version of the same story a different speaker uses S_o coding at precisely this point. My only potentially relevant observation is that this particular clause is marked in other ways, namely by the use of the contrastive special clitic *-niy*, a marked ordering of a locational phrase before the verb, and by the enclitic *-dáy* (a discourse particle whose function is still under investigation):

(19) Múú-ñiy   coodi-viimú   sa-júṵ́-dyéy.
      there-NIY snake-inside 3SG-fall-DAY
      'THERE inside the snake he fell.' (OW286)

I speculate that the speaker considered this clause to be sufficiently marked by these three features (contrastive clitic, preverbal locative, and *-dáy*) to indicate the climactic nature of the event.

Finally, there are two instances of scene switch plus unexpected action coded by S_a rather than S_o verbs. These two instances are clauses 45 and 49 of the One-Eyed Warriors excerpt. I suspect that the explanation for these apparent counterexamples lies in the use of rhetorical effect on the part of the storyteller. Scenes IIIA, B, C, E and F describe similar or identical actions, but A, B, and C are introduced with locomotion verbs with S_a coding, and E and F with S_o coding. In fact, B and C are introduced with the same verb, *rabee* 'to circle,' as E and F are. I suggest that the use of S_o coding to introduce the last two scenes in this series is because the speaker is progressively building up tension. Here we have five nearly identical scenes, the first introduced with an unmarked, unsurprising locomotion verb, and the next two with a slightly more unusual locomotion verb but with S_a coding. Finally, the last two scenes are introduced with verbs of locomotion with S_O coding, with success apparently being achieved in scene IIIF.

The examples which violate the hypotheses presented in this chapter illustrate the probabalistic nature of the discourse option between S_a and S_O coding. The environments termed "switch in locational scene" and "episodic climax" do strongly favor S_O coding when there is a discourse option, and all other environments strongly disfavor S_O coding. Competent storytellers are able to manipulate these tendencies at will in order to achieve specific stylistic effects.

6.6. Toward an explanation

In the preceding sections it has been shown that S_O coding on verbs in Yagua folkloric narratives occurs primarily in two discourse environments: (1) points of episodic climax, and (2) locational scene changes accompanied by unexpected action. Furthermore, we have seen that S_O verbs occurring at episodic climax tend to code nonvolitional actions, whereas those occurring at locational scene changes always (in my corpus) code volitional actions. In this section I pose the question: "Why should these particular discourse environments favor S_O coding so strongly?" I will approach this question from three directions: (1) semantics, drawing from the work of Keenan (1984); (2) cognition, DeLancey (1982); and (3) the use of anaphora in discourse, Clancy (1980), Givón (1983a,c,d), and Barbara Fox (1986). I hope to show how these three interrelated pressures conspire to favor the choice of S_O coding on verbs in Yagua.

6.6.1. Semantics: change in state

As mentioned in section 6.1, Keenan (1984) provides a semantic framework that may help us understand the use of S_O coding in Yagua discourse. In this work Keenan investigates the semantic properties shared by intransitive subjects and transitive objects in search of possible semantic bases for the category "absolutive" in those languages that grammaticalize this category. In his categorization of semantic properties of absolutives, Keenan lumps three properties together under the heading of "change in existence state" (p. 213). These three properties are (1) existence dependence, (2) patientivity, and (3) change in location. Existence dependence is the property exhibited by a participant whose existence depends on the action described in the predicate. If a predicate describes the bringing into existence of an entity, that entity will be either an intransitive subject or transitive object, e.g., 'a crowd gathered,' ' a fire started' (intransitive), and 'John built a house' (transitive). This is a property that is very difficult, if not impossible, to ascribe to transitive subjects. Patientivity, in Keenan's terms, is the property of undergoing a change in state, typically physical state, e.g., 'the dog died,' 'the house collapsed' (intransitive), and 'John smashed the car' (transitive). Again, this is a property which is highly atypical for transitive subjects.[5] Finally, Keenan (p. 207) asserts: "Absolutive arguments are always among those whose path of movement is specified by source and goal locatives." This statement captures the fact that in transitive sentences like 'John kicked the ball into the room' it is the object that moves into the room, whereas in intransitive sentences like 'John ran into the room' it is the subject that moves into the room. It is very difficult for a goal or source locative to describe a path of movement for a transitive sub-ject, unless the object also follows the same path, as in 'John chased Mary into the room.' Thus participants whose path of movement is speci-fied by a goal or source locative are parallel to patients, in that both are typically restricted to absolutives.

There is a stronger hypothesis that, if proven, would seem to make the case even stronger that participants that undergo a change in location are semantically analogous to patients:

> In predicates describing locomotive actions, absolutive arguments are
> always among those that change location.

Here the specification that a source or goal locative argument need be expressed has been eliminated. The hypothesis simply states that for transitive locomotion predicates the object will change location, and for intransitive locomotion predicates the subject will change location. This state of affairs would render participants that undergo a change in location parallel to patients, in that both would be restricted to the category absolutive. The problem with this hypothesis is that it simply is not true. There are many examples of transitive locomotion predicates where the subject changes location without a corresponding movement ascribed to the object; for example:

(20) a.   John passed/left/approached Mary/Mt. Rushmore.
      b.   Mary escaped prison/the wrath of God/the fire.
      c.   John walked the plank/the streets of NYC/a mile.

Therefore, of the general class of participants that change location (hereafter "locomotive participants") it is only those that move along a path specified by a source or goal locative that belong to the category of absolutive. Insofar as semantic properties shared by absolutive arguments are likely to motivate a morphosyntactic category of absolutive,[6] we can make the further claim that only those locomotive participants whose path of movement is specified by a source or goal locative are likely to motivate a morphosyntactic category of absolutive. In terms of intransitive subjects, this means that only those locomotive intransitive subjects whose path of motion is specified by a source or goal locative are likely to be identified morphosyntactically with transitive objects.

So what is the semantic difference between participants that move in general, and those that move along a path specified by a source or goal locative, such that the latter would be restricted to absolutives and the former not? I contend that the difference is that when a source or a goal locative is expressed, a *change in scene* is necessarily implied. For example, when we say 'John kicked the ball into the room' there are two locations specified, the outside and the inside of the room. Here the ball necessarily undergoes a change in locational scene. However, when we say 'John approached Mt. Rushmore,' the entire action can be perceived as taking place within one locationally defined scene. 'John' in this example, changes location, but does not move out of one scene into another.[7]

The examples of locomotive participants that do not undergo change in scene need not be restricted to transitive subjects. The same is true for 'ball' in 'John kicked the ball.' It might be said that in this sentence the ball changes location, but not that it moves from one scene to another. Similarly, 'John ran' is not specified for any scene changes, whereas 'John ran out of the kitchen' is.

The above observations lead to the conclusion that locational scenes are metaphorical extensions of physical states. A switch in scene is analogous to a change in state; hence a participant that moves from one scene to another undergoes something metaphorically similar to what happens to a patient when it changes physical state. Similarly, when something is brought into existence, the act of coming into existence can be seen as metaphorically related to an act of moving from one scene to another. This fact would not hold for simple changes in location, i.e., it is not so reasonable to imagine that the change in location embodied in a sentence like 'the ball was rolling' is analogous to a change in physical state, whereas for 'the ball rolled into the kitchen' such an analogy is more reasonable. This conclusion is also consistent with my intuitions concerning English intransitive verbs of locomotion whose past participles can modify their subjects. I contend that the difference between 'escape' ('an escaped prisoner') and 'walk' (*'a walked man') is that the action described by 'escape' necessarily implies transition from one "scene" (e.g., a prison) to another. In this respect, 'escape' is metaphorically analogous to 'grow' ('a grown woman'), in that 'grow' implies transition from one physical state (childhood) to another. These facts suggest a reasonable explanation for why *some* verbs of locomotion in Yagua receive S_O coding and others do not. It is not surprising, given the line of reasoning above, that it is exactly where there is a specific *change in scene* that S_O coding for subjects of verbs of locomotion is highly favored.

However satisfying the above explanation may be, it still does not account for all the data. First of all, there are still cases of S_O coding at points of episodic climax. Furthermore, there are cases of changes in scene coded by intransitive locomotion predicates that do not exhibit S_O coding for their subjects. These are principally those scene changes coded with the verb *jiya* 'go.' In the following sections I will propose some additional functional pressures that provide further motivations for the observed patterning.

6.6.2. Cognition: endpoint orientation

DeLancey (1982) provides a very interesting explanation for the tendency in some languages for ergative marking to occur in perfective aspect, and/or past tense, even though nonergative marking occurs in other aspects and/or tenses (Comrie 1978a, Dixon 1979, Harris 1981, T. Payne 1982b). The essence of DeLancey's hypothesis is that perfective aspect represents a view of an action as complete and bounded, and therefore places emphasis on the enduring effect of the action rather than on its initiation or internal structure. For transitive clauses, this means that perfective aspect is oriented more toward the participant with whom the action terminates than the participant with whom it begins. In the canonical transitive event (i.e., an event involving both agent and patient roles), the enduring effects of the event are more relevant to the patient than to the agent. This orientation of perfective aspect toward the temporal endpoint of an action is termed "terminal viewpoint" (DeLancey 1982:172). Insofar as ergative marking is "patient-oriented"[8] and patients are typically the endpoints of transitive actions, this notion of terminal viewpoint explains in cognitive terms the use of ergative marking only in perfective aspect.

Though the specific phenomenon DeLancey deals with is viewpoint in relation to the temporal orientation of clauses (terminal and nonterminal viewpoints are taken to be temporal notions), he asserts that this tendency is rooted in the locational notions of source and goal. That is, predicates of locomotion typically are lexicalized according to source and goal viewpoint (e.g., the difference between the members of the pairs 'come' and 'go,' and 'bring' and 'take' in English). This locational notion is carried over by cognitive analogy to the temporal notions of terminal and nonterminal viewpoint.

This notion of source versus goal viewpoint explains in a very satisfying way why some locational scene changes are coded with S_0 coding and others are not. Clauses containing the verb *jiyá* 'go' are, in general, source-oriented in the sense that they describe a locomotive event from the viewpoint of the current locational scene. There is transition, but the emphasis is on the act of leaving the old scene, rather than on the endpoint of that transition, i.e., the new scene. On the other hand, in clauses such as KT53 'they light their fires on arrival' the orientation is clearly on the endpoint of the transition. Every example of S_0 coding on verbs occurring at locational scene changes can be understood as an instance of "endpoint" or goal orientation, as opposed to "starting point" or source orientation. Insofar as direct objects of transitive events are typically endpoints of the carrying over of some action (Hopper and Thompson 1980), it is understandable why subjects of intransitive verbs of locomotion that are endpoint-oriented would be coded morphosyntactically like transitive objects.

6.6.3. Anaphora in discourse: discontinuity

Time and location are important factors in establishing the continuity (or cohesion) of a text. Events that take place in the same location and/or the same time frame have a natural cohesion that renders them all available to be mentioned in any text that concerns any one of them. Similarly, change in location or time frame is an important way of breaking up the continuity of a text when necessary. That is to say, change in location, as well as change in time, is often used as a strategy for structuring texts into various subunits, such as episodes (see, e.g., Joseph Grimes 1975:219, Givón 1983d:192).

Many folkloric narratives around the world, but in particular those of the lowland cultures of Perú, exhibit a high degree of dependence on location for the delineation of episode boundaries (T. Payne 1984b). Such narratives typically describe the travels of a character or group of characters and their adventures at various stages of a journey. Personal-experience narratives also often take this format, e.g., in lowland Perú when one arrives in a village or home it is common courtesy for a visitor to recount the story of his journey. The Kneebite Twins story is a folkloric text of this style while example 6 is from a Pajonal Campa personal-experience narrative. In this style of discourse the episodes typically coincide with locational scenes. Since locational scenes are important high-level discourse-structuring units, switch in scene entails a kind of thematic discontinuity (Givón 1983c:7), i.e., a "breaking up" of the text into thematic units, similar to what paragraph breaks do in written discourse.

Clancy (1980), Scancarelli (1984), and B. Fox (1986) have independently shown that devices used primarily for highly discontinuous participants (participant discontinuity) are also used to indicate major boundaries in the high-level structures of texts (thematic discontinuity). For example Clancy shows that in English, full noun phrases as opposed to pronouns are more likely to occur when there is a significant thematic boundary. Barbara Fox (1986) makes the same observation for logical boundaries as defined in the story grammar framework of Rumelhart (1975). Full nouns, of course, are commonly used to refer to participants whose reference is not presupposed, whereas pronouns are normally used when the reference is presupposed. However, English speakers and writers will use full noun phrases to refer to presupposed participants in order to indicate high-level thematic boundaries. Similar observations are made for Yagua in Chapter 5, section 5.2.5 - though for Yagua, thematic boundaries do not seem to be as significant a factor in motivating the use of noun phrases as they apparently are in English and in Japanese (Clancy 1980). In Yagua, only 4 out of 122 examples of unusually strong coding devices are explainable in terms of thematic boundaries. The general observation, however, is incontrovertible: speakers use coding devices normally associated with participant discontinuity to indicate thematic discontinuity as well.

In Yagua, as presumably in all languages, direct objects are typically more discontinuous, i.e., less topical, less presupposed, than are subjects. The counts for Referential Distance in Chapter 4 validate this claim for Yagua, in that O participants consistently exhibit higher RD figures than do A or S_a participants. Table 39 summarizes the RD figures for the major coding devices by semantico-syntactic role:

Table 39: Summary of Referential Distance by Semantico-Syntactic Role

	PNP	VC/E + NP	Post-NP	VC/E	|Aggregate
A	7.5	8.24		1.56	| 2.35
S_a	12.36	7.77		1.84	| 3.24
A/S_a	11.07	7.95		1.68	| 2.98
O	16.2	10.8	11.35	2.46	| 6.84

Table 39 shows that O participants exhibit a higher RD than either A or S_a participants for every coding device. The aggregate RD for O participants is 6.84, which is more than twice the aggregate RD for subjects (A and S_a), 2.98. These facts show that the O category in Yagua is typically reserved for more discontinuous, or less topical, participants than is the subject category. Subjects of S_o verbs, however, are, like other subjects, highly continuous. In the corpus used for the RD figures in table 39, there were 19 examples of S_o verbs. The subjects of these verbs have an aggregate mean RD of only 2.53. Hence, the morphosyntactic identification of O and S_o participants cannot be due to participant discontinuity. I hypothesize that one factor in the use of S_o coding to indicate locational scene changes is a generalization of the morphosyntactic category "object," normally associated with participant discontinuity, to indicate thematic discontinuity as well. This is exactly analogous to the use of full nouns to refer to highly continuous participants at episode boundaries in English.[9]

6.6.4. Climax as discontinuity

All of the above discussion centers on motivating the use of S_o coding on verbs at points of locational scene change. In this section I will offer a tentative functionally based explanation for the other major environment for S_o coding on verbs: episodic climax. I will begin by presenting some evidence from English that formal characteristics of direct objects are associated with subjects of certain intransitive verbs in situations of "counter expectation" (Gary 1978) or "surprise." Then I will show that this additional notion, along with the notion of change in state, provides a reasonable explanation for the use of S_o coding on verbs in situations of episodic climax.

In locative inversion constructions in English, intransitive subjects are treated like direct objects in that they occur postverbally:

(21)　a.　There appeared on the horizon a ship.
　　　　b.　Here comes my bus.

These two sentences actually represent two distinct construction types, for the following reason: 21a is most natural with an indefinite subject and the deictic 'there,' whereas 21b may have a definite subject and may involve any locational expression, e.g., 'around the corner,' 'lined up against the wall,' etc. Functionally, the construction type represented by 21a is commonly used to introduce participants into a discourse, whereas sentences like 21b may have subjects which are highly presupposed and tend to occur in situations of "counter expectation". Postverbal position in English is a strong morphosyntactic correlate of the semantico-syntactic role O. As observed in Givón 1979, O is the favored position for introducing participants into a discourse in English (as opposed to S or A). This may explain the use of postverbal position for the subjects of presentative constructions such as 21a. However, what about 21b? I speculate that these constructions function in a similar way to those S_o verbs used at episodic climax in Yagua. First of all, these constructions are restricted to predicates of locomotion or location, e.g.:

(22)　a.　Into the bathroom went John.
　　　　b.　*In the bathroom coughed John.

(23)   a.   Under the bed scurried the cat.
        b.   *Under the bed died the cat.

(24)   a.   Up jumped the rabbit.
        b.   *Up looked the rabbit.

(25)   a.   On the wall hung the portrait of Mao.
        b.   *On the wall burned the portrait of Mao.[10]

(26)   a.   Standing next to me was the president.
        b.   *Standing next to me spoke the president.

Secondly, the function of this construction type to indicate "counter expectation" is a possible analogy to the environment I have characterized as "climax" in Yagua. Thus we have some intriguing evidence from English that morphosyntax associated with the semantico-syntactic role O may be assigned to participants in other roles when those participants occur in the discourse pragmatic environments of counter expectation or climax.

Climax, as well as change in scene, is an instance of discontinuity in that it signals the end of a progressive build-up of tension, and the beginning of a subsequent release of that tension. This notion of release of tension is an important concept in aesthetics, often associated with "closure" (Du Bois, pers. comm.). There have been no previous studies that I am aware of showing that coding devices normally associated with discontinuous participants (i.e., "larger" or "stronger" devices) are used at points of episodic climax, but I would not be surprised if this were the case.

6.7. Summary

In this chapter we have seen that S_o coding on verbs in Pajonal Campa and Yagua is not explainable strictly in terms of semantic role. Subjects of intransitive verbs of locomotion may be coded like transitive objects, even though those subjects clearly are semantically "active" and volitional controllers of the event. A quantitative study of Yagua folkloric texts reveals that S_o coding for subjects of verbs of locomotion is highly favored in the two environments termed "switch in locational scene" and "episodic climax."

I propose that this distribution of S_o coding in Yagua folkloric narrative is explained in terms of the following three interrelated semantic, cognitive and discourse/pragmatic factors:

1. Change in state (either locational or physical)
2. Goal orientation
3. Discontinuity

These factors are all naturally cohesive, to the extent that it may be impossible to tease them apart into distinct principles. For example, a participant that changes state is most typically the endpoint of an action, hence factors 1 and 2 naturally coincide. Furthermore, insofar as the unmarked way of viewing an event is from the point of view of its inception, endpoint orientation is marked, unusual, or surprising. Hence, according to Givón's (1983c) iconicity principle of human communication, in those cases where a language avails itself of a viewpoint distinction to signal discourse continuity or discontinuity, endpoint orientation would be predicted to signal discontinuity rather than continuity.

In most "stative-active" languages, the single participant of S_O intransitive verbs is treated morphosyntactically like a transitive object because of a commonality of semantic role, namely O and S_O participants are both typically patients. According to the hypothesis advanced in this chapter, the single participant of an S_O verb in Yagua is treated morphosyntactically like a transitive object because of the commonalities of change in state, goal orientation, and discontinuity. The fact that I have isolated three factors may merely be a result of my having drawn from three distinct areas of investigation, semantics (Keenan 1984), cognition (DeLancey 1982), and discourse/pragmatics (Clancy 1980; B. Fox 1986; Givón 1983c).

Notes to Chapter 6

1   Here by the term "S_o verb" I refer to those intransitive verbs whose subjects have morphosyntactic properties of direct objects, regardless of the semantics of those verbs. The terms "unaccusative" (Perlmutter 1978) and "ergative" (Burzio 1986) have been used to refer to intransitive verbs in which the only argument is not a subject at an underlying level. The nature of the underlying level depends on the analytical framework adopted by the particular writer, e.g., for Perlmutter it is the initial stratum, for Marantz (1984) and Burzio it is D-structure, for Van Valin (1990) it is logical structure.

In the present work I do not assume that split-intransitivity is derived from a level of linguistic representation that is more abstract than the surface level. Rather, I will take the morphosyntactic distinction between S_o and S_a verbs as the observable data, and treat as a matter of empirical investigation determination of the factors that influence the choice of one morphosyntactic form or the other.

2   It might also be observed that the clauses which employ S_o coding in this excerpt are "telic," that is they describe "finishable" events, or events with well-defined endpoints (Comrie 1978b:44). This factor may contribute to the explanation of the use of S_o coding in these languages since, as has often been observed, perfective aspect and/or past tense often correlate with morphosyntactic identification of transitive objects and intransitive subjects (see, e.g., Dixon 1979:93). This correlation between "finished" acts and ergative agreement patterns is explained nicely by DeLancey (1982) in terms of "viewpoint." However, in this particular case I am not sure that the aspectual notion of telicity will correctly delimit only those clauses which take S_o coding, since it seems to me that clause a, 'We came to Obenteni,' is equally telic and yet does not take S_o coding. What clause a does not share with the S_o clauses in this excerpt is a distinct switch from one scene to another in a narrative sequence of events.

3   There is one example in the corpus of *jiyá* with no subject prefix, but with a postposed full noun phrase coding the subject:

(27)   Jiya   váriy   rá-jąą-miy   tį́įtu-ñu.
        go   then   INAN-person-PL   transform-NOM:ANIM
        'Then its people go transformed.' (or 'Then go its transformed people.') (TC452)

I have not considered this clause to be an example of S_o coding because there is no enclitic referring to the O. This fact renders the clause ambiguous as to whether this is an S_o clause exhibiting the postpredicate NP device for the subject, or whether it is an S_a clause with zero reference to the subject and a postposed recapitulating NP. In the absence of intonational data, there is no way of distinguishing between these two possibilities. However, this is the only example in the corpus that presents this problem.

4   The claim that S_o coding is possible for all verbs within the large circle of Figure 2 is made only on the basis of the 6 characteristics of S_o coding listed in section 6.4. In other words, there is no positive reason to *exclude* the possibility of S_o coding for these verbs. However, not all of the lexical verbs that occur in the blank area of Figure 2 have actually been attested with S_o coding in other environments. Hence, it may very well be the case that some of them, like *jiya*, *may not* employ S_o coding, though in the absence of a native speaker I have no way of checking each verb for its lexical coding possibilities. Nevertheless, it is clear that the difference between verbs that code their subjects as S_o and those that code their subjects as S_a is not lexically determined: many lexical verbs in the blank area also occur with S_o coding.

5   Keenan has noted that absolutives have certain properties, and has provided a nice list of such properties. We might attempt to push the chain of explanation one step further by asking "Why should absolutives have the particular properties noted by Keenan?" In answering this question, we are moving into a realm of analysis termed "ecology of grammar," by Du Bois (1987). In other words, we are no longer simply explaining particular facts about particular languages, in terms of what seem to be universal facts about language, but we are attempting to explain why language has evolved the characteristics it has. The characteristics of absolutives falling under the heading of "change in existence

state" in Keenan's work may in fact be a result of the evolution of absolutive as the relational category within which participants are typically brought onto the discourse stage (Du Bois 1987). Space limitations prohibit a full examination of the consequences of this view here. As indicated in the concluding remarks to this chapter, further research may be able to characterize the unity underlying the three approaches taken toward an explanation of the use of S_O coding in Yagua. Such research must inevitably approach the question from the point of view of the ecology of grammar.

6   This is not an uncontroversial point, but it is an underlying assumption of Keenan's work. I will not take the time to defend or refute this view here.

7   Apparent counterexamples to this claim such as 'John approached Mt. Rushmore from the north' are on the order of exceptions that prove the rule. That is, 'from the north' in such a sentence is not a source in the same sense as 'out of the kitchen' is. The difference is precisely that 'north' does not describe a locational scene, whereas 'kitchen' does. The phrase 'from the north' specifies the direction from which John is approaching Mt. Rushmore. It does not describe a specific locational scene, 'the north,' out of which John passes. Even a more specific phrase like 'Rapid City' in a sentence like 'John approached Mt. Rushmore from Rapid City' specifies direction, rather than a change in scene.

8   Ergative constructions are commonly thought of as "patient-oriented" quite apart from their tendency to occur only in perfective aspect. Traditional accounts of ergative case-marking systems nearly universally compare ergative sentences to Indo-European passives (e.g., Hammerich 1976). More recent accounts accept unquestioningly the notion that ergative constructions can develop diachronically from earlier passive constructions. These analyses are based on the fact that direct objects in ergative sentences universally have some characteristics typically associated with subjects. In other words, objects enjoy some morphosyntactic "privileges" associated with subjects in nonergative languages (see, e.g., T. Payne 1982a on Eskimo and Tagalog).

9   In the absence of adequate data, I speculate that this principle may also explain the use of S_O verbs in greetings, as mentioned by Heitzman for Pajonal Campa. Greetings and leave takings typically occur at boundaries of conversations. Since conversations are discourses, we can imagine that the same sorts of devices might occur at conversation boundaries as occur at other discourse boundaries. In Yagua, typical greetings and leave takings do not involve S_O verbs, but they do involve verbs of locomotion, e.g.:

(28)   A: Yí-ítįį-maa-víy?   'Have you arrived?'
              2SG-arrive-PERF-QP

        B: Jóóno.   Rí-ítįį-máá.   'Yes. I've arrived.'
              yes   1SG-arrive-PERF

(29)   A: Ra-ya-numáá.   'I'm going now.'
              1SG-go-now

        B: Jóó.   Ji-ya-numáá.   'Yes. You're going now.'
              yes   2SG-go-now

10   While it is true that a construction such as 25a can occur with an indefinite NP, such constructions do not typically indicate "counter expectation." They have more in common functionally with presentatives such as 21a. Since the Yagua S_O verbs in question are not presentatives, i.e., they never introduce participants into the discourse, I will claim only that they are roughly analogous to sentences such as 25a and not to the corresponding presentative constructions.

Chapter 7

PRONOUNS IN DISCOURSE

Nondemonstrative free pronouns as a coding device fill a variety of discourse functions from one language to another. In some languages, e.g., Apurinã (Aberdour 1985), pronouns occupy a position on the coding scale of topicality between agreement and full NPs as follows:

Most topical   Least topical

0   AGR   PRO   NP

In other languages, e.g., English, there are two types of pronouns: those that function on the coding scale of topicality and those that function on an intersecting scale of CONTRASTIVENESS (defined below). In English, stressed free pronouns serve the contrastive function, while unstressed free pronouns serve the simple anaphoric function (Givón 1979, 1983a).

In Hixkaryana (Derbyshire 1986), it is clear that independent pronouns are primarily sensitive to the contrastive function.[1] Characteristics of contrastive pronouns in Hixkaryana include:

1. Relatively infrequent in discourse.

2. Tend to occur in preverbal position.

3. Tend strongly to refer to arguments that have
   been mentioned in the previous clause (RD = 1).

All of these properties also hold for pronouns in Yagua. Therefore, an initial hypothesis is that preverbal pronouns in Yagua function on a scale of contrastiveness, rather than simply being sensitive to the functional scale of topicality. In order to test this hypothesis, I will take Chafe's (1976) definition of contrastiveness and apply it to the examples of pre-predicate pronouns that occur in the corpus of Yagua narrative texts. In particular, I will compare the functions of the PPRO device with the functions of the other "short-range" participant-coding devices (see Chapter 4, section 4.6).

7.1. The data base

The "pre-predicate pronoun" (PPRO) device is described and illustrated in sections 2.1.5 and 2.2.5. Oblique participants and possessors are never coded with pronouns in the corpus studied; therefore the only semantico-syntactic roles to be considered are A, S_a, O, and S_o. Nondemonstrative free pronouns referring to inanimates do not unequivocally exist in Yagua, and therefore all participants considered in this chapter are animates. The data base for this study is the same as that for Chapter 4 (see section 4.4). In Table 40, occurrences of the PPRO device considered in this study are displayed according to semantico-syntactic role:

Table 40: Occurrence of the PPRO Device by Semantico-Syntactic Role

	A	S_a	O	S_o (pred. nom.)	Total
Basic corpus	5	10	7	3	25

All quantitative measurements of pronoun usage in discourse are based on this set of examples. Other examples that serve as illustrations in this chapter were gleaned at random from the concordance of over 10,000 clauses of text.

7.2. Factors of topic continuity

In the study of topic continuity in Chapter 4, it was noted that PPRO is a "short-range" device in that it is used to code participants that have been mentioned relatively recently in the discourse. Table 41 gives Referential Distance means for the various short-range coding devices:

Table 41: Referential Distance of PPRO, VC, and E Devices

	A	S_a	O	S_o	Aggregates
PPRO	1.6	1			1.2 (A/S_a)
PPRO			1.29	1.33	1.3 (O/S_o)
VC	1.56	1.84			1.74
E			2.46	1.30	2.43

The aggregate RD for the PPRO device in all roles is 1.22. This means that the mean distance between a pre-predicate pronoun and the most recent previous mention of the participant that it codes is 1.22 clauses.

This low RD figure is comparable to findings of Derbyshire (1986) for Hixkaryana. Out of 20 examples of preverbal pronouns in Derbyshire's corpus of 1,623 clauses of narrative texts, excluding direct speech, 15 examples have an RD of 1 clause. Both the raw frequency and the percentage of examples of preverbal pronouns with RD = 1 in Yagua are comparable to Hixkaryana. In the Yagua corpus of 1156 clauses, also excluding direct speech, there are 25 examples of preverbal pronouns, 20 of which have an RD of 1.

Table 41 also shows that the RD means for both VC and E devices in Yagua are somewhat higher those for preverbal pronouns. At present I do not know any way of determining whether the difference between the RD figures for PPRO and those for the other short-range devices is statistically significant. Nevertheless, these figures indicate that PPRO codes participants that are at least as topical, in terms of RD, as those coded by the other short-range devices, if not more so. This fact appears to violate the "iconicity principle of topic continuity" (Givón 1983b:18) described in section 4.1. Since VC and E are "smaller" than PPRO, they should code more predictable, or topical, participants. Clearly there must be another factor that determines the choice of PPRO over the other short-range devices.

The first place we might look for other explanations for the use of the PPRO device is the other indices of topic continuity. Table 42 gives Ambiguity indices for PPRO:

	A	S_a	O	S_o	Aggregates
Table 42: Mean Ambiguity for the PPRO Device					
PPRO	2	1.9			1.93 (A/S_a)
PPRO			1.86	1.4	1.67 (O/S_o)

It will be recalled from section 4.2 that the range of variation for the Ambiguity index is extremely narrow compared to that for Referential Distance. Any participant mention receives an Ambiguity index of either 1 or 2; thus the range of variation for average Ambiguity indices is from 1 to 2. So, for example, an index of 1.9 is over twice as high as 1.4.

Table 42 reveals that for all roles, the Ambiguity index for the PPRO device is high (aggregate mean = 1.82), though for A and S_a participants it is especially high (1.93), almost reaching the maximum of 2. This means that PPRO is commonly used in situations where there are two or more possible referents on stage. Since ambiguity indices were calculated only for PPRO (for reasons discussed in section 4.2), we cannot directly compare it with the other devices in terms of Ambiguity. However, studies of other languages, such as Mandarin Chinese (Sun and Givón 1985) and Biblical Hebrew (Andrew Fox 1983) indicate that low RD combined with high Ambiguity is a characteristic of "contrastive" devices.[2] In these studies ambiguity indices for "noncontrastive" devices fall typically between 1.00 and 1.2, whereas those for "contrastive" devices fall between 1.4 and 2.0. Hence the combination of low RD and high Ambiguity suggests a disambiguating or "contrastive" function of the PPRO device.[3]

Table 43 compares the Persistence indices for PPRO, VC, and E:

Table 43: Persistence Indices for PPRO, VC, and E Devices

	A	S_a	O	S_o	Aggregates
PPRO	5.4	2.09			3.13 (A/S_a)
PPRO			6.71	7.33	6.9 (O/S_o)
VC	6.36	5.61			5.88
E			3.38	5.95	4.88

Table 43 shows that there is a striking discrepancy between the Persistence indices for PPRO devices used to code A/S_a vs. O/S_o participants. The PPRO device is used for relatively nonpersistent A and S_a participants (aggregate P index = 3.13), but quite highly persistent O and S_o participants (aggregate P index = 6.9). This means that O and S_o participants coded with the PPRO device are destined to be mentioned more often in the subsequent discourse than are A or S_a participants so coded. This fact contrasts with the Persistence indices for the VC and E devices, which are more similar to each other (5.88 and 4.88 respectively). As was seen in Table 27 (Chapter 4), when all coding devices are considered, the A and S_a roles are more persistent than either the O or S_o roles. Hence the Persistence figures for PPRO reverse the pattern of Persistence for all the coding devices taken together. In the following sections I will examine specific examples of the PPRO device in discourse in order to determine the significance of these preliminary observations.

7.3. Exclusive contrast: PPRO and A/S_a participants

In defining the term "contrastiveness" Chafe (1976:33-35) lists three factors: (1) the awareness (on the part of the speaker, and assumed to be shared by the hearer) that the event described by the contrastive sentence in fact occurred; (2) a set of possible candidates that might participate or have participated in that event in a particular capacity; and (3) an assertion as to which of the possible candidates is the correct one. Certainly this notion of contrastiveness is compatible with the disambiguating function of the PPRO device used to code A/S_a participants, which is suggested by the topic continuity figures in Table 42. I will now give several specific examples in order to evaluate to what extent Chafe's notion of contrastiveness is in fact a component of the environment for the PPRO device.

In the following excerpt from the Kneebite Twins tale (Appendix 1), the PPRO device is used in a situation where all of Chafe's criteria for contrastiveness seem to be met. The hero of the story, Mokayu, and his sidekicks, the Kneebite Twins, have come upon a huge boa constrictor and are debating who will be the one to do the boa in. First Mokayu speaks:

(1)   a.   "Ṛa-ạ   jaachi-dii-tyéé-níí,   kíí?"
               1SG-IRR   spear-ANTIC-INTS-3SG   huh
               "'Shall I spear him?'" (KT57)

    b.   Sụ̣-ụtay   jị́ịta   núkọvaañú,
         3SG-say JIITA   wasp
         'The wasp says,' (KT58)

    c.   "Néé. Nááy   jị́ị   rạ   jaachi-ñíí."
         NEG 1DLEX:PRO JIITA IRR spear-3SG
         '"No. WE will spear him."' (KT59)

In 1c, it is presupposed that somebody will spear the boa. There is also a limited set of possible participants that might spear him, namely Mokayu and the wasp twins. Finally, there is the assertion by one of the twins that they are in fact the ones that will do the spearing, to the exclusion of Mokayu.

If a simple prefix were used in 1c to code the twins, the use of the negative would be somewhat anomalous. Since *néé* is the regular clause-initial negative particle, when a prefix is substituted for the pronoun in 1c native speakers most naturally construe *néé* as applying directly to 1c rather than as a negative response to Mokayu's question in 1a. This interpretation is indicated in 2:

(2)   "Néé   naana-a   jaachi-ñíí."
       NEG   1DLEX-AUX:IRR spear-3SG
       '"We will not spear him."'

Extreme intonational cues (i.e., extra stress on the negative particle and a distinct pause between the particle and the rest of the sentence) are required to block this interpretation, and of course a negative interpretation of 1c does not conflict (i.e., contrast) with the possibility that Mokayu will spear the boa. If the negative were removed in 1c, the use of a prefix rather than a free pronoun would not imply that the twins were going to spear the boa to the exclusion of the possibility that Mokayu might also spear him. The twins would simply be understood as saying that they will spear the boa, without making any assertion whatsoever about whether Mokayu will also spear it or not. As the sentence actually occurs in the text, however, the free pronoun in 1c makes explicit the assertion that the twins plan to spear the boa to the exclusion of Mokayu, and this is consistent with the interpretation of the *néé* particle as constituting a negative response to Mokayu's question.

In the following excerpt, the PPRO device is used to code each of a pair of S_a participants:

(3)   a.   Núú jị́ịta   tạạry-ịị.
           one   JIITA   return-NOM:ANIM
           'One$_i$ of them returned.'
           (lit. 'One of them is a returned one.')

    b.   Níí-niy   jị́ịta   mísa-dáy.
           3SG:PRO-NIY JIITA heal-DAY
           'HE$_i$ got well.'

   c.   Núú   jį́įta   jaa-ñuvïï   tįįtájų   roorí-vïïmú-jų.
       one   JIITA   enter-ARR1   all   house-inside-towards
       'One$_j$ went right into the house.'

   d.   Níí-niy   jį́įta   dííy   tįįtájų.
       3SG:PRO-NIY   JIITA   die   all/completely
       'HE$_j$ died completely.'

In 3b and 3d, only two of Chafe's criteria for a contrastive sentence are apparent. There is a set of candidates that might have gotten well (3b) or died (3d), and there is an assertion as to which of the possible candidates is the correct one; specifically, the one who got well is the one who returned, and the one who died is the one who went right into the house. It is not clear that prior to 3b and 3d there is a common awareness that someone died and someone else got well. Rather, it is asserted in the contrastive sentences themselves that this is the case. The PPRO devices in 3b and 3d strongly assert that the participant being coded is the same as the one mentioned in the previous clause, to the exclusion of the other member of the pair. If the simple VC device were used in 3b or 3d, it is not clear that the participant being mentioned would necessarily be identified with the one mentioned in the previous clause. That is, if 3b employed the VC device, even if it were understood that the one who got well was in fact the same one that returned (and in the absence of a native speaker I cannot test this hypothesis), the identity of that participant would not be the main assertion of 3b. I venture to speculate, though with some certainty, that it would not be a necessary condition to the interpretation of 3b that the one who got well is the same as the one who returned. However, with the PPRO device such a stipulation is in fact demanded.

Excerpt 4 is from another text where the PPRO device is used to code participants filling the semantico-syntactic role A:

(4)   a.   Ra-dyéétya-rų́ų́-kyey
          1SG-know-POT-EVID
          'I want to know

      b.   níí-numáá-tiy   vátan-tán-dyé-ryéy,   mununú-niy,
          3SG:PRO-now-COND   curse-cause-DAY-1SG   savage-NIY[4]
          'if HE cursed me, the savage,

      c.   rá-ñiy   vátan-tán-dye-ryéy.
          1SG:PRO-NIY   curse-cause-DAY-1SG
          'or I cursed myself.'

In this excerpt, there are two persons who might have cursed the speaker, either 'the savage' or the speaker himself. In 4b and 4c the PPRO device is used to code each of these persons in turn, indicating that the speaker wants to know which of the potential cursers actually did the cursing *in contrast* to, i.e., to the exclusion of, the other. In this case the assertion of correct identity seems to be missing. Again, if the simple VC device were used in this context it would not be clear that the savage and the speaker were being contrasted. The passage could be translated "I want to know if he cursed me, the savage. I cursed myself," with no explicit indication that one participant must have done the cursing to the exclusion of the other. Note that there is no explicit coding of the disjunctive relation between 4b and 4c other than the use of the pronouns.

The final excerpt illustrating the PPRO device used to code A participants appears in section 2.1.5, and will be repeated here. The preceding context of this excerpt concerns a group of Yaguas who come upon a group of non-Yagua Indians. They wonder how they can speak with the nonYaguas, since they don't know each other's language. Then another participant is introduced, a Yagua who happens to be with the group of nonYaguas:

(5)   a.   Jási-jíȋta-níí   núú   nijyąąmi-ntíy,   si-isą-ntíy.
              there-JIITA-3SG   one   Yagua-REP   3COL-COM-REP
              'There is a certain Yagua person with them too.'

       b.   Níí-niy   jíȋta   dáátya-ra   máá-ñikyee-jadá.
              3SG:PRO-NIY   JIITA   know-INAN   white-speak-PART
              'HE (this new participant) knows Spanish.'

       c.   Níí-niy   nikyee-ta-ríy   nijyąą-vay . . .
              3SG:PRO-NIY   speak-TRNS-3PL   Yagua-PL
              'HE says to the Yaguas . . .'

The existential clause in 5a introduces the new participant. 5b asserts that he, as opposed to any of the other Yaguas, knows Spanish, and 5c asserts that he, as opposed to any of the nonYaguas, speaks to the group of Yaguas. Like examples 3b and 3d above, only two of Chafe's criteria for contrastiveness are evident here, namely, a set of possible referents and an assertion of correct identity.

The following example illustrates the PPRO device used to code an S_o participant:

(6)   a.   "Já-tiy   ji-jyę́ę́-byéy   jínoo-síy
              DEMO-REL   2DL-father-deceased   head-CL:seed(?)

              rą-chą́-ą́siy   sa-marííy,
              IRR-be-PROX1   3SG-necklace

              "'The one who has your father's skull as his necklace,
              (lit. 'The one who your father's skull will be his necklace,')

       b.   níí-ni-ñíí   ji-jyąąpá.
              3SG:PRO-NIY-3SG   2SG-grandfather
              "'HE is your grandfather.'"

In this example, an animal/human character is sent to search for his grandfather in order to avenge the death of his father. He is advised by his mother that of all the animals he might encounter, the one that has the skull of his deceased father around his neck is the character's grandfather. Excerpt 6 is a quote from the mother. Sentence 6b exhibits all of the features characteristic of contrastive sentences as defined by Chafe (1976): both mother and son are aware that *someone* is the son's grandfather; there is a set of possible candidates, namely, the animals the son will encounter; and, finally, 6b asserts the identity of the correct candidate. If the alternative short-range coding device (E) were used in this context, the assertion of contrast would not be as strong, though the fact that the grandfather is coded with a noun phrase modified by a relative clause in 6a would serve to contrast the grandfather with other animals that don't have the characteristic mentioned in the relative clause. The emphatic sense, however, would be lost.

The final example in this section is that of the PPRO device used in combination with a full NP within the same clause to code the semantico-syntactic role O:

(7) Níí-niy   sa-tááryį-téé   sa-są́ą́-yu.
     3SG:PRO-NIY 3SG-brother-INTS 2SG-give-REFL
     'It's HIM$_i$, his$_j$ brother$_i$, he$_k$ gives to him$_j$.' (TC506)

The context for this example (from the Twins Cycle) is the following: Placenta transforms himself into a parakeet in order to steal a special seed from Grandfather. Just as Placenta obtains the special seed, Grandfather appears and, infuriated, blowguns Placenta along with a whole flock of other parakeets. He then takes the parakeets home, and has them cooked. Elder Brother then comes visiting Grandfather. Grandfather presents Elder Brother with one of the cooked parakeets as a gift. By chance he pulls out Placenta in contrast to all the other parakeets in the pot. Without the unusual use of PPRO plus fronted object NP in 6 there would be no sense of contrast. That is, the sentence would simply mean 'he gives him his brother,' as if perhaps there were no other entities that Grandfather could have given.

The above examples of the PPRO device illustrate what I will call EXCLUSIVE CONTRAST. I will use this term to refer to the kind of contrast in which one member of a set of participants is singled out *to the exclusion of* the others in the set. Sometimes there may be a presupposed proposition (as in example 6), and an assertion that this holds for one participant, as opposed to all the others. The assertion that the proposition does *not* hold for the other participants is just as strong as the assertion of correct identity. Other times, there may be a presupposed proposition, a set of possible participants, and an assertion that the proposition holds for only one member of the set, to the exclusion of the others, but with no specific assertion as to *which* participant in the set is the correct one (as in example 4). This case may only be relevant when the contrastive sentence is in the irrealis mode. Finally, there may simply be a set of possible participants and the assertion of some proposition pertaining to one or another (as in examples 5 and 7). Again, the assertion that the proposition does *not* hold for the other participants is just as strong as the assertion of correct identity.

This analysis implies that use of the pronoun device carries more information than use of the other short-range devices (Zipf 1949). That is, when a bound form is used, the range of compatible parallel propositions is less restricted than when a pronoun is used. A pronoun specifically denies certain propositions which would be compatible with the propositional information contained in the sentence, whereas the bound forms imply no such denial. By restricting the range of compatible propositions, the pronoun imparts more specific meaning to the context in which it occurs. It is not surprising, then, that pronouns are (1) "larger" than the bound forms, and (2) less frequent in discourse.

This analysis also helps explain an anomaly in the hypothesis that pronouns serve a simple disambiguating function. The anomaly is the following: Since pronouns, enclitics, and prefixes all reference animacy, and for animates three persons and three numbers, the choice of a pronoun vs. a prefix or enclitic offers the speaker no help in terms of number or type of distinctions available by which to distinguish various participants. How, then, can we say that the pronouns are less "ambiguous" than the bound forms? All short-range coding devices are equally ambiguous in this regard. However, since pronouns have the effect of making assertions more specific (i.e., they reduce the range of possible compatible inferences), participant ambiguity is likely to be reduced just in terms of pragmatics. That is, if there are fewer possible inferences, the role of the participant being coded is more restricted, and therefore its identity is likely to be more easily gleaned from pragmatic context. Another way of expressing this hypothesis is to say that a reduction in the multiplicity of propositions compatible with a particular overtly expressed proposition also reduces the multiplicity of possible referents competing for any particular participant mention within it.

The notion of selection and exclusion (which seems to me a stronger notion than simple disambiguation) is consistent with Chafe's definition of contrastiveness, but leaves out the requirement that there be a shared awareness that the event described by the contrastive sentence in fact occurred. In an English sentence like 'RONALD made the hamburgers,' with no contrastive stress on 'made the hamburgers' it indeed seems reasonable that 'someone made hamburgers' must be a presupposition shared by speaker and hearer. However, an element can be contrastive without such a presupposition, e.g., if someone says 'SALLY made a SALAD and RONALD made HAMburgers,' the fact that someone made a salad and someone else made hamburgers is not necessarily presupposed knowledge. To the contrary, it seems most reasonable to suggest that with this particular wording these propositions are asserted, rather than presupposed. Chafe (1976:35) describes the sentence 'SALLY made the SALAD, but RONALD made the HAMburgers' as a double focus of contrast in which it is the particular pairing of participants and events that is asserted, though the events themselves are presupposed. This may be true as far as sentences of the type Chafe presents are concerned (i.e., where definite direct objects are contrasted), but it does not follow that all instances of contrastiveness must have this presupposition. It is clear here that we are dealing with two or more kinds of contrastiveness (see, e.g., Dik 1978 and Dik et al. 1981 for several different notions of what might be called contrastiveness). I introduce the term exclusive contrast here simply to distinguish the kind of contrast I perceive the PPRO device codes, at least for A and S_a participants, from that described by Chafe (1976).

7.4. PPRO and O/S$_o$ participants

All of the above examples have illustrated use of pronouns to code A and S$_a$ participants. For these roles it is clear that pronouns function primarily as special contrastive devices. Though the notion of exclusive contrast is also somewhat relevant for the O and S$_o$ roles, there is one respect in which pronouns used to code A and S$_a$ roles differ functionally from those used to code the O and S$_o$ roles. Specifically, O and S$_o$ participants coded with pronouns tend to be more persistent than A and S$_a$ participants coded with the same device (see Table 6). In this section I will suggest a possible explanation for the functional contrast between pronouns in the A/S$_a$ roles and in the O/S$_o$ roles.

The following examples illustrate the PPRO device used to refer to O/S$_o$ participants. These examples will show that Persistence is a crucial function of O/S$_o$ participants coded with the PPRO device:

(8)   a.   Mútu-súma-numaa   naaní-ítu-títyii-dye-ñíí,   múkǫǫsiy.
                agouti-large-now   3DL-carry-directly-DAY-3SG   punchama
                'A huge agouti (*dasyprocta aguti*) now she brings, punchama (*myoprocta acouchy* - unverified).'

    b.   Níí-numaa   jį́į́   naanu-mútiye.
                3COL:PRO-now JIITA   3DL-cook
                'THEM now she cooks.'[5]

In this example it is clear from the context that the two animals are not being contrasted; both are cooked. What is significant is that the animals, in their cooked state, continue to figure prominently in the discourse, as follows in English translation:

    'She gives to them (other human participants) their cooked piece of flesh. He says to his mother: "Don't eat this piece of worm meat! Do you think it's agouti?"'

There continues substantial discussion of whether the meat is worm meat or agouti or *punchama* (a rodent of the *myoprocta* genera) meat.

Other similar examples are relatively common in discourse. One more will be included here for illustrative purposes:

(9)   a.   Sa-rámuchu   jį́įta-níí   junicha,   vídya.
                3SG-swallow   JIITA-3SG   tapir   SW
                'He$_i$ swallows the tapir$_j$, gulp.'

    b.   Níí-numaa   sa-víñu-tya   rá-jachéy.
                3SG:PRO-now 3SG-twist-TRNS INAN-middle
                'HIM$_j$ he$_i$ makes twist its middle.'

Up to this point in the text the tapir has been a central character (see section 4.3), and afterward the tapir continues to figure prominently, as follows in translation:

'A long time he stays there under water. His mother comes along in hopes of seeing him. "Where can my son be? Maybe a snake has bitten him."'

And so on.

The claim that one function of preverbal pronouns is to refer to arguments that are relatively high in the topicality measure of Persistence seems to run counter to Givón's (1983a) iconicity principle of topic continuity (discussed in section 4.1). This principle states that more highly topical participants are coded with less substantial morphological marking than less topical participants. Pronouns are "larger," i.e., they involve more phonological bulk than do simple verb coding or enclitics, yet they refer to more persistent, i.e., more topical, arguments.

I believe that we must appeal to the pragmatic distinctions between the semantico-syntactic categories of subject and object in order to answer this question. Human participants are more likely to be coded as *subjects*, insofar as subject is the morphosyntactic category typically used for participants in perspective (Fillmore 1977); and speakers are likely to place human participants in perspective, since people most naturally empathize with other people, as opposed to nonhuman participants. Similarly, human participants are less likely to be coded as *objects*, since this is a morphosyntactic category typically associated with patients, nonactors, and noncontrollers.

There are many cases in language where unexpected combinations of pragmatic features are overtly marked in some way, while the expected combinations are left unmarked. For example, in Spanish, referential human direct objects are marked with the preposition a, while nonhuman and nonreferential human direct objects are not marked:

(10)   Estóy buscando a Juan.
         'I am looking for Juan.'

(11)   Estoy buscando a una empleada.
         'I am looking for a specific maid (referential).'

(12)   Estoy buscando una empleada . . .
         'I am looking for a/any maid . . . (nonreferential).'

(13)   Estoy buscando mis/las llaves.
         'I am looking for my/the keys.'

In Spanish, subjects are never case-marked, regardless of the human/nonhuman, or referential/nonreferential distinctions. Therefore in 10 and 11 above the human referential direct objects do not receive extra marking because they are more topical than the nonreferential DOs in 12 and 13 (though they normally would be), but because the collocation of humanness and referentiality with direct-object position is unusual, or surprising. Human referential participants are much more likely to be subjects than objects. Therefore, when they occur in an object role, they receive a special flag indicating an unusual collocation of pragmatic and syntactic roles (see, e.g., Comrie 1981:122ff for a more general discussion of this phenomenon). This is a general pragmatic constraint that Spanish has grammaticalized into a strictly categorical rule.

These observations may help us understand the discrepancy in Persistence indexes for the PPRO device used for A/S_a and O/S_o participants in Yagua. As mentioned above, the PPRO device is only used for animate participants, insofar as there are no nondemonstrative free pronouns referring to inanimates in Yagua. Animates are more likely to occur in the A/S_a category because of the amenability of this category to active, agentive semantic roles. Animates are less likely to be found in the O/S_o category, especially animates that figure prominently in the discourse, i.e., those that are highly persistent. It is exactly this class of O/S_o participants (animates that are highly persistent) that are coded with the PPRO device. This fact suggests the following hypothesis: the PPRO device is used to indicate *high topicality* (in terms of potential Persistence) of an O/S_o participant. It is more typical for objects to be less topical than subjects. Therefore, the assignment of more substantial morphological coding (in this case PPRO) to more topical participants in this semantico-syntactic role is understandable.

7.5. Conclusion

In this chapter I have attempted to show that the concepts of *exclusive contrast* and *deployability* are crucial to an understanding of use of the PPRO device in Yagua discourse. Unlike the concepts of *change of scene*, *unexpected action*, and *episodic climax* used in Chapter 6 to explain use of S_o coding on verbs, exclusive contrast has no independently verified definition apart from use of the PPRO device. Although this "explanation" of use of PPRO is, strictly speaking, circular, the evidence of the specific examples cited should suffice to demonstrate the empirical validity of this concept. The definition of exclusive contrast arrived at through inspection of particular examples of the PPRO device is the following:

> A short-range coding device indicates exclusive contrast if it asserts
> the identity of a particular participant to the exclusion of other
> possible referents currently present on the discourse stage.

This definition excludes the VC and E devices, since these do not inherently impart the assertion of exclusive identity. In most cases the correct identity of the participant being coded by the VC or E device is in fact understood. However, there is not the necessary assertion that this participant be the only one to have participated in the action in question. This definition seems to hold up for the instances of the PPRO device found in my corpus. Further research will reveal to what extent this condition can (1) be shown to hold for all instances of the PPRO device in Yagua and (2) be identified apart from specific instances of unusual coding devices such as PPRO.

The concept of (potential) Persistence (or *deployability*; Jaggar 1984) has been shown to be particularly relevant for the categories of O and S_o participants. The PPRO device is much more likely to code deployable (i.e., persistent)[6] O and S_o participants than A or S_a participants. This fact is understandable in terms of the typical pragmatic functions of the morphosyntactic categories of subject and object. A and S_a participants in Yagua are in general more deployable than O and S_o participants. Hence when an O or S_o participant is highly deployable, special morphosyntactic coding is induced. For short-range participants, that special coding is the PPRO device.

Notes to Chapter 7

1   Derbyshire does not use the term "contrastive," but the results of his quantitative study of use of pronouns in Hixkaryana strongly suggest this interpretation.

2   Neither Givón, A. Fox, nor Sun and Givón explicitly define the term "contrastive." For this reason, I will continue to enclose the term in quotes when referring to its use in these works. Sun and Givón (1985) virtually equate the index of Ambiguity with "contrastiveness," e.g., by calling the Ambiguity index of 1.00 the "bottom of the contrastiveness scale."

3   It may not be immediately clear how a pronoun can discriminate between competing referents with greater efficiency than a verb-coding prefix or enclitic, both of which are equally as specific as the pronoun in indicating person and number. Hopefully, the following explication of individual cases will make it clear that pronouns do in fact have this function. Contrastive pronouns simply do not function in the same domain as other coding devices.

4   The NP *munuñúniy* is an afterthought that recapitulates the subject of the sentence. It is not normal for a subject NP to occur after the object, so this NP is obviously outside the main predication. The presence of the comma in the original transcription suggests an intonational pause, thus further supporting this conclusion. The presence of *-niy* following the afterthought subject preserves parallelism between the PPRO device and the subject NP, thus further clarifying that the NP refers to the subject of the sentence.

5   This use of the pronoun *nít* to code a semantically nonsingular referent is an example of the "collective" use of 3SG forms discussed in footnote 3 of Chapter 2. Groups of nonpersonified animals are virtually always coded with singular forms. (Space does not permit inclusion of the entire, rather lengthy, portion of text necessary to justify the translation 'them' in this particular example.)

6   Persistence is an *index* of deployability. That is, it indicates whether a participant has been deployed or not; it does not constitute a *definition* of deployablity.

Chapter 8

CONCLUSIONS

This study set out to accomplish two goals: (1) to provide accurate and usable information on Yagua, a little-studied language of the Amazon basin; and (2) to test and evaluate certain hypotheses emerging within the subdisciplines of discourse analysis and functional linguistics. In attempting to reach these goals, I have explored one functionally defined area of Yagua grammar: the participant coding system. In Chapters 2 and 3 I presented the formal details of that system by describing the morphosyntactic devices used to code participants. In Chapter 4 I examined the use of a subset of those devices in terms of the framework of topic continuity developed by Givón (1983a,c,d) and others. I introduced several modifications to this framework in an attempt to more accurately isolate the functional pressures that impinge upon the choices among various coding devices in discourse. In Chapters 5, 6, and 7 I focused on particular problems raised by the findings of Chapter four, and in the process uncovered some additional factors that influence the use of coding devices. In the present chapter I summarize the key findings of the earlier chapters and attempt to discern some unity in the observations that have been made. Certain directions for further research will also be suggested.

8.1. The multidimensional nature of linguistic functions

8.1.1. Persistence and Referential Distance in conflict?

A basic assumption of the framework of topic continuity outlined in Chapter 4 is that coding devices which are in paradigmatic relationship with one another typically represent distinct points arranged along a continuous functional scale (Givón 1981). Morphosyntactic categories are necessarily discrete, whereas the functional domains they code are typically continuous. For example, if a paradigm has three members, A, B, and C, a speaker is constrained to choose one of these three, even though his or her message may involve a feature that falls most logically between A and B, or between B and C. A simplistic and oft-cited example of this phenomenon is that of basic color terminology. Language, and perhaps cognition in general, necessarily imposes discrete categories on a continuous reality.

Givón (1983a,c,d) is concerned primarily with the functional domain of topic continuity or accessibility. As discussed in Chapters 1 and 4 of the present study, topic continuity (sometimes referred to as topicality, accessibility, or availability, depending at least partly on the metaphor one uses) is a scalar domain that every language must deal with using discrete formal devices such as noun phrases, pronouns, verb agreement, etc. A speaker is constrained by the structure of his or her language to choose, for example, either a noun phrase or a pronoun to code a particular participant at a particular point in a text. That choice is based on the speaker's estimation of how accessible the participant being coded is to the hearer. Thus a binary coding choice (full noun vs. pronoun) is based on a scalar functional domain (accessibility).

It is crucial to the methodology associated with this framework that (1) the functional domain under consideration be defined and *quantified* independently of the formal devices that are used to code it, and (2) the formal coding devices used to code this domain be identified. The explanatory power of the empirical studies that result from this methodology depend on the establishment of a universal iconic relationship between the set of coding devices and the functional domain. For example, the iconicity principle of topic continuity (Givón 1983c:18) predicts that more accessible participants will be coded with "smaller" morphological devices than less accessible participants. A counterexample to this principle is easily imagined. If a language has a set of participant-coding devices including D and D,' where D is consistently "smaller" than D,' that language violates the topic-continuity hypothesis if, in an appropriately conducted quantitative study, it is shown that D typically codes participants that are less continuous than those coded by D.'

The three indices that are said to quantify the functional domain of topic continuity are Referential Distance, Persistence and Ambiguity (see section 4.1). There are several formal devices that are sensitive to this functional domain, all of which are arranged according to various "scales." One is the scale of phonological size. Phonologically larger coding devices are said to code less accessible participants, since such participants require more "work," i.e., more substantial morphological marking, in order to be identified. In Yagua the scale of phonological size is:

(1)   "Small"   -->   "Large"
       0   VC/E   PPRO   NP   VC/E + NP

If this scale directly paralleled the functional domain of topic continuity (or accessibility), we would expect that zero would code the most continuous topics, and continuity would decrease diagrammatically as the phonological size of the various coding devices increased.

In fact, however, we find that neither of the indices of topic continuity calculated in this study, Referential Distance or Persistence, directly parallels this scale at all. The clearest findings of the topic-continuity study of Chapter 4 are that full noun phrases code participants that had not been mentioned recently, and the other devices code participants that had been mentioned more recently in the discourse. Thus, the index of Referential Distance simply divides the scale of phonological size into two general areas, rather than into distinct coding points for each device, as indicated in Table 44:

Table 44: Scale of Phonological Size Divided by the
Index of Referential Distance

Scalar (?) functional domain:	Short-range	-->	Long-range
Formal coding areas	small	|	large
Devices	0	|	NP
	VC/E	|	VC/E + NP
	PPRO	|	

This finding simply reinforces the intuitions, expressed by Grimes (1975) and Chafe (1976), that "more attenuated" devices are used for participants that are more "available" in memory, and adds further substantiation to the general findings of much recent cross-language work on topic continuity, e.g., the studies in Givón 1983b. The iconicity principle of topic continuity correctly predicts the arrangement of these two areas with respect to each other in the domain quantified by the index of Referential Distance, but has virtually nothing to say with regard to the arrangements of particular coding devices within each area.

The index of Persistence, on the other hand, does not divide the scale of phonological size in the same way as RD does. The relationship of Persistence to the scale of phonological size is complicated by the fact that semantico-syntactic role is a significant factor in the ordering of the various coding devices on this scale. That is, two different scales, one for A and S_a participants and another for O and S_o participants, are distinguished by the Persistence index. These two scales are represented in Table 45:

Table 45: Ordering of Coding Devices by Index of Persistence and
Semantico-Syntactic Role

Scalar functional domain		Persistent-->Nonpersistent		
Devices (A/S_a roles)	VC	VC+NP	PPRO	NP
Mean Persistence	5.88	5.15	3.13	2.5
Devices (O/S_o roles)	PPRO	E	E+NP	NP
Mean Persistence	6.9	4.88	3.63	2.08

Neither of the arrangements represented in Table 45 parallel the scale of phonological size. However, if we consider the persistence indices of coding devices within each area defined by the RD index individually, some interesting observations emerge. These observations will be outlined in the following subsections.

8.1.2. Persistence in the long-range area

Within the "long-range" area, i.e., among the devices typically used to code relatively distant participants, we notice that for all semantico-syntactic roles simple NP is the least persistent device, while the recapitulating devices (see section 4.6) are more persistent:

Table 46: Relative Persistence Indices of Long-Range Devices by Semantico-Syntactic Role

	Recap	Simple
A/S_a	VC + NP	NP (pre-predicate)
O/S_o	E + NP	NP (post-predicate)
Persistence	higher	lower

This observation runs counter to the iconicity principle of topic continuity if we take high Persistence as an index of high continuity. It is not the case that the "larger" coding devices, VC + NP and E + NP, code topics that are less persistent. From the data in Table 46, it appears we must either reject the iconicity principle of topic continuity or reject Persistence as an index of topic continuity. In section 8.1.4 I will opt for the latter approach.

8.1.3. Persistence in the short-range area

The discussion of the use of the PPRO versus VC/E devices in Chapter 7 shows that the index of Persistence does play a role within the short-range area of the scale of phonological size as well. The situation is further complicated here, however, by the fact that the patterning of the "smaller" devices (VC and E) with the "larger" device (PPRO) is reversed for the general categories of semantico-syntactic role, as illustrated in Table 47:

Table 47: Relative Persistence Indices of Short-Range Devices by
Semantico-Syntactic Role

A/S$_a$	VC	PPRO
O/S$_o$	PPRO	E
Persistence:	higher	lower

An additional finding of Chapter 7 is that high Ambiguity is correlated with the use of PPRO, especially for A and S$_a$ participants. This fact, combined with a case-by-case analysis of individual examples of the PPRO device, suggests that the notion of EXCLUSIVE CONTRAST is the key to the use of this device, at least for the A and S$_a$ roles. It is not so clear that exclusive contrast plays such a strong role in the use of PPRO for O and S$_o$ roles. In the latter case, it appears that the PPRO device is used to indicate recently mentioned O or S$_o$ participants that are highly DEPLOYABLE, i.e., that are available to figure prominently in the immediately ensuing discourse. It is understandable that this should be a factor for the O and S$_o$ roles and not for the others in that O and S$_o$ are roles typically associated with less persistent participants (see Chapter 4, Table 25). Thus when an O or an S$_o$ participant is presented as highly deployable, special attention is called to it by the use of a larger coding device and the marked prepredicate position in the clause.

8.1.4. Continuity vs. deployability

There are several hypotheses that might be advanced as explanations for the fact that the index of Persistence does not rank the various participant-coding devices of Yagua according to the scale of phonological size. First, the null hypothesis is that the index of Persistence is not a measure of any functional domain at all. This would be equivalent to saying that whether or not a participant is going to be mentioned frequently in ensuing discourse is completely immaterial to the coding choices a speaker makes. Second, Persistence might be an index of an entirely different domain than is Referential Distance. Third, the Persistence index might be sensitive to more than one functional domain simultaneously. Although a full investigation of these and other possible hypotheses cannot be attempted here, I will suggest that the Persistence index measures a domain which is logically distinct from that measured by Referential Distance. This domain has been called "referentiality" by Du Bois (1980), "manipulability" by Hopper and Thompson 1984, and "deployability" by Jaggar (1984).

In Chapter 7 we have seen how the notion of deployability provides a reasonable explanation for the discourse patterning of the PPRO coding device. In the following discussion I will show that there is no particular reason to expect that Persistence should quantify the same functional domain as Referential Distance. I will also claim that deployability is a functional domain logically independent of topic continuity, and that the patterning of the various coding devices observed in this study is motivated given the nature of these two domains.

Jaggar (1984:113) suggests a principle which he terms the "salience:coding hypothesis," which is stated as follows:

> Prominent and persistent human referents are generally assigned more complex morphological marking than less salient, nonhuman arguments.[1]

This hypothesis can be described as an "iconicity principle" insofar as a functional domain of "prominence" or "salience" (elsewhere associated with the more overarching notion of deployability) is juxtaposed to a formal scale of "complexity of morphological marking." The hypothesis predicts that more "salient" participants will receive more complex marking and less salient participants will receive less complex morphological marking. Jaggar quantifies the functional domain by counting the number of subsequent mentions of a participant in the entire text. This methodology is similar, but not identical, to the method employed in this study for establishing Persistence indices, i.e., Persistence in this study is roughly equivalent to Jaggar's "prominence," "salience," or "deployability."

It is intuitively reasonable to suppose that "more complex" morphology should be associated with more prominent participants in discourse, however the term "prominent" is construed. For instance, an informal survey of register phenomena in English reveals that terms used for participants higher on a scale of honor or formality tend to be larger than terms used for participants lower on the scale:

> you > your honor > Madame President
> Bob > Robert > Professor Stockwell

This fact might be said to be an instance of the potentially universal metaphor "more is better" (Lakoff and Johnson 1980:22).

However intuitively reasonable the salience:coding hypothesis may be, if it is taken strictly at face value it makes exactly the opposite predictions as the equally reasonable iconicity principle of topic continuity. That is, where the principle of topic continuity predicts that the most topical participants will be coded with minimal morphological marking, the salience:coding hypothesis predicts that more salient participants will be coded with more complex morphological marking. To the extent that the notions topicality and salience overlap, these principles are in direct conflict.

I believe that the solution to this dilemma lies in the fact that deployability is a domain that relates *forward* to the subsequent text, whereas topicality is a domain that relates *backward* to previous text. That is, participants only receive reduced morphosyntactic coding *after* they have been established as "referential" (in the sense of Du Bois 1980), or deployable. Before the referentiality of a participant is established, it requires extra effort, i.e., more complex or "larger" coding devices, to call attention to that participant in order to signal to the listener that this participant is going to be important.

Note that this principle is not necessarily limited to initial mentions of participants. Participants may be mentioned in previous text, but not established as deployable. This is particularly obvious in the case of "discourse promotion" described in section 5.2.3. Here participants are introduced as full noun phrases in an oblique role, and then are recapitulated as full noun phrases in the immediately following sentence in a more central grammatical role. Only after they have been mentioned as subject or object can they be freely coded with reduced coding devices. Hence it appears that mention as an oblique (or possessor) is not necessarily sufficient to establish a participant as deployable. Another example of this fact might be the pattern of persistence indices for the PPRO device described in Chapter 7. When a participant that is going to be deployed in subsequent text appears in a role normally associated with less deployable participants, more complex marking (the PPRO device) is called for in order to alert the listener that this participant is something more than just a common, relatively nondeployable direct object. This argument is independent of how topical, in terms of Referential Distance, that participant might be.

The central point to be gleaned here is that there is no necessary reason why the indices of Referential Distance and Persistence should measure the same functional domain at all. The fact that Persistence relates to subsequent text indicates that it measures the deployability of participants, whereas the fact that Referential Distance relates to prior text indicates that it measures the continuity of participants. Continuity and deployability are two logically distinct domains that are sensitive to two different iconicity principles.

This study has only barely begun to scratch the surface of the relationships between functional domains and formal coding devices operative upon and within the participant-coding system of Yagua. The picture that emerges from this treatment, however, is one of great complexity and interrelatedness. We have observed that the same paradigmatic set of formal devices is subject to the influences of several functional domains. Particular domains that have been investigated, though not fully articulated, in this study are topic continuity and deployability, with additional reference being made to the notions of contrastiveness, climax, and thematic boundaries.

8.2. Location and discourse structure

Another contribution of this study has been to draw attention to the importance of location in the discourse-structuring strategies of Yagua, and to show how this emphasis on location has specific and universally motivated morphosyntactic consequences. It has often been observed that change in location is a component of, or represents a certain type of, thematic juncture (Joseph Grimes 1975:218, Givón 1983c:158, to name a few). In this study, particularly Chapter 6, it has been shown that, for Yagua, location plays an unusually significant role in delimiting high-level discourse units. This high degree of reliance on location has specific and unusual morphosyntactic consequences for the participant-coding system of the language: namely subjects of intransitive verbs of locomotion at locationally defined discourse junctures tend to be coded like objects. Although this particular morphosyntactic phenomenon has not previously been correlated with discourse structure for other languages, I have observed two ways in which this fact is reflected in other languages, and thereby may, under further investigation, be shown to be a significant language universal: (1) there is a tendency for certain agentive predicates of locomotion to be treated morphosyntactically like nonverbal predicates, and (2) morphosyntactic correlates of the category "direct object" are often attributed to the category "subject" under discourse conditions of discontinuity (Givón 1983b; Doris Payne 1989) or counter expectation (Gary 1978).

8.3. The importance of lowland South American languages

The final contribution of this study has been to emphasize the importance of rigorous and systematic investigation of the languages of lowland South America in order to evaluate claims made by general linguistic theory. Many previously documented "universals" of language have been shown not to hold for certain languages of South America. For example, Derbyshire (1977) and Derbyshire and Pullum (1981) show that OVS is an attested basic word order, while Doris Payne (1990) shows that Yagua violates several previously proposed universals of word-order correlates. On the other hand, this study has illuminated other possible universal tendencies that may not have been noticed were it not for close examination of South American languages. In particular, I refer to the correlation between objective morphology and predicates of locomotion, as well as the possible discourse-based motivations for such a correlation.

Though the scientific importance of the study of South American languages cannot be denied, the notion of linguistics as "pure science" is simplistic. As always, the descriptive linguistic work that will be of enduring value is that which flows out of a felt need for cultural identity in the midst of a changing and often hostile political and social reality. As communities rediscover the value of their language as a medium of education and transmission of culture to future generations, the importance of basic descriptive linguistic work, including grammars, dictionaries, and texts, will be increasingly recognized. Most of the descriptive work yet to be accomplished in this area will be done by South American linguists and native speakers of the languages themselves.

Descriptive linguistic work alone will not reverse the trend toward language death and acculturation now taking place in the Americas and elsewhere in the world. But it is a basic component of the formidable endeavor of developing language pride and the nearly universally concomitant desire for literacy. To desire literacy requires consciousness of connection to the political and social reality in which one finds oneself. The achievement of native language literacy furnishes the power to deal effectively with the larger reality without compromising cultural distinctiveness. Even with the nurturing effect of language pride and native language literacy in cultural communities, the next decades will see the extinction of many languages on the South American continent. Not only is this a loss to the community of academic linguists, but also to the community of the world, in that the loss of a language means the loss of a unique culture and its potential to enrich the experience of all members of the human family.

Note to Chapter 8

[1] For Jaggar, humanness contributes to the likelihood that a participant will be highly deployable, in the same sense that humanness (or at least animacy) contributes to the likelihood that a participant will have the role of "agent" in clause-level semantics. However, humanness itself is not a component of the definition of deployability, though the quoted passage may give this impression. The deployability of a participant is based strictly on the number of subsequent mentions of that participant in the text.

Appendix 1

The Kneebite Twins

Storyteller: Laureano Mozombite

The original recording of this version of the Kneebite Twins tale was made by Paul Powlison, and a description of the story is given in Powlison (1969). The present retranscription and translation was made by Mamerto Macahuachi and myself.

This is a story about a mythical culture hero named Mokayu and a pair of not-so-heroic identical twins. The twins are half wasp and half human, being born of a wasp bite on Mokayu's knee. The story involves a journey on the part of the three central characters, and each episode represents an adventure at a particular point in the journey. Thus the story exhibits linear locational structure as described in T. Payne 1984b. The adventures usually involve a conflict where Mokayu is initially ridiculed or victimized in some way by the twins, but in which he eventually triumphs due to his superior wisdom and cleverness. The story ends with the twins acknowledging Mokayu's superiority.

1.   Darya-niy   sa-súu̧-yada   núko̧vaañu-níí
        thus-NIY   3SG-bite-PAST3   wasp-3SG

        ta̧a̧ryi-munátyi̧-i̧.
        long:time-first-NOM

        Like this our ancestor was stung by a wasp.

2.   Rá-vicha-núú-yada   si̧-i̧tya   Mokáyu.
        INAN-be-CONT-PAST3   3SG-name   Mokayu
        His name was Mokayu.

Scene I: Mokayu's House

3.   Rá-poo   ji̧í̧   sa-súu̧-jyo̧.
        INAN-swell   JIITA   3SG-bite-NOM
        His sting swelled.

4.   Núko̧vaañu   súu̧-jyo̧   sa̧-a̧dási-ñiy,   ja̧a̧mu-rá   rá-poo.
        wasp   bite-NOM   3SG-knee-LOC   big-CF   INAN-swell
        The wasp sting on his knee swelled up huge.

5.   Tí̧i̧kii   járimyuní   sa̧a̧rá̧-ju̧   sa-tiryó̧ó̧-ta-jayá̧á̧-ra.
        one   month   extent-for   3SG-lie-TRNS-DIST-INAN
        For one month he was laid up with it.

6.   Pariché-ñumaa   sų-unúú-tye-rya,   "jiiin!"
      finally-now   3SG-look-TRNS-INAN SW
      Finally he looked at it, yikes!

7.   Néé   sa-jaachįni-tyéé   nuudá-yu.
      NEG   3SG-withstand-INTS   any:more-COR2
      He can't stand it any more.

8.   "Ra-díí-tya-rų́ų́-ñumaa   pariché-dyé-rya."
      1SG-die-TRNS-POT-now   finally-DAY-INAN
      "I'm about to die with this!"

9.   Sų-ųnúúy   jį́įta   yá-adási-ñiy   rá-dakuuy.
      3SG-look   JIITA   COR1-knee-LOC   INAN-black
      He saw that his knee was black.

10.   Rá-dakuu-tyániy   są-ądási-ñubéé.
      INAN-black-cause   3SG-knee-inside
      Inside his knee was becoming black.

11.   Sa-ryiy   jį́įta-ra   rooda.
      3SG-grab   JIITA-INAN   thorn
      He grabs a thorn.

12.   "Rą-ą   jántya-dii-tyéé   jįchitye-eda-téé."
      1SG-IRR   try-ANTIC-INTS   prick-PART-INTS
      "I'm going to try to open it."[1]

13.   Rá-richa-numaa-dee-téé-dáy.
      INAN-have:pus-now-little-INTS-DAY
      Now it has a lot of pus.

14.   Sa-niy   jįchitiy   jį́įta,
      3SG-MALF   prick   JIITA
      He pricks,

15.   sa-sąñe-yąą-níita   vari-dyéy,   "jayo!"
      3SG-yell-DIST-NEG(rhet-quest)   then-DAY   SW
      and then does he ever yell, ouch!

16.   "Nijyąąmi-ñíita   vicha-sara   rą-ądasi-ñubee-dáy,   nijyąąmíy?"
      people-NEG(rhet)   be-NOM   1SG-knee-inside-DAY   people
      "Are there people inside my knee, people?"

17.　　Naada-supáta-y　　　jíí-ra　　　váriy.
　　　3DL-emerge-DETRNS　JIITA-INAN　then
　　　So two emerge.

18.　　Naada-supáta-myáá-jíta　kari　da-nu-juy　　　vánu-ju-dyéé-ru.
　　　3DL-emerge-PERF-JIITA　swell　two-CF:ANIM-two　male-two-little-two
　　　Two emerged, two male children.

19.　　Jási-ñumaa-jíí　　sa-jáávye-chu-naadá.
　　　there-now-JIITA　3SG-grow-TRNS-3DL
　　　There he raised them both.

20.　　Taari-pyu-numáá-ti-ñiy　　　naaní-íta-jíí　　sí-íva,
　　　long:while-after-now-REL-NIY　3DL-say-JIITA　3SG-to
　　　After a time the two of them say to him,

21.　　"Váñu,　vurye-eya　ráruváá-va."
　　　c'mon　1PLINC-go　downriver-to
　　　"Come, let's go downriver.

22.　　"Váñu,　váñu."
　　　c'mon　c'mon
　　　"Let's go, let's go!"

23.　　Ri-iya-jíta.
　　　3pl-go-JIITA
　　　They go.

Scene II: Rainstorm

24.　　Múúy　jiñúva-yási-ryíy.
　　　there　arrive:late-there-3PL
　　　There they arrive late.

25.　　"Jiyu-niy　vurya-a　　mááy.
　　　here-NIY　1PLINC-IRR　sleep
　　　"Here we will have to sleep.

26.　　"Jiyu-niy　vurya-a　　sútay　　vurya-ajííju."
　　　here-NIY　1PLINC-IRR　shelter　1PLINC-in:front[2]
　　　"Here we will make shelters to protect us."

27.　　Naada-sútay　jíta　núkovaañú-juy　yá-ájííju-dáy　　　múkadi-ta.
　　　3DL-shelter　JIITA　wasp-DL　COR1-in:front-for-DAY　earth-INST
　　　The wasp twins make their shelter out of mud.

28.   Sa-sų́tạy   jį́ịta   nuu-nti-dyéy   Mokáyu-dáy.
        3SG-shelter JIITA   other-REP-DAY   Mokayu-DAY
        The other one, Mokayu, makes his shelter also.

29.   Návïï-ta   sa-sų́tạ-dyéy.
        leaf-INST   3SG-shelter-DAY
        Out of leaves he makes his shelter.

30.   Múkadi-ta   naada-sų́tạ-dyéy.
        earth-INST   3DL-shelter-DAY
        Out of mud the others make theirs.

31.   Naada-ya jį́ị   si-imu-ntíy   Mokáyu-mú.
        3DL-go   JIITA   3SG-LOC-REP   Mokayu-LOC
        The two go to Mokayu.

32.   "Jijiin! Tą́ą́-muy ji-ñiy   sų́tạ-ryų́ų́y   múkadí-ta,   tą́ą́-jụ?"
        SW   why-NEG you-NIY   shelter-POT   earth-INST   why-for
        "Ha! Why don't you want to make your shelter out of
        mud, why?"

33.   "Rá-niy   naa-ta   yu-utáy   rụụmurá.   Rá-rạạy."
        INAN-NIY   stop-NEG   y'know   rain   INAN-fall
        "That won't stop the rain! It'll fall."

34.   "Néé   da-ñumáá-jụ."
        NEG   thus-now-for
        "I don't care."

35.   Ri-mééy   jį́ịta   jásiy.
        3PL-sleep JIITA   there
        They sleep there.

36.   Tạạri-pyú   jiñúva-rya-numáá   rá-suu-tyítyiiy.
        long:while-after arrive:late-CF:NEUT-now   INAN-sound-moving:along
        After a good while, late, it comes thundering.

37.   Rų́ų́mura jááryiy   rụ-ụmú.
        rain   much   3PL-LOC
        It rains hard on them.

38.   Tạạri-pyu-dee-numáá-tiy   rų́ų́mu,
        long:while-after-little-now-COND   rain
        After it rains awhile,

39. rá-júú-yąą-numáá   naada-sútąy   yú-úva,   tipyé!
    INAN-fall-DIST-now   3DL-shelter   COR1-DAT   SW
    the wasp twins shelter collapses on them, crash!

40. Naada-sañi-yąą-jasúmiy,
    3DL-shriek-DIST-rising
    They jump up shrieking.

41. "Jéén.   Naa-pyáru-ñumáá."
    SW   1DLEX-get:wet-now
    "Yikes! Now we'll get wet!"

42. Rá-júú-yąą-mu   naada-sútąy   tįįtájų.
    INAN-fall-DIST-LOC   3DL-shelter   all
    It collapses all at once their whole shelter.

43. Parichéy   naada-sii-myaasíy   rá-vïïmu-síy.
    finally   3DL-run-exit   INAN-inside-from
    Finally they rush out.

Scene III: Mokayu's shelter

44. Sii-jéé-ñuvee-já-ąsiy   Mokáyu   sútą-jyari-ñaadá.
    run-enter-ARR2-o'land-PROX1   Mokayu   shelter-into-3DL
    They run into Mokayu's shelter on arrival.

45. "Néé-viy   rá-stay   ji-chútą-dyéy?"
    NEG-QP   INAN-leak   2SG-shelter-DAY
    "Doesn't your shelter leak?"

46. "Tama-dáy   tama.
    never-DAY   never
    "Not at all, but not at all!

47. "Rá-sta-mya   ji-ñubeeríy?
    INAN-leak-NEG   2SG-request
    Did you think it would leak?

48. "Jí-ñiy   jta-jey   néé   rúúmurá   tachara-ntí-rya."
    2SG:PRO-NIY   say-PROX2   NEG   rain   test-REP-INAN
    You thought that the water wouldn't test it!"

49. Naana-asaacha   jásiy.
    3DL-dawn   there
    They wake up there.

50.   Rą́-ą́saacha   jíį́ta.
       INAN-dawn   JIITA
       It dawns.

51.   Ri-ya   jíį́ta-ntíy.
       3PL-go   JIITA-REP
       They go again.

52.   "Vañu-numaa-ntíy."
       c'mon-now-REP
       "Let's go already again."

Scene IV: Boa

53.   Múúy   kíínchu-nuvee-já-ą́si-ryíy.
       there   light:fire-ARR2-o'land-PROX1-3PL
       There they light their fires upon arrival.

54.   Sų-ų̃núúy   jíį́ta   núkǫvaañu-ntíy,
       3SG-look   JIITA   wasp-REP
       The two wasp twins look,

55.   "Yą-ą   junúúy   koodi-chúmay,
       2SG-IRR   look   snake-large
       "Look, a huge boa!"

56.   jąąmu   koodíy   ji-ñu   muchą-kąą-mú."
       large   snake   DEMO-CL:ANIM   Lupuna-fork-LOC
       There is a huge boa in the fork of a Lupuna tree.

57.   "Rą-ą   jaachi-dii-tyéé-níí   kíí?"
       1SG-IRR   spear-ANTIC-INTS-3SG   huh
       "Shall I spear him?"

58.   Sų-ų̃tay   jíį́ta   núkǫvaañu,
       3SG-say   JIITA   wasp
       the wasp twins say.

59.   "Néé.   Naay   jíį́   rą   jaachi-ñíí."
       NEG   1DLEX:PRO   JIITA   IRR   spear-3SG
       "No. WE will spear him.

60.   "Tama   tį̃į̃   jaachi-tyąą-ta   ráñiy   junúú-rya   ji-ryúúve."
       never   anyone   spear-INST-NEG   MALF   look-INAN   2SG-spear
       Don't you know that no-one spears with your spear?"

61.   "Jóó."
        yes
        "Okay."

62.   Sa-niy   jaachiy   jį́į́   si-imú.
        3SG-MALF   spear   JIITA   3SG-LOC
        He throws his spear (probably a wasp stinger) at him.

63.   Tííy   rá-riy   pų̃ųchá-vą̃ą̃-níí.
        NEG   INAN-AUX:FRUST   penetrate-NEG-3SG
        It doesn't affect him at all.[3]

64.   Parichéy   sa-sii-ryį̃į́   Mokáyu,
        finally   3SG-run-in:passing   Mokayu
        Finally Mokayu comes attacking.

65.   "Ráy   jį́į́   rą   jaachi-ñíí,   rá."
        1SG:PRO   JIITA   IRR   spear-3SG   EXCL
        "*I* will now spear him!"

66.   Sa-jaachiy   jį́į́ta.
        3SG-spear   JIITA
        He spears.

Climax

67.   Múúy   jų́ų́-ñíí,   pų̃ų̃n!
        there   fall-3SG   SW
        There he falls, thump!"

68.   Naada-sii-ryį̃į́-numáá-ta   núko̞vaañú-jų̃y.
        3DL-run-in:passing-now-TRNS   wasp-two
        The wasp twins run to recover him.

69.   Naani-imí-ñumaa-dáy.
        3DL-eat-now-DAY
        Now they eat him.

70.   Sa-niy   vą̃ą̃ta-numaa-yą́ą́-ntya   rá-naachó̞   jį́ípu-dáy.
        3SG-MALF   want-now-DIST-right:there   INAN-towards   firewood-DAY
        The other one goes looking for firewood.

71.   Sa-niy   junúú-ñuvïï-jį́į́   rumu-síy.
        3SG-MALF   look-ARR1-JIITA   there-from
        He looks on arrival there.

72.   Tijin!   Mítya   rúkąą-dee-numáá.
       SW   nothing backbone-little-now
       Zip! Nothing is left but the backbone.

73.   "Rá-numaa-naa   sąąni-imí-myuu-ntí-ñíí,   rá."
       INAN(?)-now-wonder   2DL-eat-COMPL-REP-3SG   EXCL
       "You've already eaten the whole thing!"

74.   Ri-ya   jį́įta   jás-chi-ntíy   núú-va.
       3PL-go   JIITA   there-from-REP   path-DAT
       They go from there by trail.

Scene V: The Twins' Warning 1

75.   Múúy   maasa-nuvee-já-ą́siy   są-ajííjų   naadá.
       there sit-ARR2-o'land-PROX1   3SG-in:front   3DL
       There upon arrival the two sit waiting for him.

76.   Naada-díryey jį́įta   jási-ñíí,
       3DL-greet   JIITA   there-3SG
       They greet him there.

77.   "játiy   ji-ya   múúy, Moká."
       careful   2SG-go   there   Mokayu
       "Be careful of going there Moká!"

78.   "Tą́ą́ra-jų-ra?"
       what-for-INAN
       "Why?"

79.   "Já́ą́mu   ravichų́   są-kíínáy   Tǫkáchiy   yu-unuu-pada-mú."
       large   stone   3SG-defecate Tǫkáchiy 2SG-head-top-LOC
       "The Toncachi bird will defecate a huge rock on your head."

80.   "Sį́įteenú?"   "Jóónu."
       really   yes
       "Really?" "Yes."

81.   Naada-ya   jį́įta-ntíy.
       3DL-go   JIITA-REP
       The two go on.

82.   Sa-maachǫ   jį́įta   jásiy   naani-ibí-íva.
       3SG-remain JIITA   there   3DL-back-DAT
       He stays there where they were.

83. Sa-ya   jį́įta   ruumú núú-va.
    3SG-go   JIITA   there   path-DAT
    He goes there by trail.

Scene VI: Toncachi Bird 1

84. "Núútyi-ji-ñaa   naani-ité-ési-tyéé-níí,   núútyi-jíy?"
    how-place-wonder   3DL-say-PROX1-INTS-3SG   how-place
    "In what place did they say he was, in what place?"

85. Sa-ya-títyiiy,   sa-ya-títyiiy.
    3SG-go-directly   3SG-go-directly
    He goes along, goes along.

86. Sa-tuvą̄ą̄chu sa-nikyee,   "tǫǫká,   tǫǫká,   tǫǫká."
    3SG-hear   3SG-speak   SW   SW   SW
    He hears his call, "toncá toncá toncá."

87. Jápiichi-ñumaa-tée,   sa-nikyee-téé,   jápiichi-ñumaa-tée.
    occasionally-now-INTS   3SG-speak-INTS   occasionally-now-INTS
    Every once in a while he calls, every once in a while.

88. Váséé   są-ąri-ñumaa-téé-níí.
    straight   3SG-below-now-INTS-3SG
    Now he is right below him.

89. Jásiy   kíína-dyéy,   pų́ų́   sų-ųnúú-pada-mú.
    there   defecate-DAY   SW   3SG-head-top-LOC
    There he defecates, plop, on his head.

90. To-má-ási-tyéé   múco-jári-tyéé-níí.
    leave-down-PROX1-INTS   earth-buried:in-INTS-3SG
    He leaves him buried in the ground.

Scene VII: Toncachi Bird 2

91. Múúy   supaté-ésiy,   tá-ji-chi-nti-ñíí
            supata-y-jásiy[4]
    there   emerge-DETRNS-PROX1   another-place-from-REP-3SG
    There he emerges from another place.

92. Múú-chi-ñumaa   si-ita-ntíy.
    there-from-now   3SG-return-REP
    From there he (the bird) returns again.

93. Jási-ntya   sa-nikyéé,   "tǫǫká   tǫǫká   tǫǫká".
    there-right:there 3SG-speak   SW   SW   SW
    Right there he calls "toncá toncá toncá."

94. Sa-páta-rį̇̃   jį́íta-ra   vúdnu-kaa-dáy.
    3SG-pull-in:passing JIITA-INAN   branch-dry-DAY
    He (Mokayu) breaks in passing a dry branch.

95. "Néé   rą-ą   jaachíy,"
    NEG   INAN-IRR   spear
    "I'm definitely going to spear (him),"

96. sų-ųtá-yu-jųų.
    3SG-say-COR2-?
    he says to himself.

97. Sa-páta-rį̇̃   jį́íta-ra.
    3SG-pull-in:passing JIITA-INAN
    He breaks it in passing.

98. Sa-nikyéé,   "tǫǫká,   tǫǫká".
    3SG-speak   SW   SW
    He calls "toncá toncá."

99. Jásiy   jaachi-dyéy,   pǫ́ǫ́.
    there   spear-DAY   SW
    There he spears, zap!

Climax

100. Múúy   júų́-ñíí.
     there   fall-3SG
     There he falls.

101. Są-ąsítya-rį̇̃   jį́í   sa-múú.
     3SG-pluck-in:passing JIITA   3SG-feather
     He plucks his feathers going along,

102. Sa-túúnu-rį̇̃   jį́íta   jí-myoo-tąąsá-jų-ra.
     3SG-weave-in:passing JIITA   COR1-face-middle-for-INAN
     and weaves them going along to place on his forehead.

103. Sa-ya   jį́íta   váriy   jás-chi-ntíy.
     3SG-go   JIITA   then   there-from-REP
     So he goes from there again.

Scene VIII: The Twins' Warning 2

104.   juuun!   múúy   sarye-ñuvee-já-ásiy   naada-ntíy.
      SW   there   meet-ARR2-o'land-PROX1   3DL-REP
      Oops! *There they meet (him) on arrival again.*

105.   Naani-inúúy   jíí   sa-moo-mu-síy,
      3DL-look   JIITA   3SG-face-LOC-from
      They look at his forehead.

106.   "Rá-numaa-naa   yu-uvá-ryii̯-téé-níí   Tọkáchi-ntíy,   rá."
      INAN-now-wonder   2SG-kill-in:passing-INTS-3SG   Tọkáchiy-REP   EXCL
      "You've killed the Tonkachi bird also!"

107.   "Núú-ta?"
      how-NEG
      "Why not?"

108.   Naani-itay   jíí   sí-íva-ntíy,
      3DL-say   JIITA   3SG-DAT-REP
      They say to him again,

109.   "Játiy   ji-ya   múú-ntíy,   Moká.
      careful   2SG-go   there-REP   Mokayu
      "Be careful of going there again, Mocá.

110.   Jaséésiy   rạ   dápuuta-jíy."
      beetle   IRR   plant-2SG
      "The beetle will plant you under the ground."

111.   "Síiteenú?"
      really
      "Really?"

112.   "Sạ-ạ   jạatyọ-rii̯   ji-ñíy.
      3SG-IRR   hit-in:passing   2SG-at
      "He is going to hit at you in passing.

113.   "Tyéé̯!   múúy   ráá̯-jíy.   (*)
      SW   there   fall:over-2SG
      "Pow! *There you fall over.*

114.   Jási-tyiy   sạ-ạ   dápuuta-jíy.
      there-REL   3SG-IRR   plant-2SG
      "There where he will plant you under the ground.

115.   Nichą́ą́riy   są-ą̨   to-mu-jíy."
       deep   3SG-IRR   leave-down-2SG
       Deep he will leave you."

116.   Naada-ya   jį́įta-ntíy.
       3DL-go   JIITA-REP
       The two go again.

117.   Sa-ya   jį́įta   naani-ibí-íva-si-ntíy.
       3SG-go   JIITA   3DL-back-DAT-from-REP
       He goes after them also.

Scene IX: The Beetle

118.   "Téé-naa-téé   naani-ité-ési-tyéé-níí   jaséésiy,   téé?"
       where-wonder-INTS   3DL-say-PROX1-INTS-3SG   beetle   where
       "Where now did they say this beetle is, where?

119.   Jʉʉ!   sa-jįį-numaa-yą́ą́   jaséési-chúma,
       SW   3SG-fly-now-DIST   beetle-large
       Aha! A large beetle is flying around all over."

120.   Ję́ę́.   Jápichi-ñumaa-téé   sa-rámi-yąą-téé.
       SW   occasionally-now-INTS   3SG-circle-DIST-INTS
       O-oh. He is repeatedly circling.

Climax

121.   Jásiy   jąątyǫ-rįį   sa-ñi-ñíí,   tyę́!
       there   hit-in:passing   3SG-LOC-3SG   SW
       There he hits in passing into him, pow!

122.   Múúy   rą́ą́-ñíí,   pʉʉ.
       there   fall:over-3SG   SW
       There he falls, plop!

123.   Sa-dápuuta   jási-ñíí,
       3SG-plant   there-3SG
       He plants him there.

124.   to-má-ásiy   múkadi-nubee-níí.
       leave-down-PROX1   earth-within-3SG
       He leaves him in the ground.

125.   Sa-supáta-myaa-ntíy.
        3SG-emerge-PERF-REP
        He emerges again.⁵

126.   Múú-chi-ñumaa   si-ita-ntíy.
        there-from-now   3SG-returns-REP
        From there he (the beetle) returns again.

127.   Jási-ntya   sa-jįį-numaa-yą́ą́   sa-moo-mú.
        there-right:there   3SG-fly-now-DIST   3SG-face-LOC
        Right there in front of him he is flying circling.

128.   Sa-jaachiy   jį́įta-nti-ñíí,   pǫ́ǫ́!
        3SG-spear   JIITA-REP-3SG   SW
        He spears him also, zap!

129.   Sa-jóta-rįį   jį́įta-ra   sa-jó.
        3SG-peal-in:passing   JIITA-INAN   3SG-covering
        He deshells him going along.

130.   Sa-rúpa-ñiy   jį́į   jí-myusi-tyąąsá-ra.
        3SG-stick-TRNS   JIITA   COR1-cheek-middle-INAN
        He sticks it on his cheek.

131.   Rá-taarya   jo-ntíy   jídyéy   musi-tyąąsá.
        INAN-twin   covering-REP   other   cheek-middle
        The other shell on the other cheek.

Scene X: The Twins' Warning 3

132.   Sí-ítǫǫ   jį́įta   naadi-imu-ntíy.   (*)
        3SG-arrive   JIITA   3DL-LOC-REP
        He arrives where the other two are again.

133.   "Rá-numáá-ta   yu-uvá-ryįį-níí   jaséési-ntíy,   rá?"
        INAN(?)-now-(?)   2SG-kill-in:passing-3SG   beetle-REP   EXCL
        "Already you've killed the beetle also!"

134.   Naani-itay   jį́įta   sí-íva-ntíy,
        3DL-say   JIITA   3SG-DAT-REP
        they say to him again.

135.   "Játiy   ji-ya   múú-ntíy,   Moká.
        careful   2SG-go   there-REP   Mokayu
        "Be careful going there also, Moká.

136.   Saritíñu-ją́ą́miy   rą   tánu   jí-ncha.
       caterpillars-large   IRR   mill   2SG-upon
       "The giant caterpillars are going to mill you.

137.   Néé   jántyu-ryá   sa-vicha-sará   saritíñu-ją́ą́miy,
       NEG   merciful-NOM   3SG-be-HABIT   caterpillars-large
       "They are not merciful the giant caterpillars,

138.   ji-ryá-tiy   sa-núú   ką́ą́siy   múúy."
       DEMO-NOM-REL   3SG-path   terminate   there
       "the ones whose trail ends there."

139.   "Jo."
       yes
       "Okay."

140.   Sa-maacho̧   jį́í̧ta   jásiy   naani-imú-tąąsa-ntíy.
       3SG-remain   JIITA   there   3DL-LOC-middle-REP
       He remains behind them again.

141.   Sa-ya   jį́í̧ta-ntíy.
       3SG-go   JIITA-REP
       He goes again.

Scene XI: The Caterpillars

142.   Ju̧u̧, Ri-tyánu-vąą   sa-moo-mú,   ti   ti   ti.
       SW   3pl-mill-by:chance   3SG-face-LOC   SW   SW   SW
       Aha! they are milling in front of him, ti ti ti.

143.   Jápiichi-dyee-numaa-téé   ri-tyánu-téé.
       occasionally-little-now-INTS   3PL-mill-INTS
       Repeatedly they are striking.

144.   Núúñiy   sí-íto̧o̧-téé   rumú,
       almost   3SG-arrive-INTS   there
       He almost arrives there.

145.   jásiy   tíí-yada-tyéé-níí,
       there   pull-PART-INTS-3SG
       There they pull him,

146.   ju̧vi̧,   túnuunu-vïïmú-ju̧.
       SW   mortar-inside-towards
       Arrghhh! Inside the mortar!

147. Ri-tyánu   jíí   sa-ncha,   ti   ti   ti   ti,
      3PL-mill   JIITA   3SG-upon   SW   SW   SW   SW
      They mill on top of him, ti ti ti ti!

148. ja̧a̧miy   juru-déé-ju̧.
      person(?)   powder-little-for
      until he is fine powder.

149. Ri-jéétya   jíí   si-irú.
      3PL-throw   JIITA   3SG-powder
      They throw out his powder.

Scene XIIa

150. Sa-ti̧i̧tu-myuuy   rumu-ntíy.   Nijya̧a̧mí-ñumaa-ntíy.
      3SG-transform-COMPL   there-REP   person-now-REP
      He transforms himself into a person again.

151. Míryani-numaa-ntíy.
      complete-now-REP
      Complete he is again.

152. Múú-chi-ñumaa   sa-rupi-tyítyiiy.
      there-from-now   3SG-walk-directly
      From there he comes walking.

153. Ri-tyánu-vá̧á̧   sa-moo-mú.
      3PL-mill-by:chance(?)   3SG-face-LOC
      They are mashing in front of him.

154. Sa-tiya̧a̧-nuvïï   jííta-nti-ryíy   saritiñu-já̧á̧miy.
      3SG-pull-ARR1   JIITA-REP-3PL   caterpillar-large
      On arrival he pulls the giant caterpillars.

155. Sa-tánu   jíí   ri-nchá,   ti   ti   ti   ti,
      3SG-mill   JIITA   3PL-upon   SW   SW   SW   SW
      He mills on top of them, ti ti ti ti,

156. ja̧a̧miy   juru-déé-ju̧.
      person(?)   powder-little-for
      until they are fine powder.

157. Sa-dúú   jíí   ri-irú,   juus!
      3SG-blow   JIITA   3PL-powder   SW
      He blows away their powder, puff!

158.   "Dá-ntya-múy   dárya   jiryę́-ę́cha-sara-nuu-dyéy."
        thus-same-NEG   thus   2pl-be-HABIT-CONT-DAY
        "You will never be the same again!"

159.   Sa-tąarya   jį́į́   rumu-si-ntíy.
        3SG-return   JIITA   there-from-REP
        He returns from there again.

Scene XII: The Twins' Warning 4

160.   Múúy   sarye-ñuvee-ją́-ą́siy   naada-ntíy.
        there   meet-ARR2-o'land-PROX1   3DL-REP
        There the two meet (him) on arrival again.

161.   Rį-įñúva-ñumaa   váriy.
        3PL-arrive:late-now   then
        They arrive late.

162.   "Jiyu-niy   vuryą-ą   mááy,   Moká?"
        here-NIY   1PLINC-IRR   sleep   Mokayu
        "Here we must sleep, Moká."

163.   "Jóó."
        yes
        "Okay."

164.   Ri-mééy   jį́į́ta   jásiy.
        3PL-sleep   JIITA   there
        They sleep there.

165.   Núpora-numaa   jį́į́   sa-niy   jútay   sí-íva,
        night-now   JIITA   3SG-MALF   say   3SG-DAT
        In the night he says to him,

166.   "Játiy   yą-ąrúpan-ta-naada   jí-ñu   vátu-rų́y.
        careful   2SG-bother-TRNS-3DL   DEMO-CL:ANIM   woman-DL
        "Be careful if you bother this woman.

167.   Rá-rąącha-níí   yá-ápį.
        INAN-cut:off-3SG   2SG-penis
        "She will cut off your penis.

168.   Naada-táchiy   rą   rąącha-níí."
        3DL-vagina   IRR   cut:off-3SG
        "Her vagina will cut it off."

169.   "Síį́teenú?"
        really?
        "Really?"

170.   "Jóó.   Yạ-ạ-tiy   jarúpan-ta-rų́ų́-ñíí.
        yes   2SG-IRR-COND   bother-TRNS-POT-3SG
        "Yes. If you try to bother her.

171.   Jí-ñu-dáy   ráñiy   cha   naana-asatų́-nta,
        DEMO-CL:ANIM-DAY   AUX:MALF   be   3DL-niece-seems
        "The one that is her niece,

172.   níí-niy   jíį́   yạ-ạ   jarúpan-ta."
        3SG:PRO-NIY   JIITA   2SG-IRR   bother-TRNS
        "HER you can bother."

Scene XIII: The Vicious Woman

173.   Sa-ya   jíį́ta   naadi-imú,   núpora-numáá.
        3SG-go   JIITA   3DL-LOC   night-now
        He goes in to where she is at night.

174.   Rą́-ą́saacha-rų́ų́-ryatúúnu.
        INAN-dawn-POT-almost
        It is about to dawn.

175.   "Néé   vą́nay   juvá-chị   da-ryéy.
        not   possible   do/make-NOM   DAY-1SG
        "Nobody can make me (says the woman).

176.   Rạ-ạ   rạacha-níí   yá-ápị."
        1SG-IRR   cut:off-3SG   2SG-penis
        "I will cut off your penis."

177.   Sa-tuvạachú-tya   naadi-imú.
        3SG-hear-NEG   3DL-LOC
        He doesn't pay any attention.

178.   Si-iváy   vári-ñaadá.
        3SG-do/make   then-3DL
        He makes her.

179.   Rá-tamu-myáá   jási-ñíí,   tịị!
        INAN-squeeze-PERF   there-3SG   SW
        It squeezes him there, eek!

180.   Rá̧-á̧saacha-numáá.
        INAN-dawn-now
        It dawns.

181.   Tííy.   Núúti-chi-tya   sa̧-a̧   supáta?
        NEG   how-from-NEG   3SG-IRR   extract
        How can he get it out?

182.   Jakúva-tya   rá-tamu-ñuu-dye-ñíí.
        strongly-NEG   INAN-squeeze-DAY-3SG
        It doesn't squeeze him strongly anymore.

183.   Parichéy   su̧-u̧ta   naadí-íva,
        finally   3SG-say   3DL-DAT
        Finally he says to her,

184.   "Jadyíí-tya-ra.   Chi̧i̧rá   su̧u̧   rá̧-á̧pi̧-rúúva̧-mú?"
        wait-TRNS(?)-INAN(?)   who   sting   1SG-penis-base-LOC
        "Wait, who is stinging me at the root of my penis?"

185.   Naanu-táchi-jyasí-ñeecho̧-niy   sa-niy   júri-jye-ntíy.
        3DL-vagina-hair-towards-onto   3SG-MALF   grab-PROX2-REP
        He grabs her pubic hair.

186.   Ti̧i̧ta̧ju̧   rootye-chi-nt-tyéé-níí,   ró̧ó̧.
        all   break:loose-DEP-REP-INTS-3SG   SW
        He yanks it all out, scrape!

Climax

187.   Múúy   maasi-tyéé-níí.
        there   exit-INTS-3SG
        There he escapes.

188.   Sa-túúnu-ri̧i̧   jí̧í̧ta   jí-myoo-ta̧a̧sá-ju̧-ntí-rya.
        3SG-weave-in:passing   JIITA   COR1-face-middle-for-REP-INAN
        He weaves it in passing to put on his forehead again.

Scene XIV: Conclusion: The Twins' Surprise

189.   Múú-ñumaa   jumúsa-jo-mú   naada-maasá sạ-ạjíí-jụ-dáy.
        there-now   descend-NOM-LOC 3DL-sit   3SG-in:front-for-DAY
        There in the port the two sit waiting for him.

190.   Naada-díryey jịịta-nti-ñíí.
        3DL-greet   JIITA-REP-3SG
        They greet him again,

191.   "Jịịị,   rá-numaa-naa-téé   jí-jee-yási-tyéé
        SW   INAN-now-wonder-INTS 2SG-enter-PROX1-INTS

               naadi-imú jí-ñu   vátu-rụ́-tyéé-ntíy   rá?"
               3DL-LOC   DEMO-CL:ANIM woman-w/children-INTS-REP EXCL

        "Yikes! What? Have you gone in to that woman also?"

192.   "Jóó."
        yes
        "Yes."

193.   "Tạ́ạ́-jụ-naa-muy   vánay víchéén-chị-téé   ji-ñicha-téé,   tạ́ạ́-jụ?"
        what-for-wonder-NEG   able   harm-NOM-INTS   2SG-be-INTS   what-for
        "How is it that nobody can harm you, how?"

Notes to Appendix 1

1   The suffix *-diiy* (*-dii* in the surface representation), here glossed ANTIC for "anticipation," virtually always cooccurs with the irrealis auxiliary and seems to imply that the result of the proposed action is unknown. There is always a shading of doubt to clauses with *-diiy*, though its precise meaning is still to be determined.

2   The form *-jajííju̧* is a post position that normally implies location somewhere in the path of its object, e.g.

       Jási-ñiy   yȩ-ȩcháásiy   kítyo-mú   ra̧-a̧jííju̧.
       there-NIY   2SG-wait   Iquitos-loc   1SG-in:front
       'There you will wait for me in Iquitos.'

Here the object of the post position is the speaker, and the sentence might be rendered "there you will wait in Iquitos *in my path*," or "*towards which I am headed.*" In KT26 and KT27, however, the implication is that protection is provided for the object of *-jajííju̧*. The commonality here is hard to capture, though there is some intuitive reality to it. In other words *-jajííju̧* implies location "in front of" in the sense of blocking, or barricading.

The stem *su̧ta̧y* is used as a verb in sentences 26, 27, 28, 29, 30 and 32 to mean 'to build shelter.' In sentences 39, 42, 44 and 45, however, the same stem is used as a noun to mean 'shelter.'

3   This version of the Kneebite Twins story is unusually rich in the kinds of negation strategies used, and the uses to which those negation strategies are put. The negative *tíiy* in sentence 63 means "unsuccessful attempt." It is used as an interjection, for example, when one is trying to start a recalcitrant outboard motor. Also, it can sometimes be freely translated as 'I don't know,' as it is the usual response to a question for which the addressee does not have the answer. In this context, the addressee might be construed as saying something like 'that was an unsuccessful attempt to get that information.'

The meaning of the suffix *-va̧a̧* in sentence 63 is still under investigation. It often occurs in negative sentences, though it never occurs without some other indication of negation in the sentence.

Negative markers, of various sorts, are often used in rhetorical questions, and for other "rhetorical" effects. The form *tama* 'never' or 'impossible' combined with the enclitic *-ta* marks sentence 60 as a rhetorical question. The enclitic *-nííta* (possibly a polymorphemic form *-níí* + *-ta* NEG) in sentences 15 and 16 essentially does the same thing. In clause 95 the negative *née* plus the irrealis auxiliary is used to impart a sense of boastful certainty.

4   In this sentence the morphological breakdown is provided for the word *supatéésiy* so as to make explicit the presence of the detransitivizing *-y* suffix. The only effect this suffix has on the surface form is the vowel *éé*: without the suffix the form would be *supata̧a̧siy*, and would mean 'extracted' or 'caused to emerge' (see, e.g., clause 181).

5   In sentence 125 no source locative is expressed, so no sense of change in scene is imparted. Otherwise, this sentence is exactly parallel to sentence 91 where SO coding is used along with a locative expression explicitly marking a change in scene.

Appendix 2

The First Squirrel

Storyteller: Manungo Díaz

This text represents one episode of a larger Yagua myth entitled "Little Baldy" in Powlison (1969). This particular version was recorded in 1980 as a self-contained story. Another version of the same story appears in English translation in appendix 3 of this work, clauses 258 to 336. The storyteller, Manungo Díaz, is the traditional leader of a group of about 60 Yaguas who moved from Cahocuma, downriver from Pebas, to Urco Miraño on the Napo River (see figure 1) in 1974. Members of this group speak a dialect which I classify with the downriver dialects, though it is not as divergent from the upriver dialect (as represented by Laureano Mozombite, the teller of the Kneebite Twins tale) as are the dialects spoken around Caballococha.

The circumstances surrounding the telling of this tale were not the most natural, and perhaps for this reason the tale itself differs in some significant respects from other versions of this episode of the Little Baldy epic. The following table lists the factors I am aware of that diverge from the natural setting for taletelling in the Yagua culture:

	Normal	Actual for FS text
Time:	Night	Afternoon
Audience:	Native speakers children	One adult native speaker and the investigator (a non-native adult)
Occasion:	Party	No special occasion
Purpose:	Entertainment Instruction Socialization	To fulfill a request on the part of the investigator To be neighborly Instruction(?) Entertainment(?)
Equipment:	None	Small cassette recorder Tie clip microphone attached to storyteller's shirt

The thematic structure of this text is not as coherent as that of the other texts appearing in these appendices, and therefore the text does not provide the best illustration of some of the more interesting features of Yagua discourse structure. In particular, since this story is only part of a longer epic, the storyteller doesn't quite know where to begin. He begins in clause 1 describing how the First Deer was tricked by the First Squirrel into crossing a stream on the back of a boa. In clause 3 an allusion is made back to the previous episode, as though the teller felt he had to fill in some missing information. The Squirrel's deception is described in clauses 4 through 21. Then the teller fills in some more background material, and the deception

171

scene is recapitulated beginning in clause 29. This flashback and recapitulation is not a normal feature of Yagua discourse structure. Furthermore, the actual plot of this version of the tale differs in one significant respect from other versions, e.g. those described in Powlison (1969). For most of the present version it is the First Toucan that is swallowed by the boa, and the Toucan's brother cries in mourning, while in other versions the Toucan's brother is swallowed by the boa while the Toucan cries in mourning. This is a crucial distinction as the Toucan's brother is in fact a human being, and not a toucan at all. It is central to the plot of the larger epic that the brother (who is Little Baldy) is swallowed, while the Toucan mourns, and in fact the teller of this version is confused at several points. For instance in clause 3 he correctly says that the boa had earlier swallowed the Toucan's brother, while in clause 64 he clearly indicates that he imagines the First Toucan himself to be inside the boa. Other native speakers who have listened to and read this text have commented on this discrepancy.

Because of the somewhat unnatural circumstances for the recording of this story, and the obvious problems the speaker had in composing it, the value of this text for ethnographic and folkloric analysis is limited. As a source of initial linguistic data, and as an example of a downriver dialect, however, the text is fundamentally sound. There are two consistent dialect differences between this text and the Kneebite Twins tale (appendix 1). First, Díaz fairly consistently uses the sequence *anu* in place of the upriver *ada*. This difference is apparent in the forms for the 3DL prefixes and enclitics (*naada / naanu*) and in the PAST3 and participle suffix (*jada / janu*). Second, there is less evidence for the sound [e] as a separate phoneme in the downriver dialect, as it is much less common outside of the environments where it can be shown to arise from underlying /a/. So, for example, the form of the diminutive suffix in the upriver dialect is *-dee*, whereas for the downriver dialects it is *-daa*. Sentence FS75 illustrates the diminutive in an environment where *aa* becomes *ee*. The same sentence also illustrates the postposition *-nubaa*, which is *-nubee* in the upriver dialects. There are several other differences in lexical items, and rhetorical usages that the astute reader may notice. However, since a detailed dialect comparison has not as yet been conducted it is difficult to say whether these are true dialect differences or simply features of the individual styles of the two story-tellers.

1.   Sa-ramúti-ñúú-yanú   jánariy   munátyį-į   sí-íva
       3SG-ford-CONT-PAST3   deer   first-NOM:ANIM   3SG-DAT

       koodíy   tąąríy.
       boa   long:ago

Long ago the first deer forded upon a boa.

2.   Múkatyu   munátyį-į   kivų́ų́-chu-níí.
       squirrel   first-NOM:ANIM   deceive-TRNS-3SG
       The first squirrel deceived him.

3.   Núúva   tááryįy   sa-jǫǫtạ-ạnú   ramuchó-ónu
        toucan   brother   3SG-begin-PAST3   swallow-PART

        koodíy   munátyį-į.
        boa   first-NOM:ANIM

Beforehand the boa had swallowed Toucan's brother.

4.   Sa-kivų́ų́-chu   jį́įta   ji-ñu   múkatyu-níí.
        3SG-deceive-TRNS   JIITA   DEMO-ANIM   squirrel-3SG
        This squirrel deceived him.

5.   "Jii-síy   vuryạ-ạ   ramútiy.
        here-from   1PLINC-IRR   ford
        "From here we will ford.

6.   Jii-síy   ra-ryamúti-chará.
        here-from   1SG-ford-HABIT
        From here I always ford.

7.   Vuryạ-ạ   rą́ą́y."
        1PLINC-IRR   jump
        Let's jump."

8.   Naanu-rą́ą́y   jį́įta   jás-chiy.
        3DL-jump   JIITA   there-from
        They jump from there.

9.   Sa-rạạy   jį́įta   múkatyu   munátyį-į   sạ-ạjïï-síy.
        3SG-jump   JIITA   squirrel   first-NOM:ANIM   3SG-front-from
        The first squirrel jumps before him.

10.   "Yi-nų́ų́y   rạ-ạ   rą́ą́-kyu."
        2SG-look   1SG-IRR   jump-EVID
        "You see that I can jump."

11.   Sa-niy   suvų́ų́-nt-tyéé   ji-ñu   munátya   sụ-ụmu-tạạsá,
        3SG-MALF   afraid-REP-INTS   DEMO-ANIM   first   3SG-behind-right
        He is afraid behind the first one,

12.   já-tiy   sa-rạạ-ñíí.
        DEMO-REL   3SG-jump-3SG
        the one that makes him jump.

13.   "Rạ-ạ   júú-charatáá   jiyu-dáy   koodi-viïmú.
        1SG-IRR   fall-might   here-DAY   snake-inside
        "I might fall inside a boa.

14.   Koodíy,   sạ-ạ   saratáá-dáy.
        boa   3SG-IRR   might:be-DAY
        It might be a boa.

15.   Jínu-ni-vyíy   rá-nicha-vą́ą́?
        log-NIY-QP   INAN-be-NEG
        Is it not a log?

16.   Koodí-ñiitá   ra-dyííy   sí-íva-dáy.
        boa-NEG   1SG-see   3SG-DAT-DAY
        I see that it's not a boa.

17.   Néé   koodíy sa-níícha."
        NEG   boa   3SG-be
        He's not a boa."

18.   "Jás-chi-ñiy   yạ-ạ   rą́ą́y."
        there-from-NIY   2SG-IRR   jump
        "Jump from there."

19.   Sa-niy   rą́ą́-yanu   jíịta.
        3SG-MALF   jump-PAST3   JIITA
        He jumped (to his detriment).

20.   Sa-júú-yanú   tịịtájụ   sa-viïmú   koodíy kanekïï, jïïïï.
        3SG-fall-PAST3 complete   3SG-inside   boa   SW   SW
        He fell right inside the boa, kanekïï, jïïïï.

21.   Sa-maachọọ   rumú.
        3SG-remain   there
        There he remains.

22.   Sa-rą́ą́-tii-yạạ-sạ-ạnu   jíịta   sa-tááryịị
        3SG-jump-IT-DIST-upriver-PAST3   JIITA   3SG-brother

                yí-va-siy   nuuvá.
                COR1-DAT-from   toucan

His brother went jumping all over from where the toucan was.

23. Jásiy   sa-súų́y   si-iyú   "kua,   kua,   kua",
    there   3SG-call   3SG-above   SW   SW   SW
    There he calls above him "kua, kua, kua",

24. sa-núúvaa-yanu-mú.
    3SG-mourn-PART-LOC
    in his mourning.

25. Sa-tááryį́-įva-siy   jí-ñuuvaay.
    3SG-brother-DAT-from   COR1-mourn
    For his brother he mourns.

26. Tá-rïïda-mú-jų   sa-súų́-yásiy   tąąrimisí-jyų.
    some-day-LOC-for   3SG-call-PROX1   morning-for
    From day to day he calls.

27. Sa-tááryį́-įva-siy   jí-ñuuvay.
    3SG-brother-DAT-from   COR1-mourn
    For his brother he mourns.

28. Néé   tááryįį-tyįį   nuudáy.
    NEG   brother-NOM:having   anymore.
    He didn't have a brother anymore.

29. Si-itǫ́ǫ́-janú   jánariy   munátyį-į   si-imu-ntíy
    3SG-arrive:there-PAST3   deer   first-NOM:ANIM   3SG-LOC-REP
    First Deer comes to him again,

29b. jási-dye-ntíy   múkatyu-mu-ntíy.
    there-DAY-REP   squirrel-LOC-REP
    there again, to Squirrel again.

30. Níí-numaa   jį́įta   sa-kivų́ų́-chu-ntíy.
    3SG-now   JIITA   3SG-deceive-TRNS-REP
    This one he deceives again.

31. "Jii-síy   vuryą-ą   ramútiy.
    here-from   1PLINC-IRR   ford
    "From here we will ford.

32. Jiyú-ra   vuryą-ramútę́-ę́nú.
    here-INAN   1PLINC-ford-PART
    Here is our fording place.

33.   Néé   nikiirą́ą́y   ramúté-ę́nú   jiyú."
        NEG   bad   ford-PART   here
        It's not a bad fording place here."

34.   Vánoodyí   rąą-ryá-vay,
        quick   jump-NOM-being
        Jumping quickly,

35.   sa-niy   kivų́ų́-chu-níí   jánariy   munátyį-į̣.
        3SG-MALF   deceive-TRNS-3SG   deer   first-NOM:ANIM
        he deceives First Deer.

36.   "Jii-síy   vuryą-ą   rąą-tyéé.
        here-from   1PLINC-IRR   jump-INTS
        "From here we will jump.

37.   Yi-tá-charatá
        2SG-say-might
        You might say (or think)

38.   rípya   rą́ą́-rya-jíy?"
        far   jump-NOM-2SG
        you are a far jumper?"

39.   Múkatyu   jǫǫtá
        squirrel   begin
        Squirrel begins

40.   ramútye-enú   są-ąjïï-síy.
        ford-PART   3SG-front-from
        to ford before him.

41.   Naanu-ramútiy   jį́įta.
        3DL-ford   JIITA
        They (2) ford.

42.   Sa-sii-chíy   są-ąjïï-síy,   múúy,   koodíy   ríínu-va.
        3SG-run-DEP   3SG-front-from   there   boa   back-DAT
        He runs before him on the boa's back.

43.   Sa-rą́ą́-ñuuvá   sų-ų̣tunuvų́ų́   rámurya-mu-síy.
        3SG-jump-(?)   3SG-neck   base-LOC-from
        He jumps from the base of his neck

44. Múúy   rida-mu-síy   níín-tạạsá   sa-rą́ą́y.
    there   ?-LOC-from   tree-middle   3SG-jump
    From there right onto a tree he jumps.

45. Sa-naatyú   jị́ịta-níí   jánariy   yí-sijyụ.
    3SG-call   JIITA-3SG   deer   COR1-after
    He calls Deer after him.

46. "Néé   yạ-ạ   suvụ́ụ́."
    NEG   2SG-IRR   be:afraid
    "Don't be afraid."

47. Sa-niy   rupíy   jị́ịta   jánariy   sụ-ụsíjyụ   koodíy   ríínu-va.
    3SG-MALF   walk   JIITA   deer   3SG-behind   boa   back-DAT
    The deer walks after him on the boa's back.

48. Múúy   sa-yá.
    there   3SG-go
    There he goes.

49. Sa-niy   jutáy   sí-íva,
    3SG-MALF   say   3SG-DAT
    He says to him,

50. "Jás-chi-ñiy   yạ-ạ   rą́ą́y.
    there-from-NIY   2SG-IRR   jump
    "Jump from there.

51. Sa-jụ́-daa-tụụ-síy   yạ-ạ   rạạ-yésiy,
    3SG-mouth-little-point-from   2SG-IRR   jump-PROX1
    From the tip of his mouth jump,

52. jiryá-tiy   sụ-ụtunuvụ́ụ́   jásiy.
    DEMO-REL   3SG-neck   there
    that which is his neck there.

53. Jás-chi-ñiy   yạ-ạ   rą́ą́y."
    there-from-NIY   2SG-IRR   jump
    Jump from there."

54. Sa-niy   rą́ą́-yanú   jị́ịta   jánariy   munátyị-ị-dáy.
    3SG-MALF   jump-PAST3   JIITA   deer   first-NOM-DAY
    First Deer jumped (to his detriment).

55.   Sa-júú̯-yanú   sa-vïïmu-ntíy   kanekii,   mïïï.
       3SG-fall-PAST3   3SG-inside-REP   SW   SW
       He fell inside him also kanekii, mïïï.

56.   Sa-maachǫǫ   rumú   sa-vïïmú.
       3SG-remain   there   3SG-inside
       He remains inside him.

57.   Tąąríy   sa-maachǫǫ-janú   sa-vïïmú,
       long:while   3SG-remain-PAST3   3SG-inside
       He remains inside him for a long while,

58.   tíí̯kii   járimuní   tąąsavuurá   sará-ju̯
       one   month   half   extent-for
       for an entire half a month.

59.   Są-ąsúmi-tya-anú   jíí̯ta   siinu-mú   naanú.
       3SG-ascend-TRNS-PAST3   JIITA   shore-LOC   3DL
       He ascends to the shore with them.

60.   Tíí̯chąą-nchá   koodíy.
       sand/beach-upon   boa
       The boa is on a beach.

61.   Sa-duutú-tya   jí-tiryǫǫ   náává-jyu̯,
       3SG-belly-INST   COR1-lie   upward-for
       He lies with his belly up,

62.   já-tiy   naanu-rupí-yąą   jánari-jyú̯y   sa-vïïmú.
       DEMO-REL   3DL-walk-DIST   deer-DL   3SG-inside
       the one that had the deer and company walking around inside him.

63.   Naanu-nichá-ju̯   jí-tiryǫ   sa-vïïmú,
       3DL-be-for   COR1-lie   3SG-inside
       They (2) were there lying inside him,

64.   nuuva   munátyi̯-i̯   múúy   są-ąríy.
       toucan   first-NOM   there   3SG-underneath
       the first toucan was underneath him.

65.   Naanu-tú̯ú̯cho-onú   sa-vïïmú-yu,
       3DL-converse-PAST3   3SG-inside-COR2
       They (2) conversed with each other inside him,

66. "Muutyǫ́ǫtu   ją́ą́nu   vuryą-ą̱   jidyíy   vuryi-imú-jų̱.
    pirahna   tooth   1PLINC-IRR   grab   1PLINC-LOC-for
    "Let's grab us a pirahna tooth.

67. Rá-ta-niy   vuryą-ą̱   jinisi-tyííy   sa-páday   jáy."
    INAN-INST-NIY   1PLINC-IRR   slice-IT   3SG-stomach skin
    With it we will slice the skin of his stomach."

68. Vánukii   jínta   naanu-níy   vi-dyéy.
    heat   radiate   3DL-upon   QUEST-DAY
    They feel heat, huh?

69. "Síínu-mu-dyéétya   vų̱ų̱-vyí-charatáá,
    shore-LOC-maybe   1PLINC-QP-might:be
    "Maybe we're on shore,

70. núútyu   vánukii-ntá   jínta   vų̱ų̱-níy."
    how   heat-seem   radiate   1PLINC-upon
    since we feel such heat."

71. Jiñíí-daa   jínta   naanu-níy.
    sun-DIM   radiate   3DL-upon
    The sun shown upon them.

72. Parchéé   naanu-jaachipí-yą́ą́,
    finally   3DL-think-DIST
    Finally they think,

73. naanu-tų́ų̱cho-oní-íyu,
    3DL-converse-PART-COR2
    they converse with each other,

74. "Jii-si-dyéy   vuryą-ą̱   jinisíy   sa-kę́ę̱ni   rámurya-są́ą́rą̱ą̱-síy."
    here-from-DAY   1PLINC-IRR   slice   3SG-anus   end-across(?)-from
    "From here let's slice across from the end of his anus."

75. Naani-inise-enu   jį́íta   tápi-dyee-nubaa-síy.
    3DL-slice-PAST3   JIITA   slowly-DIM-within-from
    They sliced slowly from inside.

76. Sa-sikítya-ją̱ą̱   koodíy   váriy   tu   tu   tu.
    3SG-twitch-ITM   boa   then   SW   SW   SW
    The boa twitches repeatedly tu tu tu.

77. Naani-inisíy   sa-páday   jáy.
     3DL-slice   3SG-stomach   skin
     They slice his stomach skin.

78. Sa-párų   váriy.
     3SG-stop:work   then
     Then he stops (slicing).

79. Tąąri-pyú   naanu-párų   munátya-ntíy.
     while-after 3DL-stop:work   first-REP
     After a while they stop (slicing) again.

80. Sų-ųnsíy   jį́įta-ntíy,   saaaaaaaay.
     3SG-slice   JIITA-REP   SW
     He slices again saaaaaaaay.

81. "Núútya rá-niy   vííta-ryų́ų́-tyéé."
     how   INAN-MALF   break:open-POT-INTS
     "It's about to break through."

82. Daryajų́ų́yu jinise-enu-mu-síy   sa-sirį   nuuvá
     four   slice-PART-LOC-from   3SG-cut(?)   toucan

          sų-ųbí-íva-jų.
          3SG-in:place-DAT-for

     Slicing four times, the toucan takes turns with him.

83. Níí-numaa jį́įta   jinise-enú   sų-ųbí-íva-jų   vári-nti-dyéy.
     3SG-now   JIITA   slice-PART   3SG-in:place-DAT-for   then-REP-DAY
     Now HE slices in place of him again.

84. Sų-ųtay sí-íva,
     3SG-say 3SG-DAT
     He says to him,

85. "Jááryi-pyu-déé   yą-ą   jinisi-tyéé."
     much-hard-little 2SG-IRR   slice-INTS
     "Cut a little harder!"

86. Sų-ųnse-enú   jį́įta   saaaaaay.
     3SG-slice-PAST3   JIITA   SW
     He sliced saaaaaay.

87. "Sạ-ạ-numaa   mús-ta   jáá-mu-vúúy."
    3SG-IRR-now   descend-TRNS   water-LOC-1PLINC
    "He's going to carry us back into the water!"

88. Jii-sí-jyụ-dáy   naanu-juutyá   munátya.
    DEMO-from-for-DAY   3DL-puncture   first
    This size hole they puncture first (gesture).

89. Sụ-ụnúúy   jíịta.
    3SG-look   JIITA
    He looks.

90. "Síínu-mu-numáá   vụụ-ñícha.
    shore-LOC-now   1PLINC-be
    "We're now on the shore.

91. Néé   jáá-jaríy   vụụ-ñícha   nuudáy.
    NEG   water-under   1PLINC-be   anymore
    We're not under water anymore."

92. Sụ-ụtay   sí-íva-ntíy,
    3SG-say   3SG-DAT
    He says to him also,

93. "Juváy,   jíy   rạ   jinisíy."
    do(?)   2SG:PRO   IRR   slice
    "Now, YOU are going to slice."

94. Sụ-ụnse-enu   jíịta-ntíy   saaaaaay.
    3SG-slice   JIITA-REP   SW
    He sliced again saaaaaay.

95. ánrajúúy   jomutú   sáransará   sụ-ụnse-enú   tịịtájụ   naan-sarájụ.
    two   hand   measure   3SG-slice-PAST3   all   3DL-extent
    He sliced two hand lengths, enough for both of them.

96. Sụ-ụnse-enu-ntíy   saaaaaay.
    3SG-slice-PAST3-REP   SW
    He sliced again saaaaaay.

97. Naan-saranu-jáá-títyiiy   váriy.
    3DL-measure-ITM-directly   then
    So they keep on measuring.

98.   Núútya   tịịtájụ-numáá,   núúrya   naanu-mutụ́ụ́   sarájụ.
        how   all-now   like:this 3DL-shoulder   extent
        Up until the size of their shoulders (gesture).

99.   Pachéé   sụ-ụtay   jánariy   sí-íva,
        finally   3SG-say   deer   3SG-DAT
        Finally Deer says to him,

100.   "Váran-tą́ą́tiy   ji-myaasíy   rị́-ịsi-jyụ.
        quickly-wiggling(?) 2DL-exit   1SG-behind-towards
        "You quickly exit behind me.

101.   Néé   rą-ą   junúúchiy.
        NEG   1SG-IRR   wait
        I'm not going to wait.

102.   Néé   rą-ą   sii-myaasíy   yi-táy.
        NEG   1SG-IRR   run-exit   2SG-say
        You know I'm going to rush out.[1]

103.   Jadyííy,   yí-ínúú-jés-kyu."
        wait   2SG-see-PROX1-EVID
        Wait, you'll see."

104.   Sa-rą́ą́-yanú   sa-viïmu-síy.
        3SG-jump-PAST3   3SG-inside-from
        He jumped out from inside him.

105.   Sa-maase-enú   nóóiii.
        3SG-exit-PAST3   SW
        He exited nóóiii.

106.   Múúy   sii-myaasi-tyéé-níí   nuuvá   munátyị-ị
        there   run-exit-INTS-3SG   toucan   first-NOM:ANIM

            sụ-ụsíjyụ-dyéy   miïï.
            3SG-behind-DAY   SW

        There the first toucan rushes out behind him, miïï.

107.   Naan-sii-chíy   tị́ịchá-va.
        3DL-run-DEP   sand/beach-DAT
        They run away on the beach.

108. Naadí-íriyą́ą́-numuyąą   rí-íva   yí-ínoo.
      3DL-feel-all:over   INAN-DAT   COR1-head
      They feel all over their heads.

109. Sa-jų́ų́y jį́į́ta koodíy naadi-iví-íva-siy   váriy,   múúy.
      3SG-fall JIITA boa   3DL-place-DAT-from   then   there
      So the boa fell back where they (2) had come from.

110. Rá-pudoo-jąą-numuyą́ą́   rumú   sa-páda-vyiimu-síy.
      INAN-spew-liquid-all:over there 3SG-belly-inside-from
      Rotten liquid spews out of his belly.

111. Sų-ųtą-ąnu   jį́į́ta ji-ñú   nuuvá   sí-íva,
      3SG-say-PAST3   JIITA DEMO-CL:ANIM   toucan 3SG-DAT
      This Toucan said to him,

112. "Núútyu-dáy vuryą́-ą́   cha-táá?"
      how-DAY   1PLINC-IRR   be/live-INTS
      "How are we going to live?"

113. Mítya rurya-kę́ę́   naani-inúú-tya-numayą́ą́-ra   jí-ñiisíy,
      just   dark-CF:large   3DL-look-TRNS-all:over-INAN   COR1-eye
      Just darkness they see with their eyes,

114. já-tiy   sų-ųvųųdii-póó   jááy   naan-níísi-myú.
      DEMO-REL   3SG-stomach:contents-rotten   enter   3DL-eye-LOC
      that his rotten stomach contents had gotten into.

115. Si-iriyą́ą́   jánariy munátyį-į   rí-íva   yí-noo.
      3SG-feel   deer   first-NOM:ANIM   INAN-DAT   COR1-head
      The First Deer felt his own head.

116. "Rá-tadiita-my-áá   rí-ínoo-dáy.
      INAN-peal-DETRNS-PERF   1SG-DAY
      "Hy head is pealed.

117. Néé   jínoo jástyiy nuudáy.
      NEG   head   hair   anymore
      There's no hair anymore!"

118. Si-iriyą́ą́   nuuvá   munátyį-į   rí-íva   yí-noo-nti-dyéy
      3SG-feel   toucan first-NOM:AN   INAN-DAT   COR1-head-REP-DAY
      First Toucan feels his own head also.

119.   "Darya-ntíy   rí-ínoo-dáy.
        thus-REP   1SG-head-DAY
        "My head is the same.

120.   Núútyu   vuryạ-ạ   cha-dáy?"
        how   1PLINC-IRR   be-DAY
        How are we going to live?"

121.   Néé   varáánu   naani-inráá-yu.
        NEG   quickly   3DL-separate-COR2
        They (2) don't quickly separate from each other.

122.   Naanu-ya   jị́ịta   múúy,   rá-cạ́ạ-dáy.
        3DL-go   JIITA   there   INAN-fork-DAY
        They (2) go there to the fork of a stream.

123.   Múúy   naanu-ya   nurumu-daa-mú.
        there   3DL-go   stream-DIM-LOC
        There they go to the little stream.

124.   "Vuryạ-ạ   janááy.
        1PLINC-IRR   bathe
        "Let's bathe.

125.   Vuryạ-ạ   suuta   vuryí-íva-si-rya   sụ-ụvụụdíí."
        1PLINC-IRR   wash   1PLINC-DAT-from-INAN   3SG-stomach:contents
        Let's wash his stomach contents off of us."

126.   Jásiy   naana-nááy,   naana-nááy,   naana-nááy.
        there   3DL-bathe   3DL-bathe   3DL-bathe
        There they bathe and bathe and bathe.

127.   Naan-tuvạạchú   jị́ịta   jás-chiy,
        3DL-hear   JIITA   there-from
        Then they hear from there,

128.   "Yi-n-tyéé   sa-níí-sirá   ji-tyééryịị-dáy.
        here(?)-NIY-INTS   3SG-come-(?)   2DL-brother-DAY
        "Here comes your brother.

129.   Níí-n-tyéé   sụ́ụ-tyéé   jiyu-dáy,   nuuvá."
        3SG:PRO-NIY-INTS   call-INTS   here-DAY   toucan
        HE (is the one who) sings here, Toucan."

130. Sų-ųtay   sí-íva,
3SG-say 3SG-DAT
He says to him,

131. "Rumu-niy yą-ą   jiya   si-imú   ji-tyééryįį.
there-NIY 2SG-IRR go   3SG-LOC 2SG-brother.
"THERE you will go to your brother.

132. Múúy   rą-ą   jiya-dáy.
There 1SG-IRR   go-DAY
I am going there.

133. Múúy   rą-ą   jiya-sara-dáy."
there   1SG-IRR   go-HABIT-DAY
There I will always go."

134. Sa-ya-anu   jį́įta   ruumú.
3SG-go-PAST3   JIITA   from:there
He went from there.

Note to Appendix 2

[1] This is a rhetorical use of the negative, which implies absolute certainty of the truth of the proposition. This device always appears with either the form yitáy "you say", yinúúy "you see" or sometimes jidyéétya "you know."

Appendix 3

The One-Eyed Warriors

Storyteller: Laureano Mozombite

The story which I have titled "One-eyed Warriors" is the first 336 clauses of a 720 clause story entitled "Little Baldy" by Powlison (1969). This is a story about a band of mythical warriors out to find and destroy "the enemies" (*munuñúmiy*, also translated "savages", or "non-Yagua indians"). Their first encounter is with a giant toad, who is really a malevolent witchdoctor of sorts. All but two of the band club the toad as they pass him. Those that club the toad lose one of their eyes during the night, but the two that don't club the toad retain both eyes. Then the band tries in vain to take revenge on the toad. Finally, the one-eyed warriors transform themselves into various animals of the jungle and parade off the scene. The rest of the story deals with the adventures of the two who escape the first encounter with toad. This text exhibits linear locational structure (T. Payne, 1984b) especially beginning with scene IV.

This text was recorded by Paul Powlison in 1960. The retranslation that appears here is by T. Payne and Mamerto Macahuachi, a native speaker of the upriver dialect of Yagua represented in the text.

Since this text forms part of the corpus for the quantitative study of S_o coding on verbs described in chapter 6, I have included the Yagua transcriptions of all the verbal S_o clauses that occur in the portion of the text that appears in this appendix. However, due to space limitations I have included only the English translation for the excerpt as a whole. For purposes of illustrating the use of S_o clauses to develop the thematic structure of the text, I judge that the English clause-by-clause translation is sufficient.

15.   Múúy   máá-ñuvee-já-ási-ryíy.
       there   sleep-on:arrival:2-overland-there-3PL
       'There they sleep on arrival.'

68.   Júú   rabee-já-ási-ryíy,   jasí-jyú-da-ntíy.
       SW   circle-o'land-there-3PL   there-around-DAY-REP
       'There they circle in the same place again.'

75.   Rabi-imu-si-tyéé-nti-ryíy,   jasí-jyú-da-ntíy.
       circle-downriver-from-INTS-REP-3PL   there-around-DAY-REP
       'They circle from downriver at the same place again.'

143.   Puri-tyéé   jáánsa-já-tyéé-níí.
       dissappear-INTS   make:noise-overland-INTS-3SG
       'They disappear, and make noise going overland.'

187

258.   Múúy   jitá-ási-ñíí.
        there   alight-there-3SG
        'There he alights.'

263.   Múúy   jitá-ási-ñíí.
        there   alight-there-3SG
        'There he alights.'

269.   Múúy   jitá-ásiy   jáá-mu   ruda-myu-si-ñíí.
        there   alight-there   water-LOC   branch-LOC-from-3SG
        'There he alights on the other side of the stream
         from his branch.' (i.e. his original perch)

330.   Maasi-n-tyéé   sṵ-ṵsí-jyṵ-nti-dye-ñíí.
        exit-up-INTS   3SG-after-towards-REP-DAY-3SG
        'He exits following after him also.'

331.   Múúy   sii-myaasi-tyéé-ñíí.
        there   run-exit-INTS-3SG
        'There he escapes.'

The One-eyed Warriors: English translation

1.   This is how the ancestors went as warriors in search of the savages.
2.   Yes, they went.
3.   "Savages we will kill yet."

Scene I: The Toad

4.   They see on arrival a toad,
5.   a huge toad lying in the middle of the trail.
6.   One by one they wound him with their clubs, another also, another also.
7.   So right there he swells up.
8.   Another also.
9.   So he swells up.
10.   Another also, another also, another also, another.
11.   Just two remain
12.   that don't wound him in passing.
13.   They just pass by at a distance.
14.   When they have passed by the toad one by one,

Scene II: The Warriors lose their eyes

15.   *There on arrival they sleep.*
16.   "Here we will sleep."

17. They each make their own shelter.
18. In the middle of the night they awaken.
19. Too bad! Now they are missing an eye, all one-eyes now.
20. He (Toad) had emptied the eye-sockets of all of them.
21. One speaks to his companion,
22. "Are you the same?"
23. "Why?"
24. "Do you think that I still have eyes?
25. I have an eye on one side only now!"
26. "Oh, the same!" another also,
27. "The same also!" another also,
28. "I'm the same too!" another also,
29. "The same also am I!" another also,
30. "I'm the same too!" another also,
31. "I'm the same too!" another also,
32. "I'm the same too!"
33. He had emptied the eye sockets of all of them.
34. "Too bad!"
35. "Why did that cursed toad pick out our eyes also?"
36. It dawns.
37. They go in search of him.

Scene III: The Warrior's thwarted revenge

38. "We're going to kill him!
39. We're going to kill!
40. Because yesterday he emptied our eye sockets."
IIIA
41. They go around him, in vain.
42. His little birds see them.
43. "puñi puñi puñi puñi. One-eyed warriors! One-eyed warriors!"
44. Juví So they flee again.
IIIB
45. From there they circle again.   (*)
46. In vain, already the little birds had seen them again.
47. "Warriors! One-eyed warriors! One-eyed warriors!
48. So they flee again.
IIIC
49. From there they circle again.   (*)
50. In vain, they've already seen them again.
51. They flee again.
IIID
52. Finally they return.
53. "We can't kill anybody."
54. They arrive at their shelters again.

55. There they think,
56. "How are we going to do it?"
57. Finally they get a Bejuco vine, a long piece.
58. A long piece they get.
59. They look for a charapilla nut to be their claws.
60. They look for Chambira palm fibers (?) to be their body hair.
61. From there they look for Muena berries
62. and put them in place of their (missing) eyes.
63. The two are just observing them (the two that didn't club the frog and therefore didn't lose an eye?).
64. "What are they going to do, what?"
65. "Why should they transform themselves?"
66. They grab the Bejuco vine.
67. So they flee.

IIIE

68. *Juun! They circle in the same place again.*
69. It (the vine) soon breaks royin! Iran!
70. They go to look for a Hook Casha vine.
71. This is truly a strong vine.
72. They grab this one also.
73. "Let's try again."
74. They flee again juun!

IIIF

75. *They circle again at the same place.*
76. Circling again at the same place.
77. Circling again at the same place.
78. "There. Now it is good."
79. They throw the chambira fibers on their backs to be their body hair.
80. They say nothing more.
81. "As what shall I go?"
82. "Yes." Another also.
83. "I will be a Choro monkey."
84. He goes leaping, no dice.
85. He doesn't knock any over (branches).
86. Finally another scurries up.
87. "I will be the real Choro.
88. He leaps,
89. he breaks,
90. and goes knocking over dry branches.
91. "I, truly, will be the Choro.
92. You will be our sentinels below."
93. Another scurries up.
94. "I will be the Howler monkey."
95. He had put his carrying pouch around his neck to be his larynx.
96. Another had thrown his rattles also,

97. "From you we will know when there are savages below,
98. when this bird (figurative or another disguised warrior) shouts below us,
99. that which is transformed rattles."
100. He had thrown also his gourd purse, te, ru, ru, ru!
101. He goes as the Purmero bird.
102. "From you we will know also,
103. when these Purmeros shout below,
104. there must be savages below."
105. The howler says to the two that don't transform
106. after he had ascended running into the trees.
107. He had hidden himself well.
108. He says to them,
109. "Look from there.
110. Am I visible?"
111. They spy from various points.
112. "You are quite visible!"
113. So he hides himself better.
114. He says to them again,
115. "Look again (to see) if I am visible."
116. They look from there again, from there also.
117. "No.   Now you are not visible."
118. Now it is good.
119. So he says,
120. "Like this the Howler will not be able to be caught
121. when he hides himself in the middle of the thick leaves not very near."
122. The Boar says to them also,
123. "Take a shot at us, the Boars."
124. They take a shot there pon!
125. Ran! so they scatter.
126. There they reunite again.
127. They arrive again.
128. They speak on arrival,
129. "Like that you won't be able to kill many boar.
130. Just one you will kill.
131. Once in awhile you'll kill two.
132. They will always scatter themselves when you hunters arrive."
133. So they go.
134. The collared pecari carries the banner.
135. "Let's go now!"
136. They say to their two friends,
137. "Over there go behind us.
138. Wherever we will go there."
139. They go.

Scene IV: The animal parade

140.   Juun! One after the other they keep bumping the branches with their clubs, tye, tye, tye.

141.   That is what their call is, the call of collared pecaris in flight.

142.   The boar behind him, the choro behind him, the howler behind him, the little friars behind him.

143.   *They disappear overland noisily.*

144.   Too bad, the two stay behind them all.

145.   Finally they go.

Scene V: Toad's sinister hospitality

146.   "Is this the way we came?"

147.   Right there they come to the place of the toad again.

148.   He is pounding in front of them, con, con, con, con!

149.   "Well what are you doing?"

150.   "I am pounding ungurahui palm.

151.   Come into the house and rest."

152.   The toad goes into his house too.

153.   He gives them sweet potato, one potato to one and another potato to the other.

154.   They eat it.

155.   Again, he wants more of the same, his brother also the same.

156.   "I'm going to take a big bite of his piece of sweet potato also."

157.   "Don't touch it!

158.   He will bewitch you for doing that."

159.   He doesn't want to pay any attention to him.

160.   Finally he gets up,

161.   and bites off half of the sweet potato,

162.   Quiyon! The other screams immediately there, "Ow!"

163.   "You have bitten my heart!

164.   You have made my heart sore!"

165.   Says his brother to him,

166.   "I already told you 'don't touch it.'

167.   Too bad, now it's all over for you.

168.   Now he has to do something to you for this."

169.   The other one (toad) finishes pounding the ungurahuis.

170.   He offers them some also.

171.   "Do you want to eat pounded ungurahuis also?"

172.   The two eat.

173.   The toad eats and keeps piling up the sucked seeds.

174.   He finishes sucking,

175.   and scatters the sucked seeds, ran!

176.   "Chujun! They will always call them ungurahui,

177. even though they are the transformed eyeballs of the warriors!"
178. "It's their eyeballs that we've been sucking too!"
179. The two go from there.

Scene VI: Toad's revenge

180. "Let's go now,
181. because it's late.'
182. "With what shall we sleep?"
183. They keep looking for a hollow tree.
184. "let's sleep here in this hollow tree."
185. They gathered fibers of chambira to put in the opening against his coming,
186. because now they were wise,
187. "Well, he might follow us."
188. It gets dark.
189. He comes in the form of a bat.
190. "It must be him!"
191. Finally they sleep,
192. but they soon wake up.
193. He had tied his hammock above, the other below.
194. Suddenly his blood fell on him.
195. "Careful!" Chi, chi, chi.
196. "You are urinating on me!"
197. He wakes up.
198. "Don't say I'm urinating!
199. Do you think I still have a leg?"
200. My leg is cut off!"
201. You wished that it was untrue when I said 'don't touch it.'
202. How are you going to walk now, how?"
203. It dawns,
204. and the two of them exit.

Scene VII: The useless crutch

205. "How are you going to walk, how?
206. Seeing as you are without a leg now."
207. He says to him,
208. "Cut a branch for me.
209. With a little branch I will go hobbling."
210. He puts his leg then on the end, no dice.
211. They go.

Scene VIII: The disobedient leg

212.   On departure he throws away his cut off leg.
213.   He looks again.
214.   There in front of him is his cut off leg lying again.
215.   "Here now again is my cut off leg, here?"
216.   He grabs it again.
217.   "Maybe I should try to stick it in its place."
218.   He tries to insert it in its joint.   No dice.
219.   He throws it away again going along.
220.   They go from there again.
VIIIA
221.   He sees again.
222.   There it is lying again.
223.   "Are you here again?"
224.   There by the side of a stream he works it (tries to replace it) again.
225.   Finally he throws it in the water, tapuun!
226.   "Juun!" It speaks going.
227.   It has transformed itself into an alligator.
228.   They go from there again.

Scene IX: The fungus tree

229.   When the cripple sees on arrival a mass of fungus above,
230.   he calls his brother.
231.   "There are lots of lemurs (or night monkeys) here!"
232.   "So where are the lemurs, where?"
233.   "I'm going to collect lots of them.
234.   We won't even have to roast them either."
235.   "I don't see any lemurs.
236.   I just see a mass of fungus."
237.   Without paying attention to him,
238.   he ascends.
239.   He knocks down from there the mass of fungus.
240.   "There it is."
241.   The other didn't realize that
242.   he had gone and transformed himself.
243.   Finally he says,
244.   "I never want to get down from here, never.
245.   Now I am accustomed here."
246.   His brother doesn't answer him.
247.   "Throw me my jungle achiote pouch, and the ball of achiote with it."
248.   He throws him his jungle achiote pouch, and his ball of achiote also.
249.   He daubs this to become the base of his tail.

250. There where he daubed with achiote and jungle achiote all over the base of his tail.
251. So he has transformed himself into a toucan.
252. He is now a toucan.
253. He says to him,
254. "Let's go now.
255. There you will go right below me.
256. I will go spilling towards you chimicua berries."
257. He flies.

Scene X: The malicious Squirrel

258. *There he alights.*
259. He calls on arrival there also, "cu, cu, cu, cu!"
260. He speaks to him, "Is this where you are?"
261. "Yes, here I am."
262. He flies from there again.

XA

263. *There he alights.*
264. He calls there again.
265. From there he goes along below him.
266. He says to him again, "Are you now here?"
267. "Yes.Here I am."
268. He flies from there again.

XB

269. *There he alights on the other side of the stream from his branch.*
270. He calls on arrival there also.
271. The other speaks also.
272. "So how am I going to cross over?"
273. He goes looking for a tree bridge.

XC

274. Finally he encounters Squirrel.
275. "There you can cross on my tree bridge.
276. Right over there is my tree bridge."
277. From a good distance Squirrel leaps.
278. Yuun! Squirrel does not leap from nearby.
279. He says to him,
280. "Just from there leap!
281. Just from there I always leap."
282. He doesn't have the courage to try it.
283. Finally he goes way out.
284. He is close to the tip (of the tree bridge)
285. when he jumps cadaquin!
286. There inside a water boa he falls, too bad.   (*)
287. Right there his brother sings.

288.   From there he hears from inside the snake.
289.   There he sings.
290.   Right there he sings.
291.   He spends one day there.
292.   There he waits for his brother.
293.   Finally he quiets down.
294.   When he has gone,
295.   he tells his wife in passing,
296.   "A snake has swallowed my brother."
297.   Finally the water boa ascends (from the water) with him to dry land.

Scene XI: Inside the water boa

298.   "Ay!" It is very hot now for him.
299.   It is not a little time that he has been inside him.
300.   Right there was a little deer
301.   that had been swallowed first also.
302.   It is not just one day that he has been sitting there getting bored inside now.
303.   Finally something pricks his bottom.
304.   "What is it that is now pricking my bottom?"
305.   He grabs it.
306.   "Aha! It's a piranha jaw!"
307.   He shows it to the deer.
308.   "A piranha jaw was pricking me in the bottom, a piranha jaw.
309.   Let's cut with this the skin of his stomach.
310.   Didn't you say we are on dry land?"
311.   "Well yes."
312.   He cuts slowly diii!
313.   Tutu, it (the stomach?) gives a little twitch.
314.   He stops again.
315.   He cuts again.
316.   It gives a little twitch again.
317.   He stops again.
318.   He cuts again,
319.   until he gets tired.
320.   Finally he makes a little hole.
321.   He looks (through the hole).
322.   "Yes! We can say we are on firm land."
323.   He makes the hole larger, and larger and larger.
324.   He measures it every time now.
325.   "Now we fit."
326.   He says to the deer,
327.   "You first are going to exit."
328.   "OK."
329.   He exits, juyin!

330. *He exits following after him also, juyin!*
331. *There (he) escapes.*

Scene XI: On dry land again

332. The water boa falls back into the water chuun!
333. He goes all over the place looking for a stream.
334. "Where am I going to wash myself?"
335. The deer says to him,
336. "You have saved us!"

Appendix 4

The Non-Identical Twins Cycle

Storyteller: Laureano Mozombite

From Powlison (1969) and Dorson (1975)

The following is a retranslation (by Mamerto Macahuachi and T. Payne) of a tale that appears in Yagua in Powlison (1969:176-219), and in English in Dorson (1975:553-6). Again, all translation mistakes in this version are my own responsibility. Like many long tales, this story is a series of episodes, each of which may be told as individual stories. Powlison (1969) provides a detailed description of the various Yagua epic tales, and how the episodes and individual characters intertwine. The overarching theme of this tale is how the world came to be the way it is. Some of the specific topics dealt with in this version are, 1) the significance of the distinction between the Yaguas and the non-Yagua indians, 2) how the Yagua clans are created, 3) how the Amazon river is created, 4) why life must involve difficult labor, 5) the origins of blowguns and other hunting equipment, 6) how water turtles and land turtles came into being, 7) how Pifayo (*guilielma gasipaes*, a palm fruit) is obtained by the Yaguas, and 8) how corn is obtained by the Yaguas.

This tale forms part of the data base for the topic continuity study of chapter 4 of this thesis, and the first 153 clauses form part of the data base for the quantitative study of S_0 coding in chapter 6. Although it would be preferable to include the full Yagua transcription of this text, due to space limitations I have limited presentation to the English translation. The English is included in order to help the reader understand something of the thematic structure of Yagua discourse and to locate specific examples from this text cited in the body of the thesis in their discourse contexts. As mentioned above, this text appears in Yagua in Powlison (1969), though in a different orthography than that which is employed in this work, and without clause numbering.

1.   Yes, Creator created. Creator created long ago.

Scene I: The House

2.   The adults drink manioc beer,
3.   beer they drink.
4.   Her pregnant daughter says to the old woman:
5.   "While you weed the manioc patch, we are going to keep drinking."
6.   You don't drink anything with us.
Transition
7.   She goes.
8.   They drink in her absence.

Scene II: The Manioc Patch: Grandmother worries

9. After a while, suddenly they are quiet, silent.
10. She listens and listens.
11. "What could have happened to them again, what?"
12. They aren't laughing, they aren't drumming anymore.
13. It's almost evening.
14. Finally she goes.

Scene III: The House: Grandmother discovers carnage

15. She looks on arrival. jiii
16. The house is smoking, the ruins of the house.
17. The savages have burned it.
18. "Certainly the savages have completely killed them!
19. No wonder they're not drumming, no wonder!
20. Clearly they've all been killed!"
21. From there she is wandering around
22. when she hears crying from the trash pile:
23. "Cuway, cuway, cuway, cuway!"
24. "jiii, here clearly the savages have thrown my daughter's child!"
25. She goes.

Scene IV: The Trash Pile: Grandmother discovers the twins.

26. "I will recover him to be my companion.
27. I will raise him to be my companion."
28. She recovers him.
29. As she is going, she hears that another is crying there also.
30. "Is someone there?"
31. She returns again.
32. It is his placenta that has been transformed.
33. She recovers him also.
34. She goes, then, under her shelter again.

Scene V: Grandmother's Shelter (in the manioc patch): The Twins grow

35. She washes them there on arrival.
36. In two days they sit up.
37. In three days they walk all over the place.
38. They don't delay in growing.
39. In five days they are complete adults.
40. He asks his grandmother:
41. "How then did my deceased father die, how?
42. And my deceased mother?"

43.   "The savages just killed them."
44.   "Really?"
45.   "Yes."

Scene VI: The House: The Twins see game

46.   The two go again there in the neighborhood of the ruined house of their
        father,
47.   and they pass by all sides,
48.   and they see little toucans, everything: toucans, wild turkeys.
49.   They are eating tayra berries.
50.   "What can we use to kill them?"
51.   The two return to their grandmother again.

Scene VII: Grandmother's Shelter: The Twins learn about hunting

52.   "With what did my father hunt animals, with what?"
53.   "With just a blowgun."
54.   "It's not here, you know, the blowgun,
55.   that which is its tree (that which is the blowgun tree).
56.   From there your deceased father got his blowgun.
57.   Darts also from the fork (heart) of the inayuga palm he got them."
58.   When it dawned again,
Transition
59.   they left for the tree.
60.   "Be careful it traps you!
61.   Quickly you must snatch it from inside,
62.   if you want to get a blowgun."
63.   They go to the blowgun tree.

Scene VIII: The Blowgun Tree: The Twins get a blowgun

64.   It is yawning over and over again in front of him, po, po, po!
65.   Right close by he is now, right close by.
66.   There grabbing it he yanks, 'siyon!'
67.   There it springs out beside it.
68.   So he grabs his blowgun.

Scene IX: Grandmother's Shelter: The Twins learn about blowguns

69.   He carries it to where his grandmother is.
70.   He greets his grandmother;
71.   "Why have you ruined it again?"
72.   "Why not?"
73.   "For what purpose do you ruin it, for what purpose?"

74. "So that our offspring will have to suffer (work hard) to make their blowguns.
75. Isn't it important that they make them with their hands? (rhetorical question meaning "you know it's important that they make them with their hands").

Transition

76. They go again for darts.
77. "Be careful, the scorpions that protect it bite you!
78. It's not just one biting thing that protects it, red scorpions and snakes also."

Scene X: The Inayuga Palm: The Twins get darts for their blowgun

79. He climbs searching to the fork of the inayuga.
80. He finishes off the scorpions, the red scorpions, the snakes,
81. and collects from where they were the darts.

Scene XI: Grandmother's Shelter: The Twins learn about darts

82. She sees also that he carries a roll of darts.
83. "Why did you finish off the biting things that protected it also?"
84. "Why not?"
85. "For what reason did you finish them off, for what reason?"
86. "So that they will have to whittle their darts with a knife."
87. They go again for a dartholder,

Scene XII: The Catirina Palm: The Twins get a dartholder

88. which is in the fork of the catirina palm.
89. There are biting things that protect it also.
90. He finishes them off
91. the ones that protected it also
92. and he gets the dartholder also.

Scene XIII: Grandmother's Shelter: The twins learn about dartholder

93. His grandmother sees also.
94. "Why did you finish off the biting things that protected it also?"
95. "Why not?"
96. "So that they will have to weave their own dartholders."
97. Thus it remained there (i.e. like that).

Scene XIV: The House: The Twins hunt and grab the magic flute

98. The two of them go from there again around the neighborhood of the ruins of the house of their deceased father.
99. There they went blowgun-hunting little toucans, everything, wild turkeys.
100. There they spy on the spirit of their mother, and the spirit of their father

101.   those that dance in the middle of the ruins of the house.
102.   Another day, the same thing again.
103.   Another day, the same thing again.
104.   Finally the two think:
105.   If only we could snatch the flutes of our deceased parents,
106.   with them we could secure vengeance for our departed parents.
107.   Finally he says to his brother:
108.   "Let's go and snatch them!"
109.   The two of them get up early again.
110.   Today, yes, we are going to snatch them.
111.   They hide nearby, there where they circle (all traditional Yagua dancing involves circling).
112.   "Here is where they come circling."
113.   They put cetico leaves over themselves, the other one too.
114.   "Be careful not to let go when you grab it!
115.   If it heats up,
116.   your hand will heat up immediately also.
117.   If it shrinks to a tiny flute,
118.   your hand will shrink immediately also,
119.   If it enlarges to a huge flute,
120.   your hand will enlarge immediately also",
121.   he says to his brother.
122.   The two (spirits) descend to earth again.
123.   They are dancing on arrival
124.   'puun!' they dance.

Climax

125.   *There he jumps up suddenly against them.*
126.   Rupa! His brother has grabbed his deceased father's flute.
127.   Tanti! the two of them stick together.
128.   His brother now screams:
129.   "Now my hand is burning!"
130.   "Equally your hand will heat up immediately also."
131.   "Now it burns me!
132.   Now it burns me!
133.   Now I let go of it!"
134.   "Don't let go of it!"
135.   Finally, he yanks his flute from him completely.
136.   Only Placenta succeeds in grabbing the flute of his deceased mother.
137.   Finally he snatches it away from her,
138.   and she ascends jumping, puri.
139.   The two have snatched the flute from their deceased mother.
140.   The two go again there to where their grandma is.

**Scene XV: Grandmother's Shelter: The Twins test the flute,
Grandmother makes manioc beer**

141.　They call to their grandmother upon arrival:
142.　"Grandmother! Here, sit down."
143.　She sits down at their command,
144.　and they blow into it, "vïï, vïï, vïï, vïï, vïï, vïï"
145.　One strong blow into it, "kiiin",
146.　She falls like dead.
147.　Their Grandmother revives again.
148.　She says,
149.　she scolds her two grandsons:
150.　"Jii! What's happening with you two?
151.　Obviously you've succeeded in getting your deceased mother's flute also!"
152.　"Why not?
153.　Maybe with it you will secure vengeance for our dead father."
154.　He says to his grandmother:
155.　"Grandmother, prepare manioc beer."
156.　"Who, then, is going to drink it with you, who?
157.　There aren't any people that I see (i.e. know about) around here, none."
158.　"Just nearby there are people."
159.　"(But) the house is not large enough.
160.　Where then will the people sit, where?"
161.　"I'll just make the house larger then!"
162.　She makes the manioc beer.
163.　Jujum, she finishes making it.
164.　When she finished making it,
165.　she says to her grandson:
166.　"Here now is the manioc beer that you requested."
167.　He commands then his elder brother:
168.　"Invite!"
169.　"Where then will I go to invite, where?
170.　I have not seen any people around here, none."
171.　"But just over there are people."
172.　Finally, he goes.

Scene XVI: The Jungle: Elder Brother searches for people

173.　From there he goes circling,
174.　without seeing any people,
175.　and returns.
176.　"Aha! Many have you invited?"
177.　"I didn't see anybody to invite."
178.　He greets his brother:
179.　"Where, then, do people lack, where?.

180.   I then will invite!"
181.   Placenta goes.

Scene XVII: The Jungle: Placenta creates the clans

182.   Near the top of a heap he kicks.
183.   "Come and drink at my place!"
184.   From there on the top of a heap of Macaw feathers,
185.   jun!, "Come and drink at my place!"
186.   From there also on top of a Spotted Cavy burrow.
187.   "Come and drink at my place!"
188.   From there also upon an ant's nest.
189.   "Come and drink at my place!"
190.   From there also against the buttress root of a Pachaco tree he kicks in passing also.
191.   "Come and drink at my place!"
192.   From there on top of a bat's nest he kicks in passing also.
193.   "Come and drink at my place!"
194.   From there against the trunk of the blowgun tree he strikes in passing.
195.   "Come and drink at my place!"
196.   He turns back from there.
197.   "Enough now."

Scene XVIII: Grandmother's Shelter: The Clans arrive and drink

198.   He says upon arrival to his brother again:
199.   "Do you think I have invited (things) which you say are people?"
200.   There are no people within a great distance, none.
201.   After a long time, a long time, they now arrive in groups.
202.   Those of the Squirrel clan begin to arrive,
203.   those of the Red Macaw clan after them,
204.   those of the Spotted Cavy clan after them,
205.   those of the Ant (Isula, a large stinging ant) clan after them,
206.   those of the Pachaco tree clan after them,
207.   those of the Bat clan after them,
208.   those of the Blowgun clan after them.
209.   And the house was filled with people.
210.   They pulled out the supports of the house to make a large house.
211.   They drink all night long, all night long.
212.   It dawns.
213.   He tries it on them,
214.   (to see) if it works.
215.   He blows into it in the midst of them.
216.   He blows hard into it.
217.   They all fall then.

218. So he says:
219. "It works!"
220. So they get up early (to fight) against the savages.
221. "Let's go to the savages!
222. Let's kill them!"
223. They go.

Scene XIX: The Savage's house:

224. *They arrive near the house of the savages,*
225. Placenta transforms himself into a small hawk, beautifully speckled.
226. He ascends running along the roof on arrival,
227. because the savage's roof didn't reach the ground.
228. He ascends running along the roof on arrival.
229. The savages hear:
230. "Who then is running up there on the roof?"
231. They come out.
232. They look.
233. "Who then also?
234. How beautiful!
235. Look!"
236. He calls to his kinsmen.
237. They come running out.
238. Jiin, "Unreal!"
239. They all run out of house, all the savages.
240. One carries a blowgun.
241. "I'm still going to blowgun him!"
242. "Don't blowgun him yet!
243. We should tell the people of the other house too,
244. that they might come right away."
245. One runs to the other house
246. and tells them also.
247. They ran then also. Jiin.
248. He begins to blow into the flute of his deceased mother, "vïï, vïï."
249. He says to him:
250. "Don't blowgun him yet.
251. How is he going to play (the flute)?"
252. "OK."
253. He is blowing into it.
254. He blows. He blows. He blows. He blows.
255. Quickly he now blows.
256. With all his strength he blows into it,
257. Yun! All the savages fall over,
258. there they are laid out.

259. Not one remains (standing).
260. So the ones that were with him run in passing.
261. There they kill with clubs.
262. Juuuun. Finished!
263. "Your request.
264. That's how they killed my deceased father."
265. The matter was finished.
266. They turn back after the battle.
267. They drink the leftover manioc beer in the house again.
268. That's how all the clans remained.
269. So they all stayed outside.
270. So it was he who created the Squirrel clan, the Red Macaw clan,
271. so he created them all.

Scene XX: The Twins obtain water

272. Creator has caused the water to subside from them until it is all gone.
273. There isn't any water any more.
274. From then on they keep on getting it from their grandfather.
275. Day by day, day by day,
276. Tiiy until they are tired of it.
277. "I'm tired of this!"
278. They ask one who lives there with their grandfather,
279. "How does he get water?"
280. "I don't know."
281. "Don't you know where he bathes?"
282. "He always goes bathing over there.
283. He bathes at noon."
284. He says to his placenta again,
285. "Go see where.
286. This fellow says he bathes at noon."
287. "O.K."

Scene XXI: Grandfather's bathing place

288. He goes to the edge of the woods
289. and watches patiently from there.
290. At last he (Grandfather) speaks,
291. "Ugh! It's too hot for me!
292. I'm going to bathe first."
293. The sun is directly overhead.
294. He (Placenta) goes then
295. and changes himself into a little hummingbird
296. and flies after him.

297.   He (Grandfather) opens when he gets there in his (Placenta's) sight,
        Gush! pour!
298.   Their grandfather stands under it.
299.   The hummingbird is flying along,
300.   Tu tu tu He hits at him.
301.   "Hummingbird, Hummingbird! Why are you being a nuisance?"

Scene XXII: Back home

302.   *There he returns* Chiy! Chiy! Chiy! Chiy!
303.   He returns.
304.   *He arrives back at his brother's,*
305.   and tells his brother,
306.   "It's in that whatcha-ma-call-it water tree which is standing,
307.   that great big tree standing (there)!"
308.   "Really!"
309.   "Yes."
310.   "What shall we do?"
311.   "I don't know
312.   unless we cut it down."
313.   "OK!"

Scene XXIII: Grandfather's place

314.   They rise and go early the next morning to their grandfather's again.
315.   They say to their grandfather when they get there,
316.   "Grandpa?"
317.   "What?"
318.   "Uhh, we're going to cut down this tree which is standing."
319.   "Go ahead and cut!
320.   It isn't forbidden to cut it down."
321.   They invite (to work) with them woodpeckers, squirrels, agoutis, all,
322.   woodcreepers, those who make holes, barbets.
323.   They invite them all (to work) with them.
324.   They cut it.
325.   They begin cutting
326.   and cut and cut and cut,
327.   as far as its center.
328.   They cut and cut
329.   until the woodpecker is into its heart.
330.   Ti! It's getting late.
331.   It's late.
332.   They give up on it.
333.   It is quite thin (when) they leave off.
334.   "Tomorrow we'll fell it!"

335.   "Yes."
336.   It dawns
337.   and they go again.
338.   It stands there intact again.
339.   "No doubt he put its chips back again!"
340.   They cut again. ti!
341.   They cut and cut and cut
342.   until it isn't very thick any more.
343.   At last he sends his placenta again,
344.   "Go listen, transforming yourself into the likeness of a little bird,
345.   to what Grandfather says."
346.   Their grandfather is sitting in the yard, smoking.
347.   He (Placenta) goes.
348.   He transforms himself.
349.   He listens.
350.   He (Grandfather) smokes,
351.   he blows it around.
352.   He (Grandfather) speaks and
353.   he (Placenta) hears,
354.   "Those two children will never fell the, whatsit, water tree!
355.   They'll never be able to fell it,
356.   unless they should make a scorpion bite the tip of my little toe.
357.   Then, it would fall."
358.   Then Placenta turns back again.

Scene XXIV: Back home

358a.   He tells his elder (brother),
359.   "This is what Grandpa said,
360.   only if we were to get a scorpion to bite the tip of his little toe,
361.   then it would fall."'
362.   He says to him,
363.   "Transform yourself then!"
364.   "Into what?"
365.   "Transform yourself into a scorpion."
366.   He transforms himself again.

Scene XXV: Grandfather's Place

367.   He has gone again.
368.   He (Grandfather) smokes, and smokes,
369.   and blows it around on (the tree's) vines.
370.   There he bites him on the tip of his little toe when he gets there, siii.
371.   "Hey!" It begins to crack immediately,
372.   "Yikes! Ouch! How wise these two kids are!"

373. It stays,
374. it stays just a little bit on the lean now.
375. He says to him again,
376. "Who on earth is the most painful biter?"
377. "The red scorpion, I suppose."
378. "Transform yourself into a red scorpion."
379. He transforms himself into a red scorpion.
380. He goes again
381. and bites him the same way on arrival again.
382. He was indeed a very painful biter.
383. Sii, He falls over,
384. Pu̧u̧, It falls then,
385. Yu̧u̧u̧n, pu̧u̧.
386. It falls.
387. His grandson runs at the same time to him,
388. "What happened to you, Grandpa?"
389. He is not alive any more.
390. He had died.
391. He blows on him, ju̧u̧u̧u̧.
392. He sits up,
393. "Ha! How are you two so wise?
394. No doubt you've cut it down, too!"
395. "Of course.
396. What is our posterity supposed to drink?"
397. "O.K. Let it be so!"

Snail Episode (no scene change)

398. A little snail comes running for a leaf,
399. and grabs it for his door plug.
400. He touches (it).
401. In his view, it makes a pretty sound.
402. The first Water Snail comes running to him.
403. He says then to him,
404. "You just got that?"
405. He asks him for it.
406. "Let me see!"
407. He gives it to him then,
408. "Go ahead and look at it."
409. He handles it with his hands.
410. "How very pretty it is!"
411. He gives it back to him,
412. "Here it it is!"
413. He asks for it again.
414. He gives it to him again.

415.   He rubs it in his hands.
416.   At last he says to him departing,
417.   "I have it now!"
418.   He runs away from him to the water.
419.   He jumps with it away from him into the water.
420.   The owner of the taken object follows him for it.
421.   He has jumped with it into the water ahead of him.
422.   He jumps in after him.
423.   Tíiy, he can't submerge.
424.   He just floats around.
425.   The land snail speaks then,
426.   "Why did you impoverish me?!
427.   Now the isulillo (ants) will always bite my exposed fleshy parts."
428.   Another comes running, too,
429.   "I'll be a water tortoise."
430.   He jumps into the water, tápµµ.
431.   Yuu, he floats up.
432.   "Tíiy. You can't be a water tortoise!"
433.   Another comes running,
434.   "*I'll* be a water tortoise!"
435.   In he jumps tápµµ.
436.   Piri. He sinks,
437.   the one who says he will be a water tortoise.
438.   He lands on the bottom of the Amazon.
439.   "I'll be the water tortoise,
440.   you be a land tortoise."
441.   That one remains as the water tortoise.
442.   "*I'll* be the water tortoise,
443.   *you* be the land tortoise."
444.   "What will I eat?"
445.   "Well, fungus and tortoise fruit.
446.   You'll eat the tortoise fruit.
447.   The berries which ripen red."
448.   "O.K."
449.   Its owners (the caterpillars that "own" the water tree) are now transformed one by one.
450.   They paddled away.
451.   The white people paddled away, as whites, as blacks, all of them, Cocamas.
452.   All its owners go transformed.
453.   Its chips have been transformed into fish, which are the umbrella tree chips.
454.   All its leaves transform onto what they call mojarra fish, a long kind of mojarra fish.
456.   They all transform.
457.   Gamitana fish, arapaima, all its leaves are transformed into fish.
458.   It (the tree) became the long Amazon River then.

The Twins obtain pifayo (Still Grandfather's place)

459.   From there they (2) come for pifayo.
460.   Now for pifayo they pester him again.
461.   "Give me a pifayo seed, gramps!"
462.   He gives him a whole stalk.
463.   They cut them all in half.
464.   Tííy' None have seeds.
465.   "None of them have any seeds."
466.   He gives them another stalk.
467.   Tííy. Neither does this one.
468.   "This one doesn't either."
469.   Finally, he thinks again.
470.   "Let's steal it.
471.   Just over there is one that has seeds.
472.   He always gives us ones that don't have seeds."
473.   He goes.
474.   "Transform yourself.
475.   Transform yourself into a parakeet."
476.   "OK"
477.   He calls the parakeets to himself.
478.   Many he calls.
479.   He goes from there to his grown over garden,
479a.   there where his pifayo palm grove is.
480.   "This is really thick."
481.   The parakeets descend on it, Yụụụụ.
482.   There they are destined to be blowgunned by him.
483.   They pile into the pifayo.
484.   So there he shoots (blows).
485.   So then he shoots.
486.   So then he shoots.
487.   There now Placenta penetrates it.
488.   So then he shoots.
489.   There at last he finds its seed.
490.   When he comes out from there,
491.   there he immediately shoots him, Kịịị.
492.   ke, ke, tíye. He falls.
493.   Yụụụ. So then they scatter all over from him.
494.   He gathers his kill.
495.   Jụụụ. It's a big pile.
496.   He takes them.
497.   They defeather them when he arrives.
498.   They clean them.
499.   They cook them in pifayo peel water.

500.   Then his brother arrives.
501.   They take the parakeets from the fire now.
502.   His grandfather gives him to him.
503.   "Eat this one at your house.
504.   They are no good pifayo wreckers.
505.   He was wrecking pifayo."
506.   It's his BROTHER he gives to him.
507.   He says to him,
508.   "Quick! Hurry!"
509.   He whispers to him.
510.   "Lick my eye.
511.   Pifayo water has already entered my eye.
512.   Let's go!"
513.   He says to his grandfather,
514.   "I'm going now gramps."
515.   "OK"

Scene XXVI: The Twins' Place

516.   There at the forest edge he says to his brother,
517.   "Let's look around for my intestines.
518.   Yonder I saw them throw them."
519.   He grabs his intestines.
520.   He inserts them inside himself.
521.   Then he is transformed into a person again.
522.   He gives the pifayo seed to him.
523.   "This is the pifayo seed you requested.
524.   It is just a little bit cooked.
525.   Try planting it."
526.   He plants it.
527.   It dawns.
528.   It's already this size of tree at dawn.
529.   After three sleeps, it already gives fruit.

Scene XXVII: Grandfather's Place: The Twins obtain corn

530.   There corn is now lacking.
531.   Not just recently they keep asking their grandfather for corn also.
532.   He doesn't want to give them any.
533.   Finally they say to the grasshopper,
534.   "Can you steal one seed for me?"
535.   "Sure."
536.   He roasts coca leaves.
537.   Grasshopper roasts them.
538.   Their grandfather is just sitting outside.

539. Finally he stands up.
540. The coca leaves now stir themselves around in his absense.
541. Yǫ, yǫ, yǫ. As he shells (corn),
542. it spills all over, yųųųų.
543. "Grasshopper, Grasshopper, you are stealing again!"
544. "Not at all. I'm just here roasting coca leaves."
545. He (GF) goes after it (the spilled corn),
546. and puts it all back where it was.
547. He puts it back where it was.
548. Pųų. Another grain also, another grain also. (grain by grain).
549. "But exactly one grain is lacking!
550. You have stolen one grain!"
551. "Not at all, not at all."
552. He goes to him.
553. He looks all over him, his mouth, inside his nostril, everywhere.
554. There all over he looks, inside his ear.
555. "Did you find what you were looking for?"
556. He had inserted the corn seed inside his little penis.

Scene XXVIII: The Twins' Place

557. His two grandsons now arrive also.
558. He takes it out for him.
559. "Here is your requested corn seed.
560. Now plant it."
561. They return,
562. and they plant it also,
563. They invite their grandfather again.
564. "Drink some corn drink Gramps."
565. "It must be as I thought!
566. That Grasshopper stole corn for you also."
567. "Of course.
568. Otherwise, what would our posterity eat?"
569. "OK.
570. Let it be so.
571. But it won't grown quickly for them anymore.
572. It'll take three months for it to grow for them."

The Twins obtain the correct name for pifayo

573. After awhile they invite him for pifayo drink also.
574. "It must be that you stole the pifayo seed."
575. "Of course.
576. Otherwise what will our posterity have to drink?"
577. "OK. So be it.

578.   But it will not grow quickly for them anymore.
579.   It'll take one year for it to give fruit for them."
580.   He also wants its name now.
581.   He asks the one living with him,
582.   "What does he call this?"
583.   He does not say "pų́ų́riy" yet.
584.   He just says its name is "tą̀ąchurá".
585.   "That's not what it's called!"
586.   He says its real name.
587.   He (Placenta) says to one of his servants,
588.   "How does he say its name?"
589.   He is afraid of telling it.
590.   "Tell him only half of it."
591.   Of course he speaks its name loudly.
592.   "Pų́ų́riy", he says it.
593.   "Pų́ų́", his mouth twists then.
594.   His mouth becomes little then.
595.   "What is it?"
596.   Tííy. He can't speak anymore.
597.   Now he just babbles, "si, si, si".
598.   Tíjį. He figures out its name.
599.   "Is it 'pų́ų́riy'?
600.   Is that what he just said?"
601.   Tííy. He can't answer anymore.
602.   He has been transformed into a flounder.

References Cited

Aberdour, Catherine. 1985. Referential devices in Apurinã discourse. Porto Velho Workpapers, ed. David Fortune, pp. 43-91. Brasilia: Summer Institute of Linguistics.

Anderson, Stephen R. 1982. Where's morphology? Linguistic Inquiry 13:571-612.

Chafe, Wallace L. 1970. Meaning and the Structure of Language. Chicago: University of Chicago Press.

------------. 1974. Language and consciousness. Language 50:111-133.

------------. 1976. Givenness, contrastiveness, definiteness, subjects, topics and point of view. Subject and topic, ed. Charles N. Li, pp. 25-55. New York: Academic Press.

------------. ed. 1980. The Pear Stories: Cognitive, Cultural and Linguistic Aspects of Narrative Production. Norwood, N.J.: Ablex.

------------. 1984. How people use adverbial clauses. Procedings of the Berkeley Linguistic Society 10.

------------. 1987. Cognitive constraints on information flow. Coherence and grounding in discourse, ed. Russell S. Tomlin, pp. 21-52. Amsterdam: John Benjamins.

Chaumeil, Jean-Pierre. 1981. Historia y migraciones de los yagua de finales del Siglo XVII hasta nuestros días Lima: Centro Amazónico de Antropología y Aplicación Práctica.

Chaumeil, Josette, and Jean-Pierre Chaumeil. 1976a. Bibliografía de los yagua del nor-oeste amazónico. Amazonía Peruana, vol. I, no. 1:159-76.

------------. 1976b. Los yagua de la Amazonía Peruana (elementos de demografía). Amazonía Peruana, vol. I, no. 1:73-94.

Clancy, Patricia M. 1980. Referential choice in English and Japanese narrative. The pear stories, ed. Wallace L. Chafe, pp. 127-202. Norwood, N.J.: Ablex.

Comrie, Bernard. 1978a. Aspect (second printing). Cambridge: Cambridge University Press.

------------. 1978b. Ergativity. Syntactic Typology: Studies in the Phenomenology of Language, ed. Winfred P. Lehmann, pp. 329-394. Austin: University of Texas Press.

------------. 1981. Language Universals and Linguistic Typology. Chicago: University of Chicago Press.

DeLancey, Scott. 1982. Aspect, transitivity and viewpoint. Tense-aspect: Between Semantics and Pragmatics, ed. Paul J. Hopper, 167-84. Amsterdam: John Benjamins.

Derbyshire, Desmond C. 1977. Word order universals and the existence of OVS languages. Linguistic Inquiry 8:590-9.

------------. 1986. Topic continuity in Hixcariana. Native South American Discourse, ed. Joal Sherzer and Greg Urban. Berlin: Mouton.

Derbyshire, Desmond C. and Geoffrey Pullum. 1981. Object-Initial languages. International Journal of American Linguistics 47:192-214.

------------. eds. 1986. Handbook of Amazonian Languages, Vol. I. Berlin: Mouton de Gruyter.

------------. eds. 1990. Handbook of Amazonian Languages, Vol. II. Berlin: Mouton de Gruyter.

Dik, Simon. 1978. Functional Grammar. Amsterdam: North-Holland.

------------. 1981. On the Typology of focus phenomena. Perspectives on Functional Grammar ed. Teun Hoekstra, Harry Van der Hulst, and Michael Moortgat. Dordrecht-Holland: Foris

Dixon, R. M. W. 1979. Ergativity. Language 55:59-138.

Dorson, Richard M. 1975. Folktales Told Around the World. Chicago: University of Chicago Press.

Du Bois, John W. 1980. Beyond definiteness: the trace of identity in discourse. The pear stories, ed. Wallace L. Chafe, pp. 203-74. Norwood, N. J.: Ablex.

------------. 1985. Competing motivations. Iconicity in Syntax, ed. John Haiman. Typological studies in language, 6:343-366. Amsterdam: John Benjamins.

------------. 1987. The discourse basis of ergativity. Language 62:4.

Espinosa Pérez, L. 1955. Contribuciones lingüísticas y etnográficas sobre algunos pueblos indígenas del Amazonía Peruana. Madrid: Instituto Bernardino de Sahagún.

Everett, Daniel L. 1989. Clitic doubling, reflexives and word order alternations in Yagua. Language 65:339-72.

Fejos, Paul. 1943. Ethnography of the Yagua. Viking Fund Publications in Anthropology, 1. New York: Viking Fund.

Fillmore, Charles J. 1968. The case for case. Universals of Linguistic Theory, ed. Emmon Bach and J. Harms. Cambridge, Mass.: MIT Press.

------------. 1977. Topics in lexical semantics. Current Issues in Linguistic Theory, ed. Roger Cole, pp. 76-138. Bloomington: Indiana University Press.

Fox, Andrew. 1983. Topic continuity in Biblical Hebrew narrative. Topic Continuity in Discourse: a Quantitative Cross-Language Study, ed. T. Givón, pp. 215-54. Amsterdam: John Benjamins.

Fox, Barbara A. 1986. Discourse Structure and Anaphora in Written and Conversational English. Cambridge: Cambridge University Press.

Gary, Norman. 1978. A Discourse Analysis of Certain Root Transformations in English. Bloomington: Indiana University linguistics club.

Givón, T. 1979. On Understanding Grammar. New York: Academic Press.

------------. 1981. Typology and functional domains. Studies in Language 5:2.

------------. 1983a. Topic continuity in discourse: the functional domain of switch reference. Typological Studies in Language, vol. 2., ed. John Haiman and Pamela Munro Amsterdam: John Benjamin's.

------------. ed. 1983b. Topic Continuity in Discourse: a Quantitative Cross-language Study. Amsterdam: John Benjamins.

------------. 1983c. Introduction. Topic Continuity in Discourse: a Quantitative Cross-language Study, pp. 5-41. Amsterdam: John Benjamins.

------------. 1983d. Topic continuity and word order pragmatics in Ute. Topic Continuity in Discourse: a Quantitative Cross-Language study, pp. 141-214. Amsterdam: John Benjamins.

------------. 1987. Beyond foreground and background. Coherence and Grounding in Discourse, ed. Russell S. Tomlin. Typological Studies in Language vol. 11, pp. 175-88. Amsterdam: John Benjamins.

Greenberg, Joseph H 1960. The general classification of Central and South American languages. Men and Cultures: Selected Papers of the Fifth International Congress of Anthropological and Ethnological Sciences, ed. A. F. C. Wallace. Philadelphia: University of Pennsylvania Press.

Grimes, Barbara. 1984. Ethnologue (tenth edition). Dallas: Wycliffe Bible Translators.

Grimes, Joseph. 1975. The Thread of Discourse. The Hague: Mouton.

Halliday, M. A. K. 1967. Notes on transitivity and theme, Part 2. Journal of Linguistics 3:199-244.

Halliday, M. A. K, and Ruqaiya Hasan. 1976. Cohesion in English. London: Longman.

Hammerich, Louis L. 1976. The Eskimo language. Papers on Eskimo and Aleut Linguistics, pp. 43-80. Chicago: Chicago Linguistics Society.

Harris, Alice. 1981. Georgian Syntax: a Study in Relational Grammar. Cambridge: Cambridge University Press.

Heitzman, A. 1982. Some cohesive elements in Pajonal Campa narratives. MS 20 pp. Lima, Perú: Summer Institute of Linguistics.

Hopper, Paul J., and Sandra A. Thompson. 1984. The discourse basis for lexical categories in universal grammar. Language 60:703-52.

------------. 1980. Transitivity in grammar and discourse. Language 56. 251-99.

Jaggar, Phillip. 1984. Referential Choice in Hausa Narrative. University of California, Los Angeles, doctoral dissertation.

Keenan, Edward L. 1984. Semantic correlates of the ergative/absolutive distinction. Linguistics 22:197-223.

Klimov, G. A. 1977. Tipologia jazykov aktivnogo stroja. Moscow: Nauka

Lakoff, George. 1987. Women, Fire and Dangerous Things: What Categories Reveal About the Mind. Chicago: University of Chicago Press.

Lakoff, George, and Mark Johnson. 1980. Metaphors We Live By. Chicago: University of Chicago press.

Loukotka, Cestmir 1968. Classification of South American Indian Languages. (ed. Johannes Wilbert). Los Angeles: University of California, Latin American Center.

Mann, William C., and Sandra A. Thompson. 1986. Relational propositions in discourse. Discourse Processes 9:57-90.

Marantz, Alec. 1984. On the Nature of Grammatical Relations. Cambridge, Mass.: MIT Press.

Medina, J. T. 1934. The Discovery of the Amazon According to the Account of Friar Gaspar de Carvajal and Other Documents. (American Geographical Society, special publication 17.) New York: American Geographical Society.

Merlan, Francesca. 1985. Split intransitivity: functional oppositions in intransitive inflection. Grammar Inside and Outside the Clause: Some Approaches to Theory from the Field, ed. Johanna Nichols and Anthony C. Woodbury. pp. 324-62. Cambridge: Cambridge University Press.

Mithun, Marianne. 1987. Is basic word order universal?. Coherence and Grounding in Discourse, ed. Russell S. Tomlin, pp. 281-328. Amsterdam: John Benjamins.

Payne, Doris L. 1984. Evidence for a Yaguan-Zaparoan connection. Work papers of the Summer Institute of Linguistics, University of North Dakota, XXVIII:131-56.

------------. 1985. Aspects of the Grammar of Yagua: a Typological Perspective. University of California doctoral dissertation. Ann Arbor: University Microfilms.

------------. 1986. Basic constituent order in Yagua clauses: implications for word order universals. Handbook of Amazonian Languages, vol. 1, ed. D. Derbyshire and G. Pullum. The Hague: Mouton.

------------. 1987. Information structuring in Papago narrative discourse. Language 63:783-804.

------------. 1989. Continuity vs. discontinuity in Yagua narrative. Paper presented at the American Anthropological Association meetings, Washington DC.

------------. 1990. The Pragmatics of Word Order: Typological Dimensions of Verb-Initial Languages. Berlin: Mouton de Gruyter.

Payne, Doris L., and Thomas E. Payne. 1990. A grammatical sketch of Yagua. Handbook of Amazonian languages vol. 2, ed. Desmond C. Derbyshire and Geoffrey Pullum. Berlin: Mouton.

Payne, Thomas E. 1982. Role and reference related subject properties and ergativity in Yup'ik Eskimo and Tagalog. Studies in Language VI:75-106.

------------. 1982b. Subject in Guaymí. Estudios varios sobre las lenguas chibchas de Costa Rica, Series A, vol. 1, pp. 45-76. San José: University of Costa Rica.

------------. 1983a. Yagua object clitics: syntactic and phonological misalignment and another possible source of ergativity. The Interplay of Phonology, Morphology and Syntax, ed. John F. Richardson, Mitchell Marks and Amy Chukerman, pp. 173-84. Chicago: University of Chicago Press.

------------. 1983b. Subject inflection of Yagua verbs. MS, available from the author.

------------. 1984a. Split-S marking and fluid-S marking revisited. Papers from the parasession on lexical semantics. Chicago Linguistics Society, pp. 222-232.

------------. 1984b. Locational relations in Yagua narrative. Work papers of the Summer Institute of Linguistics, University of North Dakota, XXVIII:157-192.

------------. 1987. Pronouns in Yagua discourse. International Journal of American Linguistics 53:1-20.

Perlmutter, David. 1978. Impersonal passives and the unaccusative hypothesis. Procedings of the Berkeley Linguistic Society 4:157-189.

Pike, Kenneth L. 1971. Language in Relation to a Unified Theory of the Structure of Human Behavior. The Hague: Mouton.

Powlison, Esther. 1971. The suprahierarchical and hierarchical structures of Yagua phonology. Linguistics 75:43-73.

Powlison, Paul S. 1961. The number system of Yagua. International Journal of American Linguistics 27:158-9.

------------. 1962. Palatalization portmanteaus in Yagua (Peba-Yaguan). Word 18:280-99.

------------. 1965. A paragraph analysis of a Yagua folktale. International Journal of American Linguistics 31:109-18.

------------. 1969. Yagua Mythology and its Epic Tendencies. University of Michigan doctoral dissertation. Ann Arbor: University Microfilms.

------------. 1987. Yagua Mythology: Epic Tendencies in a New World Mythology. Dallas: Summer Institute of Linguistics.

Powlison, Paul S, and Esther Powlison. 1958. El sistema numérico del yagua (pebano). Tradición: Revista Peruana de Cultura 21:3-8.

Propp, Vladimir. 1958. Morphology of the folktale. International Journal of American Linguistics 24:4, part 3.

Reinhart, Tanya. 1982. Pragmatics and Linguistics: an Analysis of Sentence Topics. Bloomington: Indiana University Linguistics Club.

Rivet, Paul. 1911. La famille linguistique Peba. Journal de la Société des Américanistes de Paris 8:173-206.

Rosen, Carol. 1983. The interface between semantic roles and initial grammatical relations. Studies in Relational Grammar II, ed. David Perlmutter and Carol Rosen, pp. 71-113. Chicago: University of Chicago Press.

Rumelhart, David E. 1975. Notes on a schema for stories. Representation and Understanding: Studies in Cognitive Science, ed. Daniel G. Bobrow and Allan Collins, pp. 211-236. New York: Academic Press.

Sacks, H., Emanuel Schegloff and G. Jefferson. 1974. A simplest systematics for the organization of turn-taking for conversation. Language 50:696-735.

Scancarelli, Janine. 1984. Referential Strategies in Chamorro Narratives. University of California, Los Angeles master's thesis.

Seiler-Baldinger, Annemarie. 1976. Territoire et migrations des indiens yagua. Bulletin de la Société Suisse d'Ethnologie, No. spécial, pp. 143-154. Geneva: Société Suisse d'Ethnologie.

Seiler-Baldinger, Annemarie. 1979. 'Hängematten-Kunst': textile Ausdrucksform bei Yagua- und Ticuna-Indianern Nordwest-Amazoniens. Sonderabdruck aus den Aerhandlungen der Naturforschenden Gesellschaft in Basel, Band 90.

Silverstein, Michael. 1976. Hierarchy of features and ergativity. Grammatical categories in Australian languages, ed. R. M. W. Dixon. Linguistic Series 22:112-171. Canberra: Australian Institute of Aboriginal Studies.

Sun, C.-F., and T. Givón. 1985. On the so-called SOV word order in Mandarin Chinese: a quantified text study and its implications. Language 61:2.

Tessmann, Günter. 1930. Die indianer nordost-perus. Hamburg: Friedrichsen, de Gruyter & Co.

Tomlin, Russell S. 1985. Foreground-background information and the syntax of subordination. Text 5:85-122.

Van Valin, Robert D. 1990. Semantic parameters of split intransitivity. Language 66:221-260.

Voegelin, C. F. and F. M. Voegelin. 1977. Classification and Index of the World's Languages. New York: North Holland.

Wise, Mary Ruth. 1971. Identification of Participants in Discourse: a Study of Aspects of Form and Meaning in Nomatsiguenga. Summer Institute of Linguistics publications in linguistics and related fields no. 28. Dallas: Summer Institute of Linguistics.

Wise, Mary Ruth, and Ann Shanks. 1977. Bibliografía del Instituto Lingüístico de Verano en el Perú 1946-1976. Lima: Instituto Lingüístico de Verano.

Zipf, George Kingsley. 1949. Human Behavior and the Principle of Least Effort. Cambridge, Mass.: Addison-Wesley.

www.ingramcontent.com/pod-product-compliance
Lightning Source LLC
Chambersburg PA
CBHW080418270326
41929CB00018B/3079